AF660242

Patterns in Philosophy and Sociology of Religions

Patterns in Philosophy and Sociology of Religions

Edited by

Mihaela Gligor
Sherry Sabbarwal

RAWAT PUBLICATIONS
Jaipur • New Delhi • Bangalore • Hyderabad • Guwahati

ISBN 81-316-0388-1

© Contributors, 2011

No part of this book may be reproduced or transmitted in any form or by any means, electronic or mechanical, including photocopying, recording or by any information storage and retrieval system, without permission in writing from the publishers.

Published by
Prem Rawat for **Rawat Publications**
Satyam Apts., Sector 3, Jawahar Nagar, Jaipur 302 004 (India)
Phone: 0141 265 1748/7006 Fax: 0141 265 1748
E-mail: info@rawatbooks.com
Website: www.rawatbooks.com

New Delhi Office
4858/24, Ansari Road, Daryaganj, New Delhi 110 002
Phone: 011 2326 3290

Also at *Bangalore, Hyderabad* and *Guwahati*

Typeset by Rawat Computers, Jaipur
Printed at Chaman Enterprises, New Delhi

Contents

Foreword

The eight essays, besides the editors' introduction, which comprise this book, engage with a number of themes from a variety of perspectives. The authors include scholars of religion, philosophy and sociology. Some of them address substantive issues such as myth and ritual and religious symbolism; others are concerned with the role of religion in the public square no less than in the private domain in a modern, globalizing world, with particular reference to contemporary discords worldwide. These discords often have their genesis in religious identities; it is arguable, some of the authors rightly maintain, that in coping with them religious traditions themselves are a very important resource, for elements of love and hate, and war makers and peace makers, are present in every such tradition. Conceptual and methodological issues regarding the definition of religion and the approaches to its study also receive attention. Although there is no single theme running through the essays, the editors' introduction provides a useful, unifying prologue and concisely highlights the principal lines of thought and argument. The book is an interesting and thought-provoking read, distinguished by the seriousness of the authors' approach, an engagement with some basic issues, and obvious contemporary relevance.

The expectations from the writer of the foreword to a volume like the present one may well be of a set of wide-ranging, cross-disciplinary remarks, but I simply do not have that kind of knowledge. My familiarity with scholarly works on religion is confined to what cultural anthropologists and sociologists have given us. I am, of course, aware of the fact that the post-Enlightenment social science approaches to the study of religion were preceded by the intellectual exertions of theologians and the Enlightenment philosophers. David Hume (*The Natural History of Religion*, 1757) had, in fact, tried to liberate the study of religion from theology and situate it in a "science of man", and Immanuel Kant (*Religion Within the Limits of Reason Alone*, 1793) had distinguished between religion as cult and as moral action; the former stood for subservience to God and the latter for the assumption of moral responsibility for one's actions. The historical character of religions had come to be recognized, even when certain innate tendencies of the human mind were recognized. Such a double perspective had been employed to explain both the universality and the great variety of the forms of religious life. Neither Hume nor Kant could, however, be said to have had a sociological perspective.

What strikes me about the work of the founding fathers of the sociology is that, while they were convinced that, in the face of the onward march of science and technology and the rationalization of thought, work and governance, religion as a constitutive element of modern society was on the way out, they were, with the exception of Karl Marx, unsure of the overall significance of this development in the history of Western civilization. For Marx, religion was a justificatory ideology that drew a veil on the true, exploitative character of the capitalist class. The task at hand was the ending of religious and political illusions through a radical transformation of the material base of social life – the mode of production. Religion surely was a phenomenon of the past and had no future, and one could look forward to "the joy of emancipation". Actually, neither did Marx write much about religion, nor did he put forward a general theory of religion. For that we have to turn to others.

Thus, Max Weber wrote in *The Protestant Ethic and the Spirit of Capitalism* (1904) that, "The modern man is in general, even with the best will, unable to give religious ideas a significance for culture and national character which they deserve". Even as Marx had written about the "demystification" of social relations, Weber, in his seminal address on "Science as a Vocation" (1917), spoke about the "disenchantment of the world", which drove religion "into the transcendental realm of mystic life or into the brotherliness of direct personal human relations". Such a world "robbed of its gods" tends to instal instrumental values in place of ultimate values. It is faced with the burden of the "loss of meaning" of human existence. Weber's pessimism, derived in good measure from Nietzsche, stood in stark contrast to Marx's optimism about the future of Western civilization, and, under its impact, presumably of humanity at large.

Weber's contemporary, Émile Durkheim, more concerned with the *sui generis* character of society than individual orientations, was, however, confident that new religious forms would eventually arise in modern society even as the known religions declined. As he puts it in *The Elementary Forms of the Religious Life* (1912), "there is something eternal in religion that is destined to outlive the succession of particular symbols in which religious thought clothed itself".

Georg Simmel too acknowledged the incompatibility of religion and science. For him, the "real gravity" of the times (early twentieth century) was that "the object of transcendent faith *per se*" had come to be regarded as "illusory"; it had been replaced by "a *yearning*, once fulfilled by the idea of transcendence", and had been in the early twentieth century, "paralyzed by the withdrawal of the content of faith and as if cut off from the path to its own life" (*The Problem of Religion Today*, 1912).

Durkheim died in 1917, Simmel in 1918, and Weber in 1920. For the next half century or so, uncertainties about the significance of the decline of religion gave way to confidence, at times verging on hubris, in the prospect of the secular age. Mills (in *The Sociological Imagination,* 1959) prophesied that religion "shall disappear altogether except, possibly, in the private realm". Weber's pessimism about the future is here replaced by secularist triumphalism. The study of religion by sociologists and anthropologists yielded place to other, more topical themes, and the secularization thesis was in full cry during the 1950s and 1960s. A complex idea, it brought together the notions of functional differentiation, privatization (or minimalization) of religion, and rationalization (á la Weber) in a relationship of mutual entailment, which has since been deconstructed by scholars like Casanova (*Public Religions in the Modern World*, 1994).

Peter Berger stands tall, I think, among the sociologists of religion of our time. For him, religion, and indeed all social reality, is socially constructed. In his widely influential book, *The Sacred Canopy* (1967), Berger affirmed the positive significance of religion in history in bestowing order upon chaos, and transforming the socially constructed "nomos" into the sacralized "cosmos". He also attended to the challenges that religious faith faces in modern society from religious pluralism, which undermines all certainties including those provided by religion, and promotes secularization.

In a remarkable reconsideration of these views at the end of the century, Berger asserted that "the assumption that we live in a secularized world is false. The world today, with some exceptions [...], is as ferociously religious as it ever was, and in some places more so than ever" (*The Desecularization of the World: A Global View*, 1999). His argument is not that secularization is a myth, but that it is not a necessary concomitant of modernization. This conclusion now finds wide acceptance. Not only is there evidence worldwide of the coexistence of religiosity and modernity, but religiosity is often found to employ modern methods of communication and institutional organization to survive in contemporary times.

Who should know this better than the sociologists who study contemporary India? Indian secularism is modern inasmuch it is a product of the historical situation created by colonial rule in a multi-religious country of subcontinental dimensions. M.N. Srinivas (*Social Change in Modern India,* 1966) drew attention to this in his clear discussion of secularization as a multifaceted process that had become accelerated after independence. At the same time, it is Indian inasmuch as it does not stand for the privatization of religion, much less its abolition. Indian secularism is presented in the Constitution of India as the interrelated twin ideas of the non-discriminatory state (Article 15) and freedom of religion (Articles 25 to 30).

In other words, Indian secularism is a religio-secular ideal, and makes sense only in the continuing presence of a plurality of religions. The state has no religion, nor it favours any particular religious community, but it accepts the legitimacy of religion in the public domain, and, controversially, even facilitates the practice of religion. Srinivas had noticed the role of the government in modernizing religion (particularly Hinduism) through legislation. Secularization in India proceeds apace hand in hand with the growth of politicized religiosity among the majority as well as the minority communities. Hindutva and radical Islam are mirror images of one another.

India does not stand alone. Developments worldwide since the late 1970s in the definition of the relationship of religion, politics and society have challenged intellectuals everywhere, in particular sociologists, political scientists and philosophers, to turn to the study of religion in a big way. I need do no more than recall what has happened, for instance, in Iran, Poland, Nicaragua, Afghanistan, and, of course, India, in the last three decades. The new salience of religious fundamentalism in a variety of forms on a global scale (including in countries as culturally diverse as Japan and the United States) and the collapse of the communist state of the USSR are not to be dismissed lightly. It is obvious that religious resurgence finds expression as both heightened piety at the individual level and as a force for public good in some places and as a destructive force in others; these roles have often been found to coexist. As one of the contributors to the present volume points out, there are peace-makers and war-makers in every religious tradition.

The emergence of diasporic communities, who are not always welcomed in the host countries as, notably, Muslim immigrants in some European countries, has valourized religious identities in new ways. More generally, globalization draws out people everywhere from their traditional national boundaries, and incorporates them into world markets, even when they do not leave home. Simultaneously, it produces cultural homogenization on an unprecedented scale, generating a sense of participation, which many find dubious. Identity concerns thus acquire salience, valourizing ethnic and religious bonds. Diasporic communities, which are comfortable in their new habitats, also feel a pull towards "roots", resulting in, on the one hand, constructive innovations in the religious domain, and political conservation in relation to the homelands, on the other. It is arguable that Hinduism in America is a significantly different religion in terms of its pantheon, forms of ritual practice, and patterns of social interaction. On the negative side, Hindutva has a considerable following there. Similarly, earlier group animosities may acquire sharper edges away from home as has been shown in the one of the chapters of this book in the context of sectarian conflicts among Sikh diasporic communities in Europe.

The aphorism "God is dead: God remains dead" has been heard over and over again since Nietzsche first employed it, rather wistfully I think, in the mid-1880s, but today we are informed that religion is enjoying (in Jacques Derrida's phrase) an "afterlife". Sociologists have important work to do in making sense of our complex times. Needless to emphasize, the cultural, social and political significances of contemporary religiosity cannot be properly understood unless attention is also paid to the worldviews, ethics, and substantive content of a religious tradition, and its innovative ways. The religious dimension of environment protection and preservation movements in some places is a case in point.

Given the manner in which different religious traditions impact one another in today's world, the comparative viewpoint has become imperative. It is no longer meaningful to present understandings of religious movements in isolation, countrywise or religious communitywise. What is heartening is that concerned scholars everywhere are indeed turning, or returning, to these studies in our times; the present volume is just one example of this trend. Its importance should not be judged by its size, but rather by the current intellectual awareness that it represents. It is, therefore, welcome and I recommend it to the readers.

T.N. Madan
Honorary Professor (Sociology)
Institute of Economic Growth, University of Delhi and
Distinguished Senior Fellow
Centre for the Study of Developing Societies, New Delhi

Preface

Religion has been a key component of all societies and remains an institution that has vital implications for practically all facets of human existence. Any study of religion must aim at comprehension of the phenomenon in all its forms – as an institution, as a mode of life and, most importantly, as a pattern of values and practices that are both moulded by, and that themselves impact the social reality of their times. Humans have for a long time tried to understand and decode the mystery of existence. While searching for the meaning "of life" and "in life", people have resorted to philosophical exercises or indulged in some form of art. However, the greatest numbers have immersed themselves in religion in some way or the other. Consequently, the analysis of religion and the problems relating to its definition, functions and impact can be found located in an extensive array of subjects and perspectives falling under the fields of theology, humanities and social sciences.

The view of religion as a source of legitimation based on shared norms and values was posited by Émile Durkheim, who emphasized the notions of belonging and religion's function as being an integrating force in the community system, as the underlying motives of religious activities. Others like Marcel Mauss and Max Weber envisioned religion as the link between the individual and a supposed supranatural realm of power, in which sense it served as a wellspring of empowerment. The philosophy of religion, which mulled over issues arising in connection with religious beliefs and practices, was for a long time concentrated upon the exploration of the "soundness" of theist propositions. There has, however, been a shift in their focus as the attempt now is not to analyze the veracity of these propositions but to their "meaningfulness". The question confronting the philosophy of religion now is not how true or false the theist assumptions are, but to what extent are they logical, lucid and comprehensible. The sociology of religion, on the other hand, has been engaged in examining the influence of religious beliefs on the behaviour of groups, its interests ranging from studying the actual followers of a particular religion to a more tentative deliberation on the interface of social and affective influences on the beliefs of a society, to the contemplation of the origin and functions of religion, the secularization debate and the advent of the "new" religions.

To make sense of the present-day religion we need to examine theoretical ideas about the uniqueness of advanced industrial societies and the emerging world order, as well as, take into account the changes that have taken place in the ideas about the social significance of religion. The Enlightenment, by emphasizing the principles of rationality and humanism, threw up a challenge to God and the spiritual world being the focal points of religion, as well as to the view that human good is inextricably linked with religion. The notions of human and social progress that grew out of the Enlightenment – modern political ideals of liberalism, democracy and egalitarianism – gave prominence to the individual rather than the collective identities that had hitherto dictated traditional religion's social values. The advent of nationalism sidelined the identity derived from membership of a religious group and gave centre stage to ethnic or linguistic identities. Socialist beliefs in the nineteenth and twentieth centuries launched an assault on religion by debunking the canons of religion and suppressing the practice of religion in the socialist political systems.

Due to these developments, together with the concept of secularization that emerged as one of the most popular intellectual and practical ideas, it appeared to many that the end of traditional religion was near. However, on the contrary, we are witnessing a general revival of religious sentiments in all forms of religious thought – radical, fundamentalist, esoteric and numinous. Concomitantly, different responses to these changes have also emerged providing us with a polarized choice between reformism and fundamentalism, the former attempting to make religion more attuned to the contemporary world, and the latter rebuffing any signs and symbols of modernity and advocating a return to the old ways.

A major accomplishment of the philosophical and social scientific analyses of religion has been the realization that there can be no single definition of the phenomenon of religion. The trend now is not to delineate certain characteristics of religion but to look for nuances that sensitize us to the existence of a variety of religious expressions at different levels of culture. Consequently, while the earlier writers were satisfied with describing religion as a general theory of the world or belief in spiritual beings, the trend now is towards a more relativistic approach. In fact, as a result of the changes in the global religious scenario in recent times, the analysis of religion is becoming more international necessitating wide-ranging comparative inquiry of the phenomenon.

For long the theoretical assumptions have been too narrowly defined in Western terms and categories of thought and it is time to re-examine the existing assumptions. In its effort to comprehend a diverse heterogeneous and complex international picture of religion and its socio-cultural situation, contemporary study of religion is pressing beyond its narrow Western foundations and culturally specific definitions of religion. There is an effort being made to understand the complex linkages between nature and culture, individual and society, purity and pollution, sacred and profane, myths and rituals, factors fostering change and established conventions ensuring the persistence of the old ways.

The realization of the plurality of religions is another idea that has taken root in contemporary religious writings. Religion and religious diversity have long been a fact of life in the world. But since the events of September 11, 2001 not only did religion become a centre of focus but there was also a reframing of old questions about religion and its impact on democracy, peace, development, identity, etc. The emergence of a steadily differentiated universal social system has given rise to new cultural model of what signifies a religion, which underscores the notion of a plurality of religions that are mutually set apart. This new focus on the idea of contemporary religion in a globalized differentiated world has moved the study of religion beyond the restricted view of secularization and other similar narrow models. With greater number of people all over the world gradually becoming aware of a multiplicity of religions, the need to be aware of each other, to scrutinize the factors impacting all religions and to see how religions are transforming to face the emerging challenges, has become the agenda of religious studies.

Thus, in the previous millennia, religion played a vital role in people's lives and it seems quite evident that it continues to be a key factor in human life and thought. Additionally, modern religion presents us with new problems challenging the taken for granted assumptions about the modern world and religion. Further, religion presents a challenge to social order in many ways and continues to be controversial too. Overall, however, the pattern that becomes apparent is one of continuity along with change.

Through this book we have endeavoured to bring together scholars across disciplines to address some of the issues briefly touched upon above. To explore the complexities of religious expressions today, this book has gathered perspectives from sociology and philosophy and would therefore be of use not only for the studies of world religions but also for interdisciplinary courses. Admittedly, this volume is not a comprehensive anthology of theoretical ideas or empirical findings. Nor is it an account of the state of religion in the twenty-first century. Our hope is that it will enhance the reader's appreciation of and sensitivity to different points of views regarding religion in the increasingly pluralistic world.

In the end, we owe a debt of gratitude to all those who have helped us in various ways in this endeavour. First, we wish to thank to all contributors for accepting our invitation. For the book, as a whole, we have also greatly benefited from many helpful suggestions from Professor Mac Linscott Ricketts.

We would also like to express our appreciation for the general guidance we have received from discussions on the structure and content of the book with Mr Pranit Rawat, from Rawat Publications.

We have benefited as well from the comments and suggestions, and also from sincere support and close friendship of our friends from Kolkata. We thank them all for everything they have done for us: Dana Sugu, Sanjay Gopal Sarkar, Kamal Sinha, Sarunya Prasopchingchana, Atashee Chatterjee Sinha and B.K. Poddar, the Honorary Consul of Romania in Kolkata. Many thanks to our Indian friends from Romania, Ashok Dorairaja and Deepak Maheshwari, who are always ready to help us, without even knowing us in person.

In addition we would like to thank, for support and love, our families.

Mihaela Gligor
Sherry Sabbarwal

Introduction

Religion: From theory to action

MIHAELA GLIGOR

> Religions, if they were many, would be the same; but because they are *one*, they are different. And the unity of "religions" will finally be seen when each man will have his own mode of approaching God, when the Supreme Being will be revealed to each one directly, without the precedent of tradition or collective experience. Only then will there be a real, collective participation in the Supreme. When each one will have his own mode of approach, the ritual and dogma proper to his religious experience, then the unity of religions will become manifest.
>
> —Mircea Eliade, "Concerning the 'Unseen God' and Other Fragments", *Soliloquies*, 1932.

The word 'religion' comes from the Latin 'religare', which means "to bind back". We can say that the word reveals the fact that religion re-establishes one's connection to the origin. According to E.B. Tylor, "religion represents the belief in spiritual beings"[1] or, as in the 1970s J.M. Yinger had noticed, "religion is a system of beliefs and practices by means of which a group of people struggles with these problems of human life".[2] Religion is everywhere in today's world, often in quite unexpected places. We need to understand how religion works in such contexts. There are Western religions, Eastern religions, ancient religions, modern religions, monotheistic, polytheistic, and even slightly atheistic religions; too many to count, too many to master, in too many languages to learn. But, for all of them, the ultimate purpose is God, or as Hegel puts it, "the object of religion as well as of philosophy is eternal truth in its objectivity, God and nothing but God, and the explication of God".[3]

If we want to be equidistant, we could say that every religion is a way to God. No way to God is superior to the other. However, depending on one's mental temperament and cultural background, one way might be better suited to him/her than another. This difference arises due to the difference in the temperament of the person and cannot be used to judge the general efficacy of a path.

> Religion is man's earliest and also indirect form of self-knowledge. Hence, religion everywhere precedes philosophy […] Man first of all sees his nature as if out of himself, before he finds it in himself. His own nature is in the first instance contemplated by him as that of another being.[4]

And thus, we can rightly say that religion, in its three aspects – philosophy, mythology and ritual – deals with questions of life,[5] the existence of God, nature of beings, creation, goal of life, and means of attaining God. Through mythology, ostensibly with a historical basis, human beings tried to explain some phenomena of nature, such as the origin of life, customs, religious rites of a people, involving the exploits of gods and heroes. The philosophical exploration of religious beliefs and practices is evident in the earliest recorded philosophy of both East and West. More than that, "[…] Philosophy is a useful way of approaching religion – because it challenges the explanations for human life offered by the religious".[6] Philosophy and religion explores the nature of the real world, the basis of human values, and foundations of reason.

From the beginning of time, people have thought that above them there is an external almighty force that writes their destiny and rules the known universe. They called this force "God", and they attributed to this force all kind of names, images and powers.

Imagine a cave, Plato's cave. Then, imagine a group of people who have lived chained in this cave all their lives, facing a blank wall. The people watch shadows projected on the wall by things passing in front of a fire behind them, and begin to ascribe forms to these shadows. According to Plato, the shadows are as close as the prisoners get to seeing reality. Imagine that all those shadows that are seen by the prisoners are manifestation of the same external almighty force, called God. The shadows are manifestation of divinity, and each man sees on the wall what he believes to be reality, what he thinks to be the truth; each man sees a different God, even if as the manifestation of God is the same: abstract in form, but pure in content.

Plato tells us in the *Republic* that the "Form of God is Goodness itself, Being itself, Justice itself".[7] For Plato, religion is very much a concern of the intellect and not of the will, or the desire. Plato's famous disciple, Aristotle, says that the highest form of happiness lies in the activity of *theoria* or pure contemplation, and he goes on to claim that the activity which brings the greatest happiness to man must be that which imitates the activity of God.

> If the Gods have any care for human affairs, as they are thought to have it would be reasonable both that they should delight in that which was best and most akin to them [i.e., reason] and that they should reward those who love and honour this most, as caring for the things that are dear to them and acting both rightly and nobly. And that all these attributes belong most of all to the philosopher is manifest. He therefore is dearest to the gods. And he who is so will presumably be also the happiest, so that in his way the philosopher will more than any other be happy.[8]

Starting with Plato and Aristotle, a new school of thought was established and the search for God was an important part for its students and followers. The essence of religion had to be found somewhere in world's beliefs. But to trace the beginnings of the philosophy of religions and especially to try to understand what the divinity meant for people is a very hard attempt. According to Max Charlesworth,

> First [...] religion is defined as consisting essentially in the intellectual vision or contemplation of "God". The latter [...] has been variously understood as the Form of the Good (Plato); the purely and eternally actual and dynamic source of change and mutability, and the ever-active Nous or Mind (Aristotle); the one transcending

> all our finite categories (Plotinus and neo-Platonists); the creative and providential God of Islam; Spinoza's infinite substance (Deus sive Natura) of which finite beings are "modes"; and Hegel's Self-Conscious Spirit working itself out in the world. And the intellectual apprehension and contemplation and enjoyment of God, in these several senses, are held to be of the essence of "religion".[9]

Each religious tradition includes a system of beliefs or world view through which adherents understand the world and their place in it. A belief system is a way to perceive and interact in a society guided by a set of established moral rules. Our beliefs are an essential part of who we are and how we behave. A culture with a strong belief system is shaped by it. A religious world view provides a view of the whole of things (beliefs about life and the cosmos) and of what is ultimately real. In those traditions with a historical founder and master figure, an important accent lies on the life and teaching of the foundational figure (for example, Buddha, Christ, Confucius, and Muhammad).

Today, philosophy of religion is a robust, intensely active area of philosophy. The importance of philosophy of religion is chiefly due to its subject matter: alternative beliefs about God, Brahman, and the sacred, the varieties of religious experience, the interplay between science and religion, the challenge of non-religious philosophies, the nature and scope of good and evil, religious treatments of birth, history, and death, and other substantial themes. A philosophical exploration of these topics involves fundamental questions about our place in the cosmos. Philosophy of religion is therefore relevant to practical concerns.[10]

On the other hand, lived religion is not simply a matter of believing; it is something that is done, and felt, expressed out in words and gestures of what ultimately matters. Thus, each religious tradition constitutes a way of life or ethos, as well as a world view. Each religion involves moral commands or guidelines respecting how life ought to be lived and a sense of what constitutes the good life. Each religion, to one degree or another, performs rituals or ceremonies. Ritual is the element of practice that gives each religion a distinctive social and cultural personality and shapes a tradition's calendar. Each religion is a social and institutional entity with a set of values, and codes of conduct. Fundamental in all religions is the concept of a relationship. The relationship may involve one or more persons, it may be physical and/or spiritual and it may be real or imagined, dynamic or static. Within the ambit of this relationship, the persons involved used words such as "devotion", "respect", "faith", "holy", "sacrifice", or "enlightenment". Communicational channels may be formal and organized as through a priest or a shaman, a guru or a saint. People all over the world use daily this "direct line" with the Absolute. Beyond that, the social character of a religion – of any relationship with the Absolute – is reflected in the name by which it is identified as a communal entity: the Christian *church,* the Jewish *synagogue,* the Hindu *mandir*, the Buddhist *sangha,* the Muslim *umma,* and so on. Religion may dictate a set of acceptable standards and those who wish to remain in that society must adhere to those standards, within acceptable limits. For those who are unable to do this, there is the option of leaving the society or of belonging to another religion.

There can be no denying that the concept "religion" is complex, and the term is often taken to refer to a number of different concepts and practices. According to Joachim Wach, religion usually has three "expressions" or dimensions, namely, *the theoretical* (e.g., doctrines, dogmas, myths, theologies, ethics), *the practical* (e.g., cults, sacraments, meditations), and *the sociological* (e.g., religious groupings, ecclesiastical forms). According to Mircea Eliade,

> Wach's methodological position is especially relevant to our topic. He was mainly a historian of religions, or, more precisely, a student of Religionswissenschaft, of which, to him, the sociology of religion was one of four branches (with the history of religions, phenomenology of religion, and psychology of religion) […]. Wach felt the necessity of taking the sociological conditioning of religious life and the social contexts of religious expressions into serious consideration. With little success he strove to interest the sociologists of religion in Religionswissenschaft.[11]

Like many other historians of religions – for example, Raffaele Pettazzoni or Gerardus van der Leeuw – Eliade held that the discipline of the history of religions (*Allgemeine Religionswissenschaft*) is destined to play an important role in contemporary cultural life and that role consisted of two dimensions, viz., historical and systematic.

Eliade was the first who presented an astonishing variety of religious data and their basic "patterns". In his *Traité de histoire des religions (Patterns in Comparative Religion)*, Eliade examined both the "lower" and "higher" religious forms. He explained that "religious wholes are not seen in bits and pieces, for each class of hierophanies [...] forms, in its own way, a whole, both morphologically [...] and historically".[12]

Why is "patterns" an appropriate term to associate with the world's religions? In its simplest form any religion may be seen as a belief system. Each religion has a set of beliefs, symbols, practices, and traditions that forms a meaningful story and that provides guides and models for living. This system may affect values, laws, rites and general behaviour patterns. And, each religion has a distinctive pattern. These are not always easily discernible, but they may become evident through study, practice, and experience. Religion may affect the individual, group, community or nation. It may play an integral role within society. There is much to be learned about ourselves and about the others through the study of religion.

In 1961, for the first issue of *History of Religions*, the new journal on religions, published by Chicago University Press, Eliade wrote the famous article entitled "History of Religions and a New Humanism". Eliade expressed there his sympathy with young scholars who aspired to become historians of religions, but, in Eliade's view, they first must be learned generalists, in order to become specialists in one religion or even in a particular period or a single aspect of that religion. For Eliade,

> The History of Religions is destined to play an important role in contemporary cultural life. This is not only because an understanding of exotic and archaic religions will significantly assist in a cultural dialogue with the representatives of such religions. It is more especially because [...] the history of religions will inevitably attain to a deeper knowledge of man. It is on the basis of such knowledge that a new humanism, on a worldwide scale, could develop.[13]

Mircea Eliade's total hermeneutics was based on his understanding of the general scientific study of religions, known as the "history of religions". But this approach was dependent as well on various social, physical, and biological sciences; law; humanistic disciplines, especially the arts and literature; philosophy (of religion); and theologies. Eliade believed that all of these disciplines in combination must attempt to decipher the meaning of human experience in this mysterious universe.

Besides these theoretical aspects, without exception, religions from all around the world and throughout all the times have included a vital visual dimension – whether it is icons to contemplate, sacred diagrams used in ritual, powerful objects charged with the capacity to protect or heal, the creation of sacred spaces, or the use of clothing, vestments, or liturgical objects in worship. In front of the sacred, people act the same, and being Christian or Hindu or Buddhist or Muslim is just something external, something gained by birth or free will.

We usually have assumed that there is no such thing as a purely religious phenomenon. We agree that a religious phenomenon is a human phenomenon. By this it is not only religious but also social, cultural, and so on. Yet as Eliade rightly said,

> To try to grasp the essence of such a phenomenon by means of physiology, psychology, sociology, economics, linguistics, art or any other study is false; it misses the one unique and irreducible element in it – the element of the sacred.[14]

The term "religion" refers to both the personal practices related to communal faith and to group rituals and communication stemming from shared conviction. "Religion" is sometimes used interchangeably with "faith": the Catholic faith or the Muslim faith; the Hindu faith or the Jewish faith. In any case, the history of religious perceptions and religious freedoms take us to understand not only the similarities between religions, but also those points of view that make a religion so unique among the others. Returning to Eliade's words, "Religions […] because they are one, they are different", and in our globalized world this fact can be seen everywhere.

Beginning with problematizing the category "religion" and tracing its emergence historically and contextually as an analytical domain, this volume is organized to introduce the multiple, complex and sometimes opposing strands and arguments in many social science studies of religion. The "patterns" encountered speak essentially about religious identity, perceptions of self, peace (or the lack of it), fears of instability, loss of self, disorder and violent conflicts of our time, secularism, myth and ritual, images of the body, or immemorial facts that happened *in illo tempore* – all of them with deep impact on expressions and manifestations of religion in different religious systems, from Christianity to Buddhism or from Hinduism to Islam, not to forget about the Greek vision of primordial time. As theoretical models, similar patterns regarding interpretations of the empiric religious facts can be seen in works of Mircea Eliade or Peter Winch.

In this volume, we do not intend to explain the differences or the similarities between all these religions. We only propose to introduce the reader into the fascinating world of religions and faiths. Each and every one of them has something unique about it. There are a great many similarities among world's religions and yet a great many differences. As in the case of multiculturalism, a term we usually understand as a practice of giving equal attention or representation to the cultural needs and contributions of all the groups in a society (special emphasis may be given to minority groups underrepresented in the past, as through bilingual education), in case of religions general approaches are alike: the term "religion" defines internal relationships among communities relatively circumscribed, and also among people of specific provenience engaged in external, professional, cultural, linguistic, or any other relations.

With respect to the discipline of sociology, it is well known that is about patterns. Sociology of religion "aims to discover the patterns of social living associated with religion in all its diverse forms and to find explanations for the data that emerge".[15] For Durkheim, religion was a projection of social experience. We are interested, then, in describing the social worlds in which religious ideas, practices, groups, and experiences make an appearance. We are interested in describing what religion itself looks like, what "patterns" can we find in this globalized world and what these "patterns" mean – that is, in developing better definitions and indicators. The importance of philosophy of religion is chiefly due to subject matter: alternative beliefs about God, and the sacred, the varieties of religious experience, the interplay between science and religion, the challenge of non-religious philosophies, the nature and scope of good and evil, religious treatments of birth, history, marriage and death, and other substantial themes. A philosophical exploration of these topics involves fundamental questions about our place in the cosmos. Philosophy of religion is therefore relevant to practical concerns. Alan Aldridge writes:

> Religions are grounded in a source of ultimate meaning and authority; they command and demand respect. Any attempt to confine religion to a private sphere of individual belief and devotion is bound to be challenged. It is not possible, even in a society that aspires to be secular, to treat religion as a purely private affair to which the state can be indifferent.[16]

Both secularization and pluralism have been unduly exaggerated by theories of modern religion. Often, the exaggeration has to do with the social location of the theorists. Thus, the theory of secularization referred to earlier has been a projection of the European situation to other parts of the world where it turns out to be inappropriate. Conversely, a recently formulated "new paradigm" in the sociology of religion, which centres on pluralism, inappropriately generalizes from the American experience, which is not replicated elsewhere in the same way. With regard to this, the comparison between Europe, the USA and India is of particular importance for the sociology of contemporary religion. Because, as Eliade states, "the sociology of religion has brought, and continues to bring, important contributions to the general science of religion".[17] Given the place of religion among the vast percentage of the world's population, philosophy and sociology of religion have a major role to play in understanding people's values and commitments.

The essays contained in the present volume, contributed by reputed scholars from India, the United States and Europe, insist on multifaceted expressions of religiosity in the contemporary global context, appropriately grounded in a historical perspective. They explore various socio-cultural, political and economic processes, as they are today, or as they were in antiquity, or as they were theorized by important historians and sociologists of religion. Important matters are discussed here starting from the problem of religion and violence in our globalized world to the quest for peace as the ultimate solution, with which all the religions agree to some facts that resulted from changing interpretations of religion in secularism and to religious identities in contemporary India. Besides, included in this book are also a very interesting excursion to ancient Greece analyzing its myths and rituals, plus the role of the body in religious beliefs, and finally, contemporary reinterpretations of some of the most important historians of religion of the 20th century.

Thus, the genesis of the present book lies in our intention to show that there is a common ground for all beliefs and religious manifestation: the presence of the sacred.

NOTES

1. E.B. Tylor, *Primitive Culture*, Vol. I (London: John Murray, 1891), 424.
2. J.M. Yinger, *The Scientific Study of Religion* (New York: Macmillan, 1970), 7.
3. Georg Wilhelm Friedrich Hegel, *Lectures on the Philosophy of Religion together with a work on the Proofs of the Existence of God*, translated from the second German edition by the Rev. E.B. Speirs, B.D., and J. Burdon Sanderson, 3 volumes (London: Routledge & Kegan Paul, 1962). Vol. 1, *Introduction to the Philosophy of Religion,* 19.
4. Ludwig Feuerbach, *The Essence of Christianity*, translated by George Eliot (New York: Harper and Row, 1957), 13.
5. Regarding to this, we should mention Ludwig Wittgenstein's notes that "To believe in a God means to understand the question about the meaning of life. To believe in a God means to see that the facts of the world are not the end of the matter. To believe in a God means to see that life has a meaning". Cf. Ludwig Wittgenstein, *Notebooks 1914–1916* (Oxford: Blackwell, 1961), 74.

6. Robin Le Poidevin, *Arguing for Atheism* (London: Routledge, 1996), xvii–xviii.

7. Plato, "The Myth of the Cave", in *The Republic*, The Complete and Unabridged Jowett translation, translated by Benjamin Jowett (New York: Vintage Books, 1991), Book VII (514a–520a).

8. Aristotle, *Nicomachean Ethics*, X 7, 1177a, 25–32.

9. Max Charlesworth, *Philosophy and Religion: From Plato to Postmodernism* (Oxford: Oneworld Publications, 2006), 39.

10. The truth is that we own to Hegel the existence of a discipline named *Philosophy of Religion*. According to him, "It has appeared to me to be necessary to make religion by itself the object of philosophical consideration, and to add on this study of it, in the form of a special part, to philosophy as a whole. [...] The Philosophy of Religion has to consider its signification – this, namely, that God is the Idea, the Absolute, the Essential Reality which is grasped in thought and in the Notion, and this it has in common with logical philosophy; the logical Idea is God as He is in Himself. [...] Thus, in contemplating the Idea of God, in the Philosophy of Religion, we have at the same time to do with the manner of His manifestation or presentation to us; He simply makes Himself apparent, represents Himself to Himself. [...] In the Philosophy of Religion we have the Absolute as object". Cf. Georg Wilhelm Friedrich Hegel, *Lectures on the Philosophy of Religion together with a work on the Proofs of the Existence of God*, translated from the second German edition by the Rev. E.B. Speirs, B.D., and J. Burdon Sanderson, 3 volumes (London: Routledge & Kegan Paul, 1962), *Introduction*, 1, 25.

11. Mircea Eliade, *The Quest: History and Meaning in Religion* (Chicago: The University of Chicago Press, 1969), 18–19.

12. Mircea Eliade, *Patterns in Comparative Religion* (New York: Sheed and Ward, 1958), xvi.

13. Mircea Eliade, "History of Religions and a New Humanism", *History of Religions*, 1 (1961): 2–3.

14. Mircea Eliade, *Patterns in Comparative Religion,* xi.

15. Grace Davie, *The Sociology of Religion* (London: Sage Publications, 2007), 6.

16. Alan Aldridge, *Religion in the Contemporary World: A Sociological Introduction* (Cambridge: Polity Press, 2007), 7.

17. Mircea Eliade, *The Quest*, 19.

REFERENCES

Aldridge, Alan. *Religion in the Contemporary World: A Sociological Introduction*. Cambridge: Polity Press, 2007.

Bianchi, Ugo. *The History of Religions*. Leiden: E.J. Brill, 1975.

Billington, Ray. *Understanding Eastern Philosophy*. London and NY: Routledge, 1997.

Brody, Baruch (ed.). *Readings in the Philosophy of Religion*. New Jersey: Prentice-Hall, 1974.

Charlesworth, Max. *Philosophy and Religion: From Plato to Postmodernism*. Oxford: Oneworld Publications, 2006.

Davie, Grace. *The Sociology of Religion*. London: Sage Publications, 2007.

Dean, Thomas (ed.). *Religious Pluralism and Truth: Essays on Cross-Cultural Philosophy of Religion*. Delhi: Sri Satguru Publications, a division of Indian Books Centre, 1997.

Durkheim, Émile. *The Elementary Forms of the Religious Life*. London: George Allen and Unwin, 1915.

Eliade, Mircea. *The Quest: History and Meaning in Religion*. Chicago: The University of Chicago Press, 1969.

——. *Patterns in Comparative Religion*. New York: Sheed and Ward, 1958.

Feuerbach, Ludwig. *The Essence of Christianity*. tr. George Eliot, New York: Harper and Row, 1957.

Goodchild, Philip (ed.). *Difference in Philosophy of Religion*. Burlington: Ashgate Publishing, 2003.

Heelas, Paul, David Martin and Paul Morris (eds.). *Religion, Modernity and Postmodernity*. Oxford: Blackwell Publishers, 1998.

Hegel, Georg Wilhelm Friedrich. *Lectures on the Philosophy of Religion together with a work on the Proofs of the Existence of God*. Translated from the second German edition by the Rev. E.B. Speirs, B.D., and J. Burdon Sanderson, 3 volumes, London: Routledge & Kegan Paul, 1962. Vol. 1, *Introduction to the Philosophy of Religion*.

Kotakowski, Leszek. *Religion: If there is no God... On God, the Devil, Sin and Other Worries of the so-called Philosophy of Religion*. London: Fontana, 1982.

Long, Eugene Thomas. *Twentieth-Century Western Philosophy of Religion 1900–2000*. Dordrecht/Boston/London: Kluwer Academic Publishers, 2003.

Leeuw, Gerardus van der. *Religion is Essence and Manifestation*. tr. by J.E. Turner, New York: Harper and Row, 1963.

Singh, M. Kirti. *Philosophy and Religion*. New Delhi: Akansha Publishing House, 2007.

Smart, Ninian. *The World's Religions: Old Traditions and Modern Transfigurations*. Cambridge: Cambridge UP, 1989.

Tylor, E.B. *Primitive Culture*. Vol. I, London: John Murray, 1891.

Yinger, J.M. *The Scientific Study of Religion*. New York: Macmillan, 1970.

Zagzebski, Linda Trinkaus. *Philosophy of Religion: An Historical Introduction*. Oxford: Blackwell Publishing, 2007.

Wittgenstein, Ludwig. *Notebooks 1914–1916*. Oxford: Blackwell, 1961.

CHAPTER 1

Religion and Violence in the Contemporary World

Is religion more of the problem or the solution?

DOUGLAS ALLEN

We cannot understand what is happening in the world today and what will determine a very dangerous and insecure future without understanding the complex and troubling relations of religion and violence. This topic of religion and violence often dominates the daily news and the everyday lives of hundreds of millions of human beings.

The focus of our discussions inevitably turns to religion and violence when we are talking about Afghanistan and the Taliban; when we are talking about Iraq and Shia, Sunni, and other religious and ethnic divisions; when we are talking about much of what is happening in Pakistan, among India's Hindu religious nationalists, and with regard to Indo-Pakistani and communal conflicts; when we are talking about violence in the Palestinian territories, Israel, and other parts of the Middle East; and when we are talking about terrorism.

This topic of religion and violence is also the key to understanding what is happening politically, culturally, economically, and militarily in the United States today. In fact, it is my position that some of the most violent, dangerous, religious forces in the world exist within the modern, pluralistic, anti-theocratic United States.

I have done a lot of work on religion. I am specialized in philosophy, and the area where I have done the most publishing is in the phenomenology of religion (the nature of religion and religious experience, interpreting religious meaning, religious language, religious symbolism, religious myth). Therefore, I am very concerned with trying to understand "religion". In addition, as a peace and justice scholar-activist, who has focused during the past decade on the philosophy and practice of Mahatma Gandhi, I have been more concerned with understanding the nature of "violence" and exploring non-violent methods for resolving situations of violent conflict.

There are many confusing, contradictory questions that arise when trying to understand the relation between religion and violence. For example, there is no major world religion that has commandments such as "Thou shalt kill", "Thou shalt be violent", "Thou shalt be full of hate", or "Thou shalt be intolerant". In fact, you find the exact opposite. I have heard a number of lectures, especially in India, in which scholars gave long presentations documenting that every major religion has some version of the Golden Rule.

No religion has a narrow restrictive version of the Golden Rule claiming that we should do unto others of our own religious group as we would want them to do unto us, but this does not apply to other religious and non-religious beings that we should hate, treat violently, and kill. Nevertheless, what we actually find in the history of religions is that the unfortunate application of the Golden Rule toward religious and non-religious others has often taken the form of do unto others before they do unto you or, to provide a second historical illustration, whoever has the gold rules.

So the difficult questions are the following: If religions preach peace, why have most wars in history been given a religious justification? If religions believe in non-violence, why do we have thousands of years of so much religious violence? If religions preach love, why do we have thousands of years of so much religious hate, especially toward those who do not agree with one's religious beliefs and practices? If religions preach tolerance, why are some of them major sources of intolerance toward others? If religions preach justice, why do we have religions so often justifying and supporting unjust, exploitative, oppressive, class, race, and gender relations of domination?

Not only are such questions puzzling and difficult to unpack, analyze, and comprehend on theoretical, philosophical and sociological grounds, but they are also of the most practical urgency and significance, since they raise concerns that relate to the death, unnecessary suffering, and oppression of billions of human beings and the future of human life on this earth. In short, the major issue in this chapter is whether religion in the world today is more of a major source of the problems of violence or whether it can be part of constructive solutions to the crises of so much escalating violence that threatens to destroy us and our planet.

Violence

There are two key terms in the title of this chapter – "religion" and "violence" – and these terms are often thrown around in very uncritical and self-serving ways. We first take the term "violence".

There are two standard meanings of "violence" that one finds in all dictionaries. Violence is a force that is rough, fierce, intense and immoderate. Many philosophers, especially some major political philosophers, sociologists, anthropologists, and various scholars of religion and adherents of diverse religious faiths, often regard violence in this first sense in neutral or even positive terms. For example, many religious creation myths, apocalyptic myths, and other sacred narratives, rites of initiation and other rituals, missionary expansions and conversions, religious conquests, and other phenomena are very violent and are viewed by many believers as necessary and even glorious. In addition, there is a second, clearly negative meaning that violence is not only such a rough, intense, immoderate force, but it also involves aggression, assault, infringement, and violation. It is this second meaning that people usually have in mind when they claim to be against violence.

In my work, I use the term "violence" in ways that really broaden and deepen the meaning of violence and make the discussion of religious violence much more interesting and relevant to our contemporary world. Most people restrict violence to overt physical violence: bombing, shooting, killing, torturing, beating up, rape, bullying, etc. This is why, these people easily claim that they are opposed to violence. In the history of religions, such explicit overt violence has been manifested in such forms as holy wars and religious justifications for other wars, Crusades, Inquisitions, burning witches at the stake, sexual violence, executions, chopping off limbs, lashings, and other forms of physical punishment for alleged sins. In my opinion, such expressions of blatant, overt, physical violence are important, but they represent a small part of total violence. In fact, most people who claim to be non-violent, including most leading politicians and corporate executives and many religious leaders, are in fact very violent.

I would like to introduce two other concepts crucial to understanding violence and religious violence. The first concept is of violence as multidimensional. In addition to overt physical violence, we have inner violence. You can be filled with great hatred and thus be a very violent person, even if you do not physically assault another human being. Your repressed inner violence will make you a very violent hateful person, and this will be expressed in how you relate to yourself and to others. So, we have inner violence, or psychological violence, where we have to look at feelings, thoughts, motives, and intentions.

Different religious traditions disagree on what constitutes psychological violence and how to evaluate it. For example, Buddhists typically claim that anger is violent, is something entirely negative, and should be eliminated and avoided. By way of contrast, Hebrew Biblical prophets and even Jesus in many New Testament passages endorse a positive and necessary view of legitimate anger, righteous indignation at how human beings are behaving and mistreating others, and this is an appropriate response to injustice, not as an end in itself but as a constructive force of transformation.

Another dimension of violence essential to religious and other forms of violence is linguistic violence. Language can be very violent. It can be used as a tool to control, dominate, intimidate, humiliate, and oppress other human beings. Despite all of its teachings about non-violence, love, compassion, and peace, religious language is in fact often extremely violent. It is frequently used in a hierarchical manner of control and domination expressed through class, caste, gender, tribal, racial, ethnic, and national relations, is employed to instil guilt and shame and to dehumanize others as sinners as well as evil, and functions in ways that incite believers and legitimatize war and violence against non-believers.

One of my main concerns is economic violence. Violence is often equivalent to exploitation. We have violent economic relations in which some people have the power through the control of the industrial and the financial capital, the land, the oil and other natural resources, the technology, the media, etc. They can use such economic power in asymmetrical unjust relations of domination to exploit and oppress other human beings. For thousands of years to the present, religions of the world have established mutually beneficial relations with those with such economic power and have provided religious justification for unequal power relations that express structures of economic violence. In this regard, religions have been used to pacify the exploited and oppressed. They have been instructed not to revolt against their oppressors and told that their acceptance of their unfortunate situation in the world will be rewarded in heaven or in their next earthly existence. Of course, religions have also included those who rebelled against the conditions of economic exploitation, slave labour, poverty, hunger, and homelessness and saw it as a religious obligation to resist such economic violence.

We can also talk about cultural violence, social violence, political violence, and educational violence. And, as is evident from the history of religions and also religions in the contemporary world, one can draw a long list of diverse forms of specific religious violence.

We are socialized into a world in which linguistic, social, psychological, economic, educational, religious, and other dimensions of violence interact and mutually reinforce each other. We are thus socialized to accept religious and non-religious violent modes of being in the world; violent ways of relating to ourselves, to others, and to nature. Therefore, the multidimensionality of violence is one concept to keep in mind as we go through the analysis of religion and violence today, since religion shares and incorporates all of these varied dimensions of violence.

The second concept is of the violence of the status quo as expressed through structural violence. This is violence that we usually do not even recognize as being violent. It is part of our "normal" economic, political, cultural, religious, ideological world; it is business as usual. Hundreds of millions of human beings suffer from this passively and silently. They do not actively resist or actively assert themselves because they live in fear, feel powerless, feel hopeless, and often accept their suffering as the result of some religious or secular justification. But this is not a non-violent situation. As Martin Luther King, Jr. repeatedly tells us, there is no peace without justice. A seemingly passive, unjust, oppressive situation is in fact very violent. As the Buddha, Marx, Gandhi, and countless others have pointed out, our normal, ordinary, everyday, structural world of status quo relations is usually a world of alienation, dehumanization, powerlessness, domination, humanly caused suffering, lack of ethical and spiritual development and well-being, and, in short, of great violence.

The status quo systemic economic relations, when they are functioning smoothly without internal or external disruption, are very violent. Similarly, the status quo technological relations, when they are instrumentally functioning effectively to provide the means for domination and control over other beings and nature, are also very violent. The status quo social, cultural, psychological, educational, legal, religious, and other dominant relations, when they are functioning effectively to produce a surfacial structured context of apparent law and order, peace and non-violence, disguise what is in reality a very violent situation. Indeed, tension, conflict, and disruption of the status quo of structural violence may be much closer to the realization of non-violence, peace, justice, and liberation than the ordinary socialization and unquestioning acceptance of the dominant, religious and non-religious, multidimensional, violent orientations and worldviews.

So, once again, this is crucial for a deeper analysis of religion and violence. For thousands of years, traditional religions – with their religious, hierarchical, institutionalized arrangements – have been an essential part of the violent status quo and have provided ideological justifications for the violence of the status quo. As was noted, they frequently tell religious followers that if you have faith and suffer silently, "peacefully", without resistance and struggle, you will go to heaven or be reborn to a better karmic situation in the next life. There are numerous diverse kinds of religious teachings, techniques, rewards and punishments that function to justify the dominant, violent status quo.

Of course, as was pointed out with the multidimensionality of violence, there is also a long religious history in which reformers, revolutionaries, prophets, and other adherents saw it as essential to their religious commitment that religion critique and challenge the violent status quo as unjust, evil, and ungodly or anti-religious. These are some of the most admired figures in the history of religions, even if their followers and institutionalized religions usually ignored or marginalized their radical messages and made their peace with the multidimensional violent status quo.

Religion

The other key term in the chapter title is "religion". I worked very closely with a famous, controversial scholar of religion named Mircea Eliade, and I wrote extensively about his phenomenology of religion and his interpretation of religious symbolism and religious myth. There was a period, especially in the 1960s and 1970s, when Eliade was often described as the world's most influential theorist of religion. Here, I will present very briefly a universal model of religion, influenced greatly by Eliade's writings, which will be helpful for analyzing the topic of religion and violence today. I would not restrict my formulation to the word "God" or several other terms central to the Hebraic and western religious traditions because there are other religious traditions that use different religious language.

What follows is a necessarily oversimplified, universal, structural model of religion that is useful for distinguishing religious from non-religious or secular approaches and views. From this religious perspective, non-religious human beings live in a one-dimensional world. Secular human beings define themselves as spatial, temporal, historical, natural, finite, conditioned, limited, imperfect human beings. Religious people, by contrast, recognize another, qualitatively different, sacred dimension of reality that they distinguish from that secular or "profane" world. "Profane" is used here in the descriptive sense, as used by Durkheim, Caillois, Eliade, and other scholars, to denote what is secular or not religious and not in the normative sense of impure and defiled. Religious people recognize a transcendent dimension of reality that is described in terms of God, soul, heaven, immortality, and in numerous other ways.

This sacred transcendent dimension of reality is viewed as supernatural not natural, eternal not temporal, infinite not finite, and absolute not relative. Sociologically, all religions have taboos and other prohibitions and punishments to separate and keep pure the sacred transcendent dimension of reality.

The key point is that religion always has this two-dimensional view in which it affirms the qualitatively different, sacred, transcendent dimension of ultimate reality. It is important to note that such religious terms as the devil, Satan, and evil are not secular or profane terms. They are sacred. Sacred does not necessarily mean good. There are negative, violent, sacred forces that transcend our normal spatial, temporal, empirical, natural, historical categories; they express supernatural evil power beyond the ordinary natural and human.

In this study, the central focus on transcendence, on the mode of being and structures for transcending the secular or profane and gaining access to the transcendent sacred, is meant to be descriptive and not to endorse some theological or metaphysical claim about the nature of worldly existence and ultimate reality.

Religious believers, of course, do have such normative views; otherwise they would not be religious. However, this study is meant to suspend all such value judgements about the truth and falsity of religious claims and to be descriptive. It is formulated in the sense of a sociological description of the human existence of religious persons in this world and in the philosophical sense of a phenomenological description of the essential, general, defining structures of religious experience and religious phenomena.

In the religious model, the sacred always transcends the profane, but the two dimensions have to be brought into some integral dialectical relation in order to have religious experience and religion. In other words, the sacred has to be made accessible to our finite, empirical, cultural world; otherwise it is just an irrelevant abstraction with no existential relation to our worldly needs, crises, and economic, political, psychological and cultural modes of being. That is what religion is.

Religio points to this way of relating – of relating the transcendent sacred to our ordinarily finite, natural, limited, secular world. In other words, the transcendent sacred must always be mediated, made imminent, and brought into an integral existential relation with our everyday contextualized world. In this regard, religious language, as seen in religious symbolism and myth, provides such a mediating function, serving as a bridge between the transcendent sacred and imminent secular phenomenal world.

This universal sacred-profane, dichotomous, mediated structure expresses a kind of paradoxical relationship true of any religion. It is paradoxical and rationally incomprehensible to the ordinary, secular, spatial, temporal, historical, natural, logical mind. The familiar model of Jesus as the Christ – how can we understand God becoming man, i.e., how can we understand eternal and infinite God as the absolute taking a human form that suffers, appears in time and history, etc.? – is true structurally of every religious manifestation. Structurally, it is just as paradoxical, mysterious, irrational, or illogical to the non-religious mind to try to comprehend how the transcendent supernatural sacred reality could appear in a stone or tree or other limited natural phenomenon, in a human vision or dream, or in finite limited human language. How could something eternal take temporal form? How could something transcendent become imminent and assume a limited incarnational form? Or, what amounts to the same paradoxical relation, how can some limited, finite, spatial, temporal, natural, relative, historical phenomenon reveal that which is infinite, supernatural, eternal and absolute?

In sum, the transcendent sacred, the supernatural, the divine, etc., have to be brought into some existential meaningful paradoxical relation with our finite world as an essential structure in all religious experience and in all religions.

I will just add one of several other structures of this universal phenomenological model. If you are a religious person, you not only recognize the distinction between these two dimensions of experience that are paradoxically mediated. There is also a built-in evaluation. The really real, the ultimate reality, is the sacred, whether this is God, Allah, Brahman, Soul, Nirvana, or some other description. The sacred and the profane are not symmetrical structures that exist on the same level of reality. The sacred provides religious people with the ultimate truths about transcendent reality. This can be revealed through the Bible, the Koran, the Vedas, the Pali Canon, cosmological and eschatological myths, or other scriptures; through a founder, prophet, mystic, or other transmitter of sacred truths; through miracles, through nature, and in numerous other ways.

In all cases, that sacred dimension for the religious believer is something special, transcendent, revealing the nature of ultimate reality. So, there is an evaluation of the sacred as the really real and as providing the standards for how you should live your life in this world of imperfection, suffering, evil, and violence.

Religion as a destructive and negative force with regard to violence

We are all conscious – from hearing our politicians, reading the daily newspaper, watching television, and using the internet – of the violent threatening forces of militant Islamic fundamentalism portrayed as fanatical terrorism. We consistently hear about violent *jihad*. It is important to recognize that there are forms of militant Islam today that are very violent. One can interpret and evaluate them in different ways, but everyone agrees that they are very violent, even if some provide a religious explanation and justification for such violence.

This violent religious form is true of all militant fundamentalisms. The fastest growing religions throughout the world and in the United States are forms of religious fundamentalism and certain other militant, evangelical, and other conservative religious approaches.

For example, one could present the situation in India with militant *Hindutva* forces, violent Hindu-Muslim communal riots, and violent attacks by Pakistani and Kashmiri Muslims. One could present the three decades of violent civil war in Sri Lanka, ideologically explained and justified on religious grounds by the warring Sinhala Buddhist and Tamil Hindu sides. One could present the ongoing religious violence in Iraq, Iran and Afghanistan. And, of course, there are so many examples of such religious violence in Israel-Palestine and throughout the Middle East. I will simply discuss very briefly religious violence in the United States, since US politicians, religious leaders, and media usually exclude this from their frequent alarming presentations of religion and violence in the world.

Some of the most violent and powerful religious forces in the world today are located in the United States. One can analyze fundamentalist and other militant political and religious influences shaping violent political, economic, and cultural priorities and policies. The often-dominant US view – shared by some politicians and economic and religious leaders and by many of their followers and typical of religious-political views found throughout the world – assumes that we, the believers, have an exclusive pipeline to the truth, goodness, and reality.

The religious and non-religious others are not just wrong but evil and are a threat to the truth, goodness, and the survival of our faith. In addition, such an approach, often with a militant, western, Christian foundation, not only does not fear violence and war, but it even welcomes them as part of a necessary eschatological path toward an apocalyptic vision of salvation. It is most revealing that in the US today, the strongest lobby for war and violence is the militant Christian Right. These believers have often served as the most loyal and dedicated foot soldiers for the Republican Party. They really believe that they are on a mission from God. It is a present-day Crusade.

This is no mystery. If you look at what the Pat Robertsons, the Jerry Falwells, and others who are leaders in the multi-billion-dollar Christian Right empire say and write, they are very open about the necessity for and virtue of political and religious violence. They are the strongest supporters of US nuclear superiority. They are the strongest supporters of the death penalty. They are the strongest supporters of the invasion and occupation of Iraq and Afghanistan and nuclear or other military strikes against Iran. They are the strongest supporters of a militant Israel as a divinely ordained, necessary, preliminary stage in their Christian theology. They are the most explicitly anti-Muslim in their orientation, defining Islam in the most ungenerous and degrading terms as a false religion and as a violent threat.

The most alarming thing, in terms of the topic of religion and violence, is that most threatening prospects that would trouble or scare most of us – such as genocide, global war, nuclear holocaust, unimaginable conflagration, rapid climate change with the destruction of life on this planet – they welcome. They often cite their peculiar interpretation of some passages in the *Book of Revelation* and other theological sources to proclaim that we are going to have to go through hell, to endure the deaths of hundreds of millions of innocent human beings, because that is a precondition of the Second Coming. They use terms like "End Time" and the "Rapture".

This is not something to be feared or dreaded. As with other illustrations from the history of religions, such extreme violence is viewed as glorious, blissful, and ecstatic, since it is necessary for personal and worldly purification and ultimate salvation. That is because true believers know that they will be among those chosen for eternal salvation; they will go to heaven, while the rest of us will go to hell. One finds other versions of this religious narrative in some forms of contemporary Islam, various religious constructions that present exemplary models of martyrdom, and diverse indigenous and worldly religions that embrace other violent religious accounts.

What needs to be emphasized when examining religion as a destructive negative force is the following major danger, evident throughout the history of religions and increasingly on the rise today: Hundreds of millions of religious people have faith and are absolutely certain that they have the only pipeline to the sacred, and they are prepared to use any means necessary, including violence and war, to defend and spread their belief in their one true reality. They know what the sacred is, the true infallible nature of the divine, and what God has decreed and commanded us to do. The rest of us, who are not the true believers, do not possess such truth of ultimate reality. Such faith and certainty about exclusive, absolute, sacred truth can then be used to justify violence. One recalls the old Bob Dylan song "With God on Our Side". If you know that God is on your side and not on the side of the other, and you have a direct and even perfect channel to God, this allows you to justify all kinds of violence that you would not be able to justify in ethical and other human or secular terms.

In such religious approaches, one finds an analysis with a sharp Manichean dichotomy – religiously and politically – between good and evil. Any religion that makes such a clear-cut, absolute dichotomy between good and evil invariably rejects the view that it is evil and instead upholds the view that we the religious believers are good, and the other, not believing what we do, is evil.

Now, with such a worldview, how does one relate to the forces of evil? It was very important for President George W. Bush to coin the term "axis of evil" in his influential State of the Union Address on January 29, 2002. You can deal with disagreement, hate, conflict, etc., but evil is a theological term focusing on the sacred ground of reality. How do you deal with evil? Do you compromise with evil? Do you assuage evil? Do you tolerate evil? Or, do you destroy evil? In such a religious framework, evil is usually viewed as a kind of cancer that not only threatens religious purity but also destroy the true religion unless it is eradicated. If you do not destroy this cancer, it will destroy you.

This is not a necessary move even among religious, social and political positions that embrace this model of our diseased or cancerous condition that needs to be rid of its impurities. For example, no religious tradition has placed more emphasis on ritual purity than Hinduism. Unlike various Hindu idealizers and apologists, as well as interpreters, I do not accept that real, historical, contextualized Hinduism is simply and only a philosophy and religion of non-violence, peace, love, and compassion. One can find the strong central affirmation of such concepts and virtues in

Hinduism, but at the same time one can also find considerable violence expressed through sacred myths and rituals, class and caste domination, gender oppression, military conquests and coercive political rule, oppressive family and other social relations, and hierarchical systems of rewards and punishments. Nevertheless, even with their model of the human worldly condition as diseased with impurities and requiring religious purification, Hinduism, Buddhism, Jainism, and other philosophical and religious traditions of India have been remarkably tolerant, pluralistic, inclusivistic, and non-violent when, say, compared with dominant religious traditions in the West.

An excellent, dramatic, more recent illustration of this can be found in the philosophy and religion of Mahatma Gandhi. In his writings, especially in his most influential book *Hind Swaraj*, Gandhi even classifies the modern civilization that has dominated the West as a violent, impure, diseased condition. No political and social thinker and activist focuses more on the need for purification than does Gandhi, both his own self-purification and the purification of his followers (*satyagrahis*, or adherents holding firm to truth force, soul force, love force) as essential for ethical and spiritual practice. This commitment to truth and non-violence requires control of the body, the passions, and the mind, courage, fearlessness, and tremendous sacrifice.

But for Gandhi this purification process of sacrifice, eliminating impurities in the transformative overcoming of our diseased or cancerous condition, involves non-violent self-sacrifice and not the violent sacrifice of others.

It is possible to show that even among religions that claim to have the one, exclusive, absolute truth and the only solution to our diseased world of evil, such religious violence does not necessarily follow. We have long traditions in the history of religion in which such believers are socialized to feel pity for those unfortunate beings lacking the religious truth and living lives of sin and evil. One may reach out to them with tolerance, non-violence, and love, with the goal of converting them by showing them the obvious truth, goodness, desirability, and promised eternal reward if they only embrace one's absolute, exclusive, sacred truth.

Nevertheless, throughout history, religions that have adopted such a clear-cut dichotomous position of we, the possessors of truth and goodness, versus the others, the possessors untruth and evil, have all too easily resorted to intolerance, violence, and war in the name of their God or sacred reality. This is the mindset that is dominating so much of religion in the world today. It is a major force contributing to the perpetuation of escalating violence.

It is important to recognize that the illustrations in this section – religion as a destructive and negative force with regard to violence – have tended to bring out examples of overt, explicit, physical violence in their violent language, myths, rituals, ideologies, theologies, and practices. These illustrations have the advantage, not only in being so dramatic and influential in the contemporary world, but also in illustrating in clear-cut terms examples of religious violence.

However, in recalling the analysis in the section on violence, we must recognize that most violence in the world does not take such a clear-cut, overt, physical form. The overall situation of religion, violence, and religious violence is much more subtle, nuanced, contradictory, and complex. Most religious believers will still affirm that they and their religion believe in peace, love, and non-violence, and violence, by way of contrast, is what other traditions, religions, nations, and people endorse.

This is why, it is necessary to expand our view of violence in general and religious violence in particular. When we include the many dimensions of linguistic, psychological, economic, social, political, educational, and environmental violence and the dominant structural violence of the status quo, then, we greatly expand and deepen our analysis of religious violence as a destructive and negative force in the world.

At this point, it is tempting to conclude that religion is an essential part of the problem, the crisis, of so much violence in the world today; it is not part of the solution. However, we must now consider the question as to whether religion can also be a positive constructive force with regard to violence in the world.

Religion as a constructive and positive force with regard to violence

One can certainly find numerous resources in the history of religions that criticize violence, war, humanly caused suffering, greed, selfishness, hate, intolerance, injustice, oppression and exploitation. The Bible, the Koran, the Hindu scriptures, the teachings of Buddha and Confucius, and other scriptures and sacred texts are full of ethical and spiritual passages praising peacemakers and promoting non-violence, justice, compassion, loving kindness, tolerance, charity, and selfless service to overcome poverty and suffering. One can cite recent leaders, such as Mahatma Gandhi, Martin Luther King, Jr. and the Dalai Lama, who were and are deeply religious and have lived remarkable lives inspiring millions of people to embrace constructive and positive values with regard to non-violence.

For example, the Jewish Bible contains the profound teachings of the prophets emphasizing the imperative of living our lives based on a commitment to justice and to end war, to turn swords into plowshares, to serve those in need, and to achieve harmonious, just, and peaceful relations on earth. The Sermon on the Mount contains some of the most profound teachings on love, how unearned suffering can be both transformative and redemptive, and how we should identify with the needs of the poor and the downtrodden. The Koran repeatedly upholds the importance of justice and charity in our human relations. The Buddhist Four Blessed Dispositions emphasize profound ethical and spiritual teachings on loving kindness, compassion, sympathetic joy, and equanimity or balanced serenity. In all of these key religious teachings, as well as numerous other examples, there is a strong and clear warning about and rejection of the kinds of religious violence that are so prevalent in today's world.

In recent years, I have been doing much of my research and lecturing on the philosophy of Mahatma Gandhi, so I will just share a little of what Gandhi says relevant to our topic. Gandhi, the best-known proponent of non-violence in the twentieth century, writes at length about religious violence and is very critical of much of historical, traditional, hierarchical, institutionalized religion responsible for causing and justifying so much violence and suffering.

For Gandhi there is much truth in religion, especially at its heart or essential foundation, and one should be proud of what is best in one's own religion. But one must recognize that all religions contain both negative and positive features in their historical and institutional forms, and one should be humble while reflecting critically on one's own religion, acting to correct its defects, and working for its ethical and spiritual development.

Gandhi upholds an organic, holistic view emphasizing the interrelatedness of all of life. Truth, which he often equates with God, is that unifying ethical and spiritual force that allows us to engage in meaningful relations with other living beings, nature, and spiritual reality. For Gandhi, true philosophy and religion must be grounded in *ahimsa* or non-violence, which he often equates with love.

Religious, economic, political, and other forms of violence lead to more violence and trap us in endless causal cycles of violence. This is similar to Hindu and other Indian views of the cause and effect relations of the law of *karma*. This is similar to the Buddha's foundational teaching of the Doctrine of Dependent Origination (Conditioned Genesis) in which every phenomenal spoke or element in this impermanent worldly wheel of causation is itself caused by relative antecedent conditions and itself becomes a causal factor leading to new effects. Religious and other forms of non-violence and love break the vicious destructive cycles of violence.

According to Gandhi, violence is not only unethical since it leads to more violence, but it also violates truth, God and reality. It emphasizes essential differences, since the dehumanized other, who is evil and is the target of My violence, is falsely viewed as fundamentally unlike Me and my religion or group and as a threat to our true faith.

Non-violence and love, on the other hand, are not only ethical since they embrace positive moral values and intentions and lead to more positive moral results, but they are also consistent with truth, God and reality. Non-violence, love, compassion, responses to suffering, and egoless service to meet the needs of others, are the unifying forces that not only hold us together but also bring us into relations emphasizing the interrelatedness of life and the view that what unites or unifies us as part of the meaningful organic whole is more fundamental than what divides us. Gandhi, of course, recognizes that in the history of religions, as well as in para-religious and pseudo-religious political and social phenomena, there are numerous illustrations of how religious, non-religious, nationalistic, and other forms of violence can also be a bonding and unifying force.

However, for Gandhi, such violent bonding produces negative consequence – not only for the harmed others who are the target of the violence but also for those believers who embrace the violence – and such violent bonding is based on illusion and ignorance, a false sense of unstable unity, since it is based on a worldview constructed from a fundamental division and dichotomy in which the other is inferior, unethical, evil, and not like us. Such a violent illusory bonding contradicts the true, underlying, metaphysical, ontological, and spiritual reality of the essential interrelatedness and unity of all human beings and all of life.

Gandhi makes a basic distinction between the absolute truth and the relative truth. As a religious or spiritual human being, Gandhi certainly upholds absolute ideals, such as truth, God, self or soul, non-violence, love, and religion.

However, Gandhi submits that human beings – including himself – as finite, limited, fallible beings with embodied consciousness in a socialized contextualized world, at most have "glimpses" of the Absolute. We are relative beings moving at best from one relative truth to greater relative truth. No one fully knows truth or God or the Absolute, including absolute non-violence and love. Even when we uphold absolute ideals of non-violence, we cannot avoid all violence, especially when we regard it as multidimensional and as expressing the structural violence of the status quo. A major danger, as seen in the history of religions, is to turn our relative truths into the absolute truth. Anyone who then rejects our view of "the Truth" has false views, is a sinner, is evil, and must be opposed, even if this sometimes requires war and violence.

For Gandhi, religious persons should uphold their higher ethical and spiritual ideals and should be proud of what is best in their relative formulations, but they should also recognize that other people and other religions have their own relative truths; their own relative imperfect paths to the Absolute. This is the basis for Gandhi's famous non-exclusive, non-violent tolerance, which involves not just tolerating but respecting what is admirable in other ethical and religious positions, and which emphasizes legitimate diversity and pluralism that is grounded in an underlying interreligious and intercultural interrelatedness and unity.

Indeed, for Gandhi, other religious paths have truths that we do not have, and we can even learn from them in the sense that our openness in relating to others can serve as an invaluable catalyst in allowing us to rethink and deepen our own ethical and spiritual position and in allowing us to work cooperatively with others for a more harmonious, non-violent, and peaceful future.

Conclusions

Where does this leave us with respect to the complex relations of religion and violence and the prevalence of so much religious violence in the contemporary world? There are no simple answers. I will end by formulating two general interpretive models or frameworks that are helpful for comprehending major relations and points regarding religion, violence, and religious violence today. I will then suggest five concluding proposals for relating to the crises of religion and violence.

The *first* general framework incorporates the previously outlined universal, philosophical, structural, phenomenological model of religion. As was proposed, religion always reveals some specific religious structure of transcendence. This qualitatively unique transcendent sacred is distinguished from the normal, everyday, spatial, temporal, natural, historical, finite, limited, relative, profane or secular dimension of our worldly mode of being and consciousness. In all religious experience and phenomena, there is also the existential human need to connect or relate these two dimensions of the sacred transcendent reality and our worldly profane or secular phenomena.

This sacred-profane dichotomy and connection, necessary for any religion and for any religious phenomena to be humanly accessible and relevant, are expressed through complex, unique, paradoxical relations. In such dichotomous, paradoxical relations, religious believers evaluate the sacred transcendent as the ultimate reality and as providing the exemplary model and norms for how to live and assess our worldly existence.

In such a phenomenological and sociological framework, all religions and religious believers encounter the following key questions: What is the nature and status of the transcendent sacred? What is the nature and status of the human, natural, secular or profane, phenomenal world? What is the nature and status of the "bridges" or structural connections between the sacred and the phenomenal world as expressed through foundational teachings, scriptures, myths, rituals, institutionalized arrangements, moral codes, social structures, and dreams, visions, ecstatic and other religious experiences? Put in different terms, what are the acceptable means, allowing religious believers to approach and realize the acceptance ends, and how do we formulate the dynamic means-ends relations?

If we examine the history of religions and the presence of religion in the world today, we find a tremendous variation in how traditional religions and individual religious believers answer these questions. This is insightful when trying to unpack the endless patterns, complexities, and contradictions in religious responses revealing different ideals, attitudes, intentions, and practices with regard to violence and religious violence.

With such variations, I cannot overemphasize the following conclusion at the heart of our topic on the relation of religion and violence: There is nothing inherent in or entailed by our universal phenomenological model of religion that would allow us to claim that religions must necessarily be non-violent or violent. This applies to all of the major structures and patterns in our phenomenological model. This means that instead of prejudging whether religion is essentially violent or essentially non-violent, one must always contextualize the general phenomenological structures and patterns and analyze their complex, dynamic interactions and relations with the numerous, particular, economic, social, cultural, religious, and other contextualized variables.

Consider the transcendent sacred. Religions can embrace a view of the sacred transcendent reality as absolute non-violence, peace, love, compassion, tolerance, and inclusiveness, or they can embrace a view of the sacred transcendent as expressing considerable violence, war-like virtues, destructive power, anger, jealousy, and intolerant exclusivism. One can find numerous variations of these views of sacred transcendent reality, as well as mixtures of them, as contextualized in all kinds of ways in scriptures, myths, rituals, and institutionalized constructions throughout the history of religions and the contemporary world.

Consider our human, worldly, natural, temporal, historical, profane or secular mode of existence. In various religious conceptions, human nature, as reflected in human existence, may be formulated as inherently or essentially evil, as basically good, or as a mixture of good and evil. We cannot prejudge this in some essentialized a priori manner based on a universal phenomenological model. Different religions and religious believers will provide different answers, and their real religious beliefs and practices will be integrated within and shaped by their specific contextualized variables.

For example, if a religion views human beings as essentially sinful and evil, then it will be more likely to uphold the necessity and legitimacy of violence – in socialized interacting multidimensional forms, as part of the normal structured status quo, and as involving overt physical responses and punishments – both internally toward the evil temptations and transgressions of its own members and externally with aggression and defence against the threats of non-believing evil others.

Consider the paradoxical connections or bridges relating the sacred and the profane, the supernatural and the natural, the transcendent and the worldly imminent. Based on the phenomenological model, one cannot prejudge whether such religious connections, necessary for rendering the transcendent sacred accessible and relevant in responding to our existential crises and human needs, will be violent or non-violent.

In some religious traditions and contemporary illustrations, the connecting language, symbolism, myths, rituals, rites of passages, initiations, and economic and social practices may be strongly shaped by a religious commitment to peace, love, compassion, serving the needs of the most unfortunate, etc., and they tend to be very non-violent. In other religious traditions and contemporary illustrations, all of these connecting bridges may be very violent, reflecting the structural violence of the status quo, expressing multi-dimensional violence, and even in terms responding to overwhelming displays of overt supernatural and natural violence.

Using such an approach for interpreting and applying the first phenomenological and sociological framework is helpful for addressing many of the major issues and debates regarding religion, philosophy of religion, sociology of religion, and religious violence. For example, if a religious tradition conceives of God, the transcendent sacred, as the absolute, perfect, omniscient, omnipotent, omnibenevolent reality and if it also conceives of our limited, finite, worldly existence as partially or totally evil, how do we reconcile these two religious claims in a coherent and plausible way?

This is the traditional problem of evil, with a long history of religious attempts to provide connections or relational bridges between these two conceptions of the sacred and the profane, God and evil in the world, and which sometimes involves modifying the sacred or the profane formulations. This can be formulated in a similar way as a religious problem of violence. If a religious tradition conceives of such an absolute, perfect, all-knowing, all-powerful, and all-good God, as the sacred transcendent reality, how can this be connected consistently and convincingly with the existence of so much destructive, religious and non-religious violence in the world?

The *second* model or framework focuses on patterns of causal relations. Recognizing that there is considerable violence, in general, and religious violence, in particular, what is the causal relation between religion and violence in the contemporary world?

Such a question can be expanded in the following manner: What is the causal relation between religion and religious phenomena and economic, political, state, military, social, cultural, media, and other violent, non-religious phenomena in today's violent world? Is religion the basic cause, with religious violence an essential determinant of worldly violence, or is religion more of a symptom and an effect of more fundamental economic, political, and other causal, non-religious violence?

One usually finds extremely polarized responses expressing inverted asymmetrical causal relations. On the one hand, there is a long tradition in the history of religions, continuing in religions today, that abstracts the real or true religion from all worldly violence. In such common apologetic and idealized responses, religion has to do with peace, love, compassion, kindness, justice, and other virtues and ideals.

Worldly phenomena of violence, war, hatred, intolerance, selfishness, injustice, even when practised by so-called religious believers, are really perversions of religions and opposed to the religions' essential ideals and moral and spiritual teachings. In this sense, to use an extreme but common example, religious believers repeatedly claim that Muslim, Christian, Jewish, Hindu, Buddhist, and other terrorists have nothing to do with Islam, Christianity, Judaism, Hinduism, Buddhism, and other religions. Their terrorism and other forms of violence can be attributed to worldly, secular, political, nationalist, economic, and other non-religious causes, and such violence has nothing to do with what religion really is.

On the other hand, there is a strong tradition, especially prevalent in the post-Enlightenment modern world of scholarship, that views religion as a dangerous cause of ignorance, superstition, illusion, pre-modern and anti-modern backwardness and irrationality, leading to so much humanly-caused violence and suffering in the contemporary world. Those who interpret religious violence as a primary relational cause often point to religious wars, religious communal conflicts, religious terrorism, militant religious fundamentalism, religious hierarchical gendered and other relations of domination, religious educational indoctrination or socialization models and practices, and the like.

Such contemporary illustrations of violence lead to the conclusion that religion, with its diverse powerful forces of religious violence, is a basic causal determinant of so much violence in today's world.

My own view is that these two antithetical responses to the causal relations of religion, violence, and religious violence tend to be overly simplified, one-sided, reductionistic, non-dialectical, inadequate accounts. They fail to recognize how the dynamic, real, contextualized relations between religion and violence, with the recognition of real religious violence, are very complex, often hidden, contradictory, multidimensional, and transformative.

My own interpretation of the causal pattern is that the basic relations are indeed asymmetrical, but they are not static or invariable in the religion-violence phenomenal structures. On the one hand, if you examine violence today, the most basic and powerful determinants are economic and also political, military, and other non-religious or worldly causes. These primary causes are not religious or specifically, irreducibly, or uniquely religious. Even when examining the difficult cases of, say, self-professed Islamic or other terrorists identifying with religious orientations, it is usually most instructive to ask why other human beings, who are so much like us as human, turn to terrorism that we find so unethical, inhumane, and destructive. It is only when one examines basic contextual causes, forces, and conditions of poverty, lack of education, health care and decent work, sense of cultural humiliation by more powerful outsiders and occupiers, sense of hopelessness with no meaningful alternatives, etc., that we begin to understand why these often intelligent, sensitive, and proud individuals turn to terrorism. The usual alternative, which is often self-serving and not very instructive, is simply to categorize and dismiss them as evil.

This does not mean that religion is irrelevant in this dominant, non-religious, causal relation determining violence in the world. Religion, for example, in many contexts of such dominant worldly violence, provides solace, escapes, hopes, and at times ideological and theological explanations and justifications for the violent suffering of believers, the violent self-sacrifice of resisters, and the infliction of violence on others.

On the other hand, in this dynamic, asymmetrical, causal, relational model, what is usually a secondary force can, under specific contextual conditions, become the primary causal determinant. In other words, religion can become the primary cause of violence that most influences economic, political, state, educational, environmental, and other forms of violence.

Religious violence can become the major causal form of violence. This is most apparent in relations in which religious believers are willing to act in such ways as to sacrifice their worldly economic, political, and other interests. For example, because of certain scriptural and other religious teachings, religious believers may engage in religious violence involving their own self-sacrifice, suffering, and death, to reject economic and social and educational opportunities offered by their dominant societies, and to inflict suffering and even death on family members, neighbours, homosexuals, other races, class and caste victims, and others violating their religious beliefs and values.

What this means is that in a complex, causal, dialectical framework, one must view religion and violence neither as detached abstractions nor as generalized categories to be evaluated positively or negatively. In dealing with real contemporary religion and violence, one must always examine real, dynamic, ever-changing situations and contexts with multiple complex relations, problems, and solutions. In most situations, it is instructive to view religion and religious violence as symptoms and consequences of more basic, non-religious causal determinants of violence. In other situations, with transformations that can be analyzed and understood, religion and religious violence may be viewed as the major or primary causal determinants of contemporary violence. And, in all such contexts of religion and violence, it is important to analyze the dynamic, complex, interacting, and mutually defining and influencing relations between religious and non-religious phenomena, in general, and between religious and non-religious violence, in particular.

We may end with five concluding proposals. *First*, religion in the US and throughout the contemporary world is more of a negative and destructive force when it comes to conflicts of violence and war. Religion is more of the problem than the solution. However, as seen in the previous section, religion can also be a positive and constructive force emphasizing non-violence, love, compassion, tolerance, respect, freedom, human rights, non-violence, and peace. What we find in every society, culture, and religion is the dynamic, contradictory, creative and destructive tensions that involve contestation, resistance, and struggle. Every religion has war makers and peacemakers: those who promote religious intolerance, hatred, and violence and those dedicated to religious tolerance, non-violence, compassion, and loving kindness; those who use religion to justify injustice, exploitation, and the destruction of nature and those dedicated to the struggle for justice, freedom from exploitation and oppression, and the sanctity of all life and the planet earth. In short, every real religion contains both negative and positive features, even if the violent and destructive religious forces have been predominant in the contemporary world.

Second, if we are to relate to real religion and real religious violence, we must have a dynamic, flexible, open-ended approach for analyzing the complex relations that hold between texts, contexts, and interpretations of meaning. Such relations involve religious and non-religious texts, religious and non-religious contexts, and religious and non-religious interpretations of meaning. In such an approach, we find that all religions in the world involve numerous real contradictions, including contradictions involving violence and non-violence. When we contextualize religion, which is necessary for analyzing real religion and real religious violence, and when we do not treat religion as a collection of detached, non-contextualized, abstract, absolute, spiritual and ethical truths and ideals, we can then address all kinds of economic, class, caste, gender, racial, ethnic, environmental and other contradictions that shape real religions. Using such an approach, we find that religions use and manipulate all kinds of sacred, transcendent ideals and teachings as justifications for class exploitation, wealth and power, domination, sexism, homophobia, racism, injustice, violence, and war.

Third, we face the most urgent personal, existential, and global crises related to the topic of religion and violence. These crises provide numerous opportunities for contradictory responses by religious and non-religious persons. Unlike my experiences in the Civil Rights Movements, in which religious voices were central, and in the Vietnam/Indo-China Anti-war Movement and other struggles, in which religious voices were important, I have found that progressive religious peace and justice voices in the United States have usually been barely audible, marginalized, or completely silent in the context of the aggressively violent post-9/11 War on Terror, the Iraq and Afghanistan invasions and occupations, and other illustrations of violence and religious violence cited in this chapter. By way of extreme contrast, the violent, warmongering, religious voices have been loud, aggressive, and central to the economic, political, and military power structure. For those who are religious or work with people who are religious around issues of violence and who do not want simply to dismiss religion as a negative force in the world today, we must contextualize in the real world the positive religious and non-religious values of non-violence, love, compassion, peace, and justice. As part of this process, we must use these positive values to engage and resist those negative religious forces promoting violence, hatred, greed, injustice and war.

Fourth, what this means is that those who are religious, or are non-religious but are concerned about religion and violence, can be part of the problem or part of the solution. One can be part of religions that are perpetuating violence, justifying violent conflict and war, all over the world today and threaten to destroy humankind. Or one can choose to do nothing and thereby be complicit in perpetuating the life-threatening religious violence of the status quo and religious violence as part of linguistic, economic, political, cultural, militaristic, imperialistic violence that dominates so much of our lives and our world. Or, one can identify with religious and non-religious orientations with pro-active positions that are dedicated to exposing and resisting religious violence throughout the world and in providing constructive non-violent alternatives

Finally, Mahatma Gandhi offers a profound view of human and cosmic evolution that provides guidance when dealing with religion, violence, and religious violence. As human beings, we have a lower nature and a higher nature; values, motives, and actions that represent our brute nature and others that bring out our ethical and spiritual potential.

History books and media reports falsely emphasize that ends justify means, that might makes right, and that the survival of the fittest is determined by those with the most economic and violent power. Gandhi submits that human beings have developed and survived because of our capacity to be touched by and respond to the suffering and needs of others; to live lives full of compassion and loving kindness; and to base our lives on ethical and spiritual principles and actions committed to truth and non-violence.

Religion can tap into our brute nature, our worst nature, and thus become part of the problem of so much violence, hatred, intolerance, and war that causes and justifies so much preventable death and suffering and threatens the survival of humankind and the earth. Or religion can tap into our best nature, dimensions of our higher ethical and spiritual development, and thus become a constructive force in dealing with religion and violence in the contemporary world.

CHAPTER 2

Changing Interpretations of Religion and Secularism*

SHERRY SABBARWAL

The study of religion has enjoyed the attention of philosophers from the beginning. However, when it comes to sociology, the earliest and illustrious writings came from the founding fathers of sociology itself: Marx, Weber and Durkheim. All three thinkers' writings were reactions to the economic and social turmoil occurring in late nineteenth and early twentieth centuries, on account of the terrible consequences that speedy industrialization had caused in their respective societies. At this juncture, the study of religion became almost imperative as religion was seen as an essential part of the society that appeared to be transforming beyond recognition (O'Toole, 1984). Each writer, however, tackled the subject from a different perspective.

This essay focuses upon the secularization debate that basically puts forward two major arguments. The first point of view contends that the secularization thesis tends to marginalize the religious phenomenon, both theoretically and in the substantive sense. The second line of thinking emphasizes the "privatization of faith" view which provides an individualistic, non-institutional representation of religion. It is my endeavour here to show that not only do both the secularization and privatization approaches to religion, despite their opposing but compelling arguments, undersell the relevance of religion in society but actually misconstrue the secular phenomenon itself.

---

* This paper is an extended version of an earlier article published in *Social Science Research Journal*, Vol. 9, No. 2, 2001.

The sociology of religion: its various phases

The task of the sociology of religion has been described as being three-fold: first, to further the understanding of the role of religion in society; second, to analyze its significance in and impact upon human history; and, third, to understand the social forces and influences that in turn shape religion (Hamilton, 1994). Religion did not become a topic of sociological analysis with the advent of sociology in the mid and late nineteenth century. This phenomenon, in fact, has occupied the attention of thinkers for a long time, but it is in the Judaeo-Christian culture that it was focused upon as a sociological issue. There has been a continuity between the pre-modern and modern thinking about the social aspects of religion, as the seeds of ideas and questions found in the so-called scientific sociology can be found in the works of scholars even in the periods of Late Antiquity, Reformation and Enlightenment.

There have been three major theories in sociological literature and all have one thing in common: each has regarded religion as an important key in understanding the structures and processes of human society. For the first group, the functionalists, religion performs the role or *function* of holding societies together. Its main proponent, Émile Durkheim, working on his study of totemic religion among Australian Aborigines, saw only the binding character of religion. In his words, religion celebrates, and thereby, reinforces, the fact that people can form societies (Beckford, 1989). When asked whether traditional forms of religion would collapse as the long-established forms of society begin to change rapidly, Durkheim responded by saying that the religious aspects of society should also be allowed to evolve, so that the symbols of solidarity suitable to the developing social order (in this case, just beginning industrial society) may emerge. His theoretical stance was clear. Religion as such will always be present for it performs a necessary *function*. The exact nature of that religion will, however, differ over time as also between one society and another. Durkheim (1965) claims that the very formation of society is a religious process in the sense that it involves the establishment of categorization of people (clans, tribes, nations) and the sacred and profane aspects of the world. The implication is that as long as there are societies, the sacred-profane distinction will keep on serving as the symbolic reminder of individual and collective subjection to them. Even in the age of Enlightenment writers such as Comte (1969), de Tocqueville (1945), Mill (1843), etc., despite considering much of the *content* of religious ideas and sentiments as outdated and a hindrance to development, emphasize the social *functions* of religious institutions, namely, the more or less harmonious social and cultural integration of societies on the threshold of the industrial era in the early nineteenth century.

The second school of thought, influenced by Marxist reflection, holds that both the content of religious ideas and the supposedly integrative functions of religion in the industrial societies are obsolete. Marxian perspective on religion has two dimensions – the first is descriptive, while the second is evaluative. In the first sense, Marx described religion as a dependent variable stating that its constitution and character were dependent on economic and social relations – a thought that forms the core of his social theory. In his opinion, nothing could be understood apart from the economic order and the relationship of the capitalist/worker to the means of production. The second evaluative aspect follows from this view. Marx felt that religion is a form of alienation and an indicator of social distortion that will cease to exist with the arrival of a classless society. For him religion could be understood only in the context of the social reality of which it is part. Marx and his followers saw religion as the mask that obscures the real (economic) driving forces of societal progression and change. Thus, scholars like Marx and Engels (1958), and Feuerbach (cited in Marx and Engels, 1958) etc., see the endurance of religion in both cultural and organizational forms as the indication of a deep-rooted disinclination to social change. They connect religious persistence to the exploitative and alienating aspects of the class-ridden capitalist order.

The third perspective regards religion as a symbolic and organizational recourse, and resource, which is used by a particular, or all sections of society to suit their interests. Weber (1930) and Simmel (cited in Abercrombie et al.,1984), for instance, in their own way, studied religion as a reservoir of fundamental cultural meanings through which individuals and collectivities interpret their conditions of existence. The key to Weber's thought is the belief that religion can be established as something other than, or separate from, society. This implies three things – one, the relationship between religion and "the world" is conditional and changeable; two, their association can only be understood in its historical and socio-cultural specificity; and three, this relationship develops in a determinate direction (Beckford, 1989). These three assumptions form the foundation of Weber's masterwork in this area, his comparative study of the major world faiths and their impact on everyday behaviour in different parts of the world. The precise effect of religious decisions in any society, however, cannot be assumed and needs empirical examination, since religion may either provide legitimation to an established order or challenge it. Additionally, religion may even stop having the sway that it previously had, thus giving rise to the likelihood of the decline of religious authority within any given society, the process that has come to be known as *secularization*.

It is clear that despite their differences, the founding fathers recognized the integral position of religion in the human enterprise. Also, none of the three theoretical positions isolates religious, from the other phenomena but situates them in the context of other social processes and structures. And yet, it is noteworthy that slowly religion became progressively marginalized in sociological works in general, and the writings of the modernization theorists in particular and, according to them, from social order itself. It took almost half a century for a new wave of sociology of religion to re-emerge. At first it came from within the churches themselves. In the United States, where religious institutions were relatively thriving and religious practice was growing, sociologists of religion in the early twentieth century were, very largely, inspired by and involved with the Social Gospel. Some writings (Niebuhr, 1929, 1984; Demerath, 1965) also focused on the association of religion with the social divisions of American society.

The 1950s and 1960s, with the principal focus of American Sociology being situated in the normative functionalism of Talcott Parsons (1966, 1977a), who stressed above everything the integrative role of religion, sociology of religion was back in business. Religion was considered a functional prerequisite and became central to the intricate models of social systems and social action given by Parsons. The influence of his writings can still be observed in succeeding generations of American scholars, particularly Robert Bellah (1967, 1970). It would be pertinent to remember that the functionalism of Parsons surfaced in a serene and affluent social order (post-war America) which was quite dissimilar to the social upheavals faced by Durkheim, Marx and Weber. When Parsons was writing, America was experiencing an advanced phase of industrialism where consensus was not only desired but could actually be achieved. Hence, the importance of religion as the bedrock of the society.

But the 1970s were a different era marked with insecurities of various kinds and the sociology of religion took a new form again. The Parsonian model was turned on its head by the approach of social construction of meaning systems exemplified by the work of Berger (1974a) and Luckmann (1967), who held that social order exists but it is produced from below. The later part of the decade witnessed a period in which it was not consensus, but conflict, especially religious conflict that dominated the world and thus religion became a controversial issue. Interestingly, in Europe, the weakening position of the church gave rise to the concept of "lived religion".

Nevertheless, religion was increasingly becoming invisible in theoretical terms, firstly, as it was described as a part of the central value system without any regard to its distinctiveness. In other words, it was studied as a phenomenon indistinguishable from other normative phenomena. In a way, the very insistence on the functional indispensability of religion deterred scholars from undertaking a serious examination of this phenomenon.

It was, as Berger (1974a) puts it, "flattened out" so that it was no longer even perceived. Even the concept of "invisible religion" given by Luckmann (1967) or "civil religion" by Bellah (1967) only served to disguise the distinctiveness of religion. They show that religion is a social force, which transcends the boundaries of formal organizations like the church, but in doing so, they further diffuse the presence of the "real" religion in society. Secondly, and more importantly, the sociological inquiry by the modernization theorists into religious phenomena became preoccupied, even obsessed with the topic of *secularization.*

The process of secularization

Most, if not all, modernization perspectives started emphasizing the secularization process in the nineteenth and twentieth century industrial societies in which religious ideas, beliefs, practices and organizations gradually lose their authority in the face of scientific and other modern forms of knowledge. Modernization thesis holds that secularization is an inevitable feature of the rise of industrial society and the modernization of culture, since science has made traditional belief less credible, urbanization has resulted in an individualistic and anomic world and rationalization has broken the monopoly of religious symbols. The point being made is that secularization is an integral part of the culture of a capitalist society as the thought and behaviour of members of a society are less influenced by religious concerns, symbols and institutions and more by practical, even selfish considerations.

Secularization is the process by which domains of society and culture are removed from the domination of religious institutions and symbols. The process has two dimensions – social-structural and cultural. In *social-structural* sense, it indicates a substantial reduction in the respect, privilege and power of religion as an institution in society due to the separation of church and the state. Secularization has been associated, directly or indirectly, with economic change, industrialization and capitalism, i.e., it is viewed as a part of modernization. It is claimed that religion has lost authority over one institution after another. It was formerly a major consideration in decisions about government, medicine, crime and punishment, mental health etc. But, all these aspects have increasingly been taken out of religious control. On the other hand, *culturally*, it implies a change, towards secularization of our view of reality, as well as, of the reasoning that sustains our values. In other words, supernatural beliefs become less widely accepted and there is a notable decline in attachment and commitment to traditional and orthodox religious convictions. That is, in a secular society, the thought and behaviour of members are less influenced by religious concerns and symbols and more by a "this-worldly" disposition.

Weber (1930) was the first to bring into focus the ongoing process of secularization. His works described a dual association between religion and society. On the one hand, he held that the relationship between the two is historical, culture-specific and variable. On the other, he treated them as independent of each other, at least in analytical terms, since in the new rational order religion was no longer required to provide the legitimizing functions in society. In fact, religion itself became rationalized with the development of an intellectual strand in theology. By disengaging religion and society, Weber laid the foundation of the secularization approach.

His differentiation approach has been followed by many others (Bellah, 1970; Berger, 1967; Casanova, 1994; Gauchet, 1997; Parsons, 1966). Different scholars have emphasized different effects of this partition of society and religion. Some like Comte (1969) and Saint-Simon (1975) talked about the complete disappearance of religion from a rational society. Others like Bruce (1996) described only the decline of religious dominance. Yet others like Parsons (1977a) also discuss the corrosion in religious authority in society but stopped short of talking about its disappearance. Wilson (1982), too, anticipated religious decline along with the emergence of new religions. Thus, although secularization theory is not a compact one and has various strands, yet all versions hold that modernization of society results in secularization which itself implies religion-society dissociation.

While discussing the process of secularization, Fisher (1999) mentions various processes, such as modernization and globalization, which are supposed to have impacted the definition, practices and the relevance of religion differently. Fisher holds that religion had a key role in all societies before the advent of modernization which as is often said contributed to its relegation to a more separate specialized role. No more does religion influence the economy, the polity, the educational system and the policy making of modern societies. The new take on religion was that religious beliefs are subjective choices and not absolute laws. It is further pointed out that industrialized societies, free from the influence of religion, are now ambivalent about ethical questions. Fisher goes on to add that the globalization process and the technological revolution that accompanied it resulted in the shrinking of the globe and the interlinking of people from all over the world making geographic distances between cultures unimportant. Not only economies and polities got interlinked but there has also been an unprecedented mixing of cultures. Religious cultures are no longer isolated from each other and are exposed to multiple belief systems. Diana Eck (1994) holds that it is precisely the interpenetration and proximity of ancient civilizations and cultures that is the hallmark of the late twentieth century. This is the new geo-religious reality. Sections of the world cannot be categorized as Christian, Muslim or Hindu as each area is now speckled with people belonging to a variety of faiths. Digital and virtual technology, along with advances in the satellite television, have transcended the geographical base of religions.

The secularization issue is to an extent based on the debate regarding the definition of religion, namely, the Weberian emphasis on the substantive definition which describes what religion is as against the Durkheimian functionalism that is concerned with what religion does. Understandably, those like Bruce (1995a) who view religion in substantive terms are more likely to believe that modernizing societies become increasingly secular, for what they perceive as religion is diminishing in a way that can be convincingly measured. Those, on the other hand, who define religion in the functional sense, are naturally less convinced about its demise, as taking a cue from the Durkheimian description of the sacred they believe that the sacred set of phenomena shows a far greater degree of resilience.

Secularization or privatization of faith?

This brings us to questions such as has religion given way to total secularization? Are religious phenomena outdated now that new ways of understanding social and physical life have been developed and continue to be developed? Or, is there a special realm of knowledge that science will never influence? The response to these questions has come in two steps. Firstly, it is asserted that religion cannot disappear, nor even decline significantly, since every society requires some set of common values whose function is to resolve ultimate problems and provide meaning for the world of everyday life. Human beings require, in the words of Luckmann (1967), a sacred canopy in order to make sense of the world. Secondly, it is also averred that religion in contemporary societies is taking on a new, less institutional, less theistic and more individualistic form. It has become a matter of personal choice rather than a dominant feature of public life. In other words, it is privatization and not secularization of religion that is an integral part of life in the contemporaneous society.

Weber, for instance, believed that even if religion is separate from the world but both still, by necessity, impinge on each other. No doubt, the intellectualized and calculative reason has gained predominance over the traditional values which had given meaning to human affairs, yet the pursuit of value, meaning and direction in life would continue. However, it would now be at the level of the individual person. In other words, a more personal and private type of faith is being cultivated alongside the progressive rationalization of other spheres of life. The increasing impersonality in the world is accompanied by, if not actually becomes the cause for, the emergence of spiritual autonomy. The boundary between the religion and the world remains but its socio-cultural locale has moved.

In his writings, in the 1960s and 1970s, Parsons describes the two-fold changes occurring in the society. In the first place social control is exercised through new and more specialized normative agencies. Side by side, however, a more generalized system of cultural values also emerges which engenders a moral consensus. In other words, to a large extent, religion becomes a personal and private affair. The relations between religion and society get re-institutionalized so that religion is given a redefined place in the social setting as well as in an individual's life. This does not mean that religion disappears from public life. The basic values of people, which have their origin in the religious traditions, experience only minor conversion in the process of modernization. In fact, "modern" religion is itself located in life in the secular world marked by alienation. It is a response to the overly rationalized and utilitarian individualistic existence in an industrial society, and does not imply secularization. The pervasive hold of the religious institutions on public life may have weakened; instead moral values of even higher generality take over the task of directing social progress. However, its imprint is visible chiefly on individual identity, motivation and everyday morality.

Luhmann (1984) relates his views on religion to the general evolutionary theory propounded by him, which describes how the principle of social differentiation has shifted from segmentation to stratification to specialization, leading to related changes in the institution of religion. Luhmann holds that when the principle of differentiation was segmental, religion functioned by making everything sacred at the societal level and it was practised through rituals, cults, myths, etc. When the principle of differentiation became stratification, religion took the form of intellectualized truths or dogmas. But, when the principle of differentiation became functional specialization in the present social scene, the practice of religion has taken the form of individual option of the available faiths, i.e., the emergence of what is called the denominational form of voluntary religious obligations, which are marked by personal and emotional closeness of the individual to his conception of divinity. Religion no longer remains a "given" of social life; rather now it may or may not be practised, or if practised, could take any form. It has become optional, of course, with the option being made in accordance with the kind of choices made in other spheres.

In a similar vein, Beyer (1998) states that in the new era, the religious system tends to take the form of a differentiated assortment of religions on a global scale. Instead of religion as a single and singular entity, there are "religions" involving an ever-increasing profusion of religious organizations aligning themselves to one religion or another. One also witnesses a boost in reflexive religious pursuits. In fact, there is the off chance that religion may turn into something undetectable by becoming highly individualized, substantially flexible disdaining the social frontiers that are generally associated with it so much so that it becomes difficult to distinguish it from practices of individual development.

Fisher (1999) too has pointed out that along with the other views on religion, there are those who do not identify themselves with any religion and in fact may reject religion itself. Some of them may wonder about the meaning of reality and the purpose of existence but find no scientific answer to their questions. Scholars like Nietzsche and Marx saw nothing divine in religion and found it something that was created by humans for certain gains and which was displaced by the advent of science. This orientation called "scientific atheism" was highly valued in the communist societies where scientists were revered but religion found no veneration. Another intellectual movement, namely, humanism emerged in the modern era stressing human ethics rather than belief in the supernatural. Fisher also mentions that in the post-modern era another twist has occurred. Faced with the crisis of modernity leading to powerlessness, disorientation, loneliness, abandonment and a feeling of "nothingness" people are moving towards a post-modern spirituality marked by an openness in religious expression. The religious groups at this point are so many and diverse that the fable about the six blind men and the elephant, in which each man describes the elephant differently by grabbing its different parts, has come true.

Hence, religion has neither disappeared nor secularized; it has only privatized and personalized. The individual person is now the operative unit in terms of which religion is practised involving a conscious self-reflection on the meaning of life and is expressed in the form of *faith*. Berger (1974a) adds that any attempt by the religious organizations to regain dominance in the modern industrial society would endanger the foundations of the now rational society. However, it must also be realized that the voluntary form of religion poses no problems for modernity. It only reinforces the separation of personal meaning or identity from activities in the public sphere. In truth, the proliferation of personal religious ideals is not necessarily the sign of the declining dynamism and potency of religion. Rather, it signifies the inception of a non-institutional form of religion in response to, and may be as a result of, the declining importance of church-oriented religion in modern society. Again, this does not mean that the new form will replace the old. The church-oriented religion will endure, but alongside there is its new form characterized by the lack of an overarching unity or structure. In its new *avatar*, religion consists of a mélange of sacred motifs selected by the individual, the selections representing a flexible system of personal preferences, which have little or no sanction or endorsement from public institutions. It is merely the transformation of the official model of church-oriented religion into an unofficial, personal form of religiosity. As Luckmann (1967) puts it, these themes originating in the *private* (emphasis mine) sphere are primarily rooted in personal sentiments. Individuals can now choose whether or not to embrace religious leanings. These choices denote consumer dispositions and fit the individual's autonomous status and location in modern society. The new form of religion is in tune with the modern industrial society without categorically legitimating it. Rather, the religious consciousness that is found in the industrial societies epitomizes the ultimate meaning in terms of personal identity, not a dogmatic ideology.

Thus, while religion and religious organizations may have lost much of their erstwhile authority, existential questions requiring religious answers still remain and, as a result, new religious forms emerge, which are private and personal in nature. This inconspicuous and introversionist form of personal religiosity is ideal in a world characterized by instrumental rationality. Thus, the advent of modern society, marked by secularization, cannot, and does not, dislodge religion from society; it merely nurtures a type of religion which reflects the mood of the times, a kind of 'partial' religion having no major function for the entire society.

The privatization view goes a step further and adds that the crystallization of a capitalist world system may actually produce fresh religious awareness of human existence, which is truly global in nature. Issues, such as human rights, life chances, equality, quality of life etc., become salient, the common thread running through all these being "humanity", i.e., the concern with the ultimate meaning of human existence. There is, thus, a secular alternative to religion, which, however, functions like a religion without involving a belief in the sacred, suggesting the emergence of a sort of neo-sacred phenomenon.

It would be pertinent at this point to make a brief reference to the concept of "popular religion". Christian Parker (1996), citing the case of Latin America, discusses why twentieth century modernization did not lead to the kind of secularization there as was envisaged by the sociologists from North America and Europe. His contention is that although dependent capitalist development did bring about a secularizing logic, yet at the same time, local and folk religious beliefs persist due to which lay people are able to rebuff the dehumanization, instrumental rationality, reduction of life's meaning to capitalist consumption, and further commodification of popular labour caused by modernity. Hence, religion remains central to the determining of popular culture. Popular religion includes the customs of a blatantly religious nature observed by the lay population at particular places and times, in thickly populated urban and rural areas; for instance, celebration of the "official birthdays" of saints in Italy or gods in India. It implies a situation where there has been an incomplete social differentiation of religion from other components of culture, such as the arts, entertainment and commerce.

As Parker puts it, "unlike the religion of reason characteristic of the intellectual elites and the clergy, popular religion is a religion of rites and myths, dreams and emotion, of body and the quest for this-worldly well being [...] It is a manner of *feeling* and *expressing*" (1998: 205). It includes the dialectics between official ecclesiastical religion and popular religion; bourgeoisie and intellectual forms of religion and non-enlightenment/illiterate forms of faith; and the official and dominant (elite) culture and the culture of the lower strata, especially in developing societies.

In fact, Parker looks at popular religion as a counter-culture to modernity that has changed religion in so many ways. It affirms life in a world increasingly characterized by violence and insecurities. It acknowledges the fundamental forces like God, omens, healing powers, spirit of good etc., in times defined by rationalism and intellectualism. It roots for the carnivals and the festive celebrations in a society dominated by officialdom and commerce. Most importantly, it celebrates "survival" in periods of hunger, misery and exploitation with an underlying hope among the common people for intervention by some supernatural element(s). In short, it involves the idea that people in different situations and surroundings can create and recreate religious meaning on the basis of their common sense.

A critical look at secularization and privatization perspectives

Both the secularization and privatization views of religion make some assertions that can be contested. In the first place, both tend to view conventional religion as an endangered species. It takes only a look around us to realize the fallacy of this belief: First, (a) while in more traditional societies people are as, if not more, religious than ever, even in the western societies, membership and attendance in religious organizations remains high; (b) the prevalence of rational beliefs in the contemporary societies is overstated ignoring the continued evidence of irrationality and magic in them. For instance, still operative in many modern societies is the belief in various pseudo sciences like astrology (this, in fact, is one of the most popular columns in any newspaper and magazine) and superstitions still continue to endure; (c) cults like "Hare Krishna" or "Divine Light Mission" are quite predominant in the so-called modern societies; (d) majorities of the members of even the most developed societies continue to maintain belief in religion, although there may be a decline in elaborate religious practices (although the spurt of *yajnas* and papal masses does not indicate this); and (e) to treat conventional or real religion as a thing of the past is not correct as there is a fundamentalist revival being registered in many parts of the world, the established sectarian movements continue to flourish everywhere and a confounding assortment of new religious movements have begun to gain notice.

Secondly, in both perspectives, it seems to be a foregone conclusion that the onset of secularization implies, if not a complete disappearance of religion, then at least its marginalization since religious displays in the public domain are discouraged confining religion mainly to the private domain. However, there is another side to this story as scholars like McClay (2001) point out that it is secularism whose authority is diminishing. In the modern-day chaotic and soulless existence, marked by exploitative multi-national corporations, corrupt and apathetic bureaucracies and a complete disregard for an ethical code of conduct in most secular societies, it is religion that fosters social solidarity and safeguards morality. Casanova (1994) goes a step further and holds that modernity itself is imperilled due to the inflexibility of the "inhuman logic" and needs to re-establish a "creative dialogue" with those very religious ways that it has questioned. For these scholars, secularism has lost its dynamism and its very initiative. It becomes vitalized only in the face of an opposite force – or foe, in this case, religious fundamentalism. It has no agenda of its own and is more of a defensive move to counter Right Wing religious movements. Its fading glory is clear from the fact that whereas at one time it was fashionable to be secular, now it is hip to be religious and spiritual.

A third assumption of both secularization and privatization theses is that the process of differentiation has tended to disconnect religion from other kinds of institutions. The argument is that as institutions become more specialized, religion has been progressively divorced from politics, law, education, economics etc. Once again, what we see around us does not confirm this. We are well aware of the link between religion and politics. Similarly, religion is not only associated with, but may even interfere with the modern institution of law (the debate on personal law, *fatwa* being more powerful than any other modern law and so on). Also, the influence of religion on other spheres like education, entrepreneurship, etc., is well researched and recorded (Weber, 1960; Singer, 1972). Thus, religion continues to be closely linked with the different institutions of modern societies.

Fourthly, it is often believed that the processes of modernization and globalization have contributed significantly to the rise of secularization. But we must not forget that both modernization and globalization have been accompanied by the trend of exclusivity whereby some religious groups closed their ranks and restricted the contact of their members to other groups. In its extreme form this exclusivity became reactionary fundamentalism which is described as an effort of the members of the religious groups to check and counter the ill-effects of outside influences on their culture and their members. Such groups are against the various selected aspects of modern life – pluralism, consumerism, materialism – and do not believe in gender equality. They are absolutists, exclusivists and separatists and may use their fundamentalism as a political tool to gain power or secede from a nation.

Fifthly, both the secularization and privatization views distinguish between the *content* of religion and the *functions* of religion. They also assert that the content of religion may vary but the (integrative) functions remain constant. In my view, the exact opposite is true. The contents of religion have not changed significantly but its functions have. Religion can challenge, and is challenging, the taken for granted basis of social order in society. It has come to represent a source of *disorder* in most parts of the world. It is becoming a direct threat to the prevailing order in the form of fundamentalism in all major world religions – be it Zionism, militant Islam, radical Catholicism in Latin America and nearer home, the resurgence of Hindutva. Thus, the allegedly timeless and constant functions of religion are undergoing changes and it is being deployed for a great variety of purposes. I am not saying that religion has only a dysfunctional role in the present times. It is still one of the main mediums of continuity and stability in society. It also provides the individual with a meaning of life. It may still convey ideas of national integration. Nevertheless, the unrest that is characteristic of the world system of states should caution us regarding religion's potential to threaten or challenge the existing order.

Sixthly, both secularization and privatization approaches to the understanding of religion are ethnocentric. In the first place, both views are based on, and describe essentially, the western (American and European) experiences and not that of other societies. Moreover, both try to sell the post-Enlightenment western account of advancement that entails the idea of the inescapable weakening of religion in a modern progressive world. This assumption has been countered earlier as we have already mentioned that there is ample evidence to prove that most of the world today is as, if not more, religious than ever. Moreover, by focusing basically on the religious experiences of the West, they seem to indicate that the western societies alone are central to the world religion history while the rest of the world is peripheral. The truth, however, is that religion is part of a larger domain, namely, knowledge, which is concerned with the meanings and definitions of existence held by the members of a society. This "universe of meaning", as Berger and Luckmann (1969) call it, containing lofty philosophical notions as well as everyday taken for granted wisdom, is constructed by the society and is as much part of a so-called traditional or even primitive society as it is of a modern one.

Conclusion

Speculations about the transformations of societies in the nineteenth century have raised questions both about the future and usefulness of religion and secularism and have given rise to conflicting answers. Religion still presents a problem both in the theoretical and substantive sense. The existing perspectives in the sociology of religion do not offer plausible explanations of religion's increasingly controversial character and some fresh insights into the new sociological significance of religion are required. Religion may have strayed away from its former pride of place, but is no less potentially powerful as a result. In its most basic sense, it is a human response to things, which concern us most, and in that sense all human beings are religious. Thus, religion remains an effective cultural expedient that may act as the source of change, challenge or preservation. As Beckford (1989) puts it, it is nowadays better to conceptualize religion as an unpredictable and flexible cultural resource than a social institution since its capacity to mobilize remains strong, but the mobilization takes place in unanticipated ways and unexpected places.

On the other hand, secularization itself has come in for a lot of bashing. For instance, it is pointed out that secularization need not necessarily go hand in hand with modernization as the so-called modern societies are still very much religious. Criticism also comes from the post-colonial and post-modern schools, which treat secularism's assertion that it alone is the guardian of universal truth and rationality, as a form of cognitive imperialism. Instead, these schools feel that since learning is linked to the wisdom of specific groups, religious expressions also have a claim to being the 'truth', and advocate the idea of autochthonous faiths.

The harshest criticism of secularism comes from those who liken it to the tyrannical and oppressive religions of the middle ages. Scholars, such as Marsden (1997), feel that gradually secularism itself has assumed a position of orthodoxy becoming a "substitute religion" which is intolerant of any opposition. This tendency is clear when we see how secular ideology is used to regulate academia, media, courts, in short, all civic dialogue. If religion was at one time accused of repression and nullifying individual autonomy, secularism seems to be doing the same, controlling what, where and when (politically or should we say secularly correct) discourses are allowed (McClay, 2001).

Thus, the significant issues ultimately are not only whether religion is disappearing or weakening, or whether its replacement is secularization or privatization, but also the very desirability of secularism itself. Actually, all these posers can be dealt in an effectual fashion if we remember to use cultural contexts to define secularism since the term may have different connotations in different societal settings. For a westerner, it implies demystification and disenchantment, but for an Indian, it may simply mean equal respect for all religions. In other words, it may not involve marginalization of the religious beliefs but equal *preservation* of all faiths. This view is echoed by McClay (2001) who, following Berlin's (1977) two concepts of liberty – positive and negative – also describes secularism as being positive and negative. Positive secularism, guided by the ideas of self-mastery and self-governance, may become rigid and sometimes even coercive since it gives the licence to the "truly liberated" souls to intimidate and tyrannize others considered less enlightened than themselves, thereby paving the way for an authoritarian set-up. Negative secularism, on the other hand, implies openness to manifold divergent views – religious as well as non-religious. It is more about *freedom to* inquire and *freedom from* controls, even from what is called militant or aggressive secularism. It is also different from privatization as the latter implies individualization and decoupling of religion from an established church whereas negative secularization makes no such claims but, in fact, advocates the concept of multiple churches.

Every religious tradition has transformed itself in the face of the traumatic experiences of the past two centuries – be it colonialism, industrialization, nationalist movements, revival of old religions, emergence of new religions, modernization, globalization, exclusivism, fundamentalism, humanism, post-modernity etc. What does religion look like in the twenty-first century? Difficult to say. If people were to define it from singular points of view, they would give very different descriptions. A liberal person living in a society in the grip of religious and ethnic turmoil would define it differently from a dislocated person in a camp being fed and clothed by a religious institution. And, a new age IT professional living in the consumeristic "mall culture" in a developed country would probably find the institution of and the discussion on religion irrelevant. Nevertheless, it would be safe to state that religion will continue to exist, and so will secularism. What would be required, however, will be moderate forms of both. Religion must allow inquiry into its fundamental elements and secularism must prevent itself from becoming dogmatic. What is required is a change in perceptions, namely, from the idea of "religion *versus* secularism" to that of "religion *and* secularism".

REFERENCES

Abercrombie, N. et al. (eds.). *Dictionary of Sociology.* New York: Penguin Books, 1984.

Beckford, James. *Religion and Advanced Industrial Society.* London: Unwin Hyman, 1989.

Bellah, R.N. "Civil Religion in America". *Daedalus*, Vol. 96, No. 1 (1967): 1–21.

——. *Beyond Belief.* New York: Harper & Row, 1970.

Berger, Peter L. *The Sacred Canopy: Elements of a Sociological Theory of Religion.* Garden City, NY: Doubleday, 1967.

——. "Some Second Thoughts on Substantive versus Functional Definitions of Religion". *Journal for the Scientific Study of Religion*, Vol. 3, No. 2 (1974a): 125–133.

Berger, Peter L. and T. Luckmann. "Sociology of Religion and Sociology of Knowledge", in *Sociology of Religion*, edited by R. Robertson. Harmondsworth: Penguin Books, 1969.

Berlin, Isaiah. "Two Concepts of Liberty", in *The Study of Politics: A Collection of Inaugural Lectures*, edited by Preston King. London: Frank Cass, 1977.

Beyer, Peter. "The Modern Emergence of Religions and a Global Social System for Religion". *International Sociology*, Volume 13, No. 2, June 1998.

Bruce, Steve. "The Truth about Religion in Britain". *Journal for the Scientific Study of Religion.* Vol. 3 (1995a): 417–430.

Bruce, Steve. *Religion in the Modern World: From Cathedrals to Cults.* Oxford: Oxford University Press, 1996.

Casanova, Jose. *Public Religions in the Modern World.* Chicago: The University of Chicago Press, 1994.

Comte, Auguste. *Course in Positive Philosophy* (reprint). Brussels, Belgium: Culture and Civilization, 1969.

Demerath, N. Jay. *Social Class in American Protestantism*. Chicago: Rand McNally, 1965.

Durkheim, Emile. *The Division of Labour in Society*. New York: Free Press, 1964.

——. *The Elementary Forms of Religious Life* (translated by Joseph Ward Swain). New York: Free Press, 1965.

de Tocqueville, Alexis. *Democracy in America*. NY: Vintage Books, 1945.

Eck, Diana. "A New Geo-Religious Reality". Paper presented at the World Conference on Religion and Peace, Sixth World Assembly, Riva del Garda, Italy, November 1994.

Fisher, Mary Pat. *Religion in the 21st Century*. London: Routledge, 1999.

Gauchet, Marcel. *The Disenchantment of the World: A Political History of Religion*. Princeton: Princeton University Press, 1997.

Hamilton, M. *The Sociology of Religion*. London: Routledge, 1994.

Luckmann, Thomas. *The Invisible Religion.* New York: Macmillan, 1967.

Luhmann, Niklas. *Religious Dogmatics and the Evolution of Societies.* New York: Edwin Mellen Press, 1984.

Marsden, George. *The Outrageous Idea of Christian Scholarship*. Oxford: Oxford University Press, 1997.

Marx, Karl and Friedrich Engels. *Selected Works*. Vol. 1 and 2. Moscow: Progress Publishers, 1958.

McClay, W.M. "Two Concepts of Secularism". *SPAN*, January-April 2001: 7–11, 25–27.

Mill, J.S. *A System of Logic*. London: Longmans (8th edition), 1843.

Niebuhr, H. Richard. *The Social Sources of Denominationalism*. Gloucester, MA: Peter Smith Pub., 1984.

O'Toole, R. *Religion*. Toronto: McGraw-Hill, Ryerson, 1984.

Parker, Christian. *Popular Religion and Modernization in Latin America: A Different Logic* (translated by Robert R. Barr). Maryknoll, NY: Orbis Books, 1996.

——. "Modern Popular Religion: A Complex Object of Study for Sociology". *International Sociology*. Vol. 13, No. 2, June 1998.

Parsons, Talcott. *Societies: Evolutionary and Comparative Perspectives*. Englewood Cliffs, NJ: Prentice-Hall, 1966.

——. *The Evolution of Societies*, edited by J. Toby, Englewood Cliffs, NJ: Prentice-Hall, 1977a.

Saint-Simon, Henri. *Selected Writings on Science, Industry and Social Organization*, K. Taylor (ed.), New York: Holmes and Meier, 1975.

Singer, Milton. *When a Great Tradition Modernizes*. New York: Praeger, 1972.

Weber, Max. *The Protestant Ethic and the Spirit of Capitalism*. London: Allen and Unwin, 1930.

——. *The Religion of India*. Glencoe Ill.: The Free Press, 1960.

Wilson, Bryan. *Religion in Sociological Perspective*. Oxford: Oxford University Press, 1982.

CHAPTER 3

Globalization and Religious Identities in India

Understanding the subaltern context of contestations

SANTOSH KUMAR SINGH

> Roots make me think of my forefather …
> His roots are flowing in my veins.
> I am the seed of that root.
> Roots remind me of root infinite,
> The source of everything.
>
> —**Amarjit Chandan**
> (London-based Punjabi poet,
> from his bilingual work, "Sonata for four hands")

If the ideal of modernization was assimilation of diverse identities into a monocultural melting pot, the era of globalization is marked by an unprecedented upsurge in identity articulations largely fomented by primordial ascriptive impulses of various communities and groups. Globalization, in a sense, therefore marks the return of the "native" and the "nativism" in the social sciences discourse. The increasing invocation of the roots, localism and frayed ethnocentric collective behaviour, as displayed by various groups in our body politic and public life in general, represents the mood of changing times. This is despite the fact that globalization, unlike modernization, appears to have been more deferential to local cultures, which is what has been variously described as "glocalisation" or what the controversial writer Salman Rushdie called "chutneyfication".

The process of modernization, we may recall, emphasized merger of identities, what was ostentatiously articulated by the modernists as "convergence theory". It was argued that the twin processes of industrialization and urbanization will bring about a world where all the differences and autonomy of cultures will be coloured in one shade. Riding on the hype of techno-scientific arrogance, the architects of the grand design of modernity declared the end of religion, spirituality and faith. Clearly, nothing of the sort happened. Instead, the contemporary world is experiencing an unprecedented revival of religious and symbolic elements in the public domain.

The "unsecularisation of the world", as George Weigel remarked, "is one of the dominant social facts in the late twentieth century" (Weigel, 1991: 27). There are reports indicating phenomenal rise in the number of religious visitors to the temples, churches, mosques and gurudwaras across the globe. The market for spiritual goods has grown multifold.[1] The pathologies of science and modernity and the loss of its emancipatory ideals in collusion with highly appropriative, speculative and profit-driven market forces seem to have created conditions for people's faith in the invisible and even in unreason. For people do not live by reason alone. Primordial identities, such as religious, ethnic and caste groups, here work as a unifier and a formidable rallying point for identity crystallization processes.

A new era, in the meantime, dawned, facilitated by the unprecedented boom in mass media and other information technology (IT) enabled services. The new world promised to compress time and space, the two critical barriers of communication in yesteryears to bring about what Marshall McLuhan (1964) called a "global village". The logic of globalization undermined the role of the nation-states and its totemic fixation to territory. In principle, globalization also meant free movement of people, goods and services across the national borders regulated and governed by the market forces. Globalization of course carries many streaks of modernization. Yet it is qualitatively different. The premises on which it is built differ substantially from modernization in terms of both its eidos and ethos. Globalization is as much about migration, mobility, dislocation and deterritoriality as it is about interdependence and interconnectedness. It is not to suggest that these features were not there earlier, but it is the speed, instantaneity and intensity of interaction across cultures that makes the era of globalization different from modernization, making some commentators refer to it as "second modernity" or new modernity (Beck, 1992).

The grand narratives of modernity and then globalization processes, however, could not make much difference to the paradoxes, contradictions and asymmetries of human societies. The globalizing world appears to have spawned serious economic, political and, of course, cultural questions. The critique of globalization has variously referred to it as "Americanization", "McDonaldization" and "Wallmartization", pointing towards its hegemonic traits (Friedman, 1999, 2005). It is being argued that globalization which was created with the imagination of an open discourse of integration, interaction and harmony based on principles of symmetry and equal participation has failed to triumph over discord, differences, demarcations, discrimination and dissonance of local villages (Dasgupta, 2004: 19).

Zygmunt Bauman (1998) argues that being local in a globalized world is a sign of social deprivation and degradation. If the world were a global village, it is being contended, of a 100 people, 70 of them would be unable to read, and only one would have had any college education. Over 50 would be suffering from malnutrition and over 80 would live in what we call substandard housing. If the world were a global village of 100 residents, six of them would be American. These would have half of the village's income while the other 94 would exist on the other half. How would the wealthy six live "in peace" with "their neighbours"? (Huizer, 2003).

Ideally, globalization was expected to create conditions that will connect the different nations of the world in an organic whole and thereby establishing a mutually beneficiary "global village" based on the premise of equality and reciprocity. Sadly, the resultant impacts of global processes so far have been fraught with glaring inequalities and discriminations. Hence, "globalization creates a world of winners and losers, a few on the fast track to prosperity, the majority condemned to a life of misery and despair" (Giddens, 2000: 33). Giddens further argues that the world today is a "runaway world" and considers globalization as little more than "global pillage" (Giddens, 2000: 34, 37). He comments:

> This is not – at least at the moment – a global order driven by collective human will. Instead it is emerging in an anarchic, haphazard fashion [...]. It is not settled or secure, but fraught with anxieties as well scarred by deep divisions. Many of us feel in the grip of forces over which we have no power (Giddens, 2000: 37).

Nothing captures the paradox of existing gross inequality today more powerfully than the two sets of reports which appeared simultaneously in the Indian media recently. First came from Forbes declaring that "India's billionaire list has nearly doubled" giving details as to how the net worth of the promoter of the largest listed Indian company is put at $32 billion, an increase of 54 per cent from nearly $21 billion last year. The list also indicates how India's billionaires have done better than their counterparts in others parts of the world.[2] This piece of news was followed by another but chilling reminder from the same world and territory. The special edition of UNICEF's state of the world children report was released to mark two decades of the historic convention signed on November 20 which tracks the progress made over the years. The report says that in India 5,000 kids die every 24 hours and each year 1 million new-born die during the first month of life while another million die before they reach the age of five.[3]

The mist of utopian romanticism around the idea of a global village facilitated and induced by neo-liberal ideology and premised on the concept of self-regulated market economy therefore seems to be evaporating against such formidable negative consequences. The UNDP report on globalization also highlights this point:

> Globalization expands the opportunities for unprecedented human advance for some but shrinks those opportunities for others and erodes human security. It is integrating economy, culture and governance but fragmenting societies. Driven by commercial market forces globalization in this era seeks to promote economic

efficiency, generate growth and yield profit. But it misses out on the goals of equity, poverty eradication and enhanced human security (UNDP, 1999: 43–44).

Other than the staged celebrations of localism and cultures, globalization has shown strong universalizing streaks which aim to make the rest of the world – those who are at the margins of the globalizing discourse – bereft of its traditional moorings and history. This is why, some critics have considered cultural globalization as malignant, manifesting itself in the form of the ever-increasing electronic culture and ever-proliferating fast food outlets, the process that George Ritzer refers to as McDonaldization. These restaurants have been considered by Ritzer as the new "cathedrals of consumer culture" which result in a clash between new cultural spaces and traditional cultural spaces (Ritzer, 2001). Similar conflicting spaces have mushroomed in various forms across the world. The entry of politics further sharpens these flash points. For instance, the US sponsored "global war against terror" has created many fissures instead of cementing them. Tragically, the trends of international political polarization of nations give credence to Huntington's clash of civilization theory.

In other words, even though globalization has created and propelled enormous tides of mobility and migration, it has also created a vacuum for the majority for want of avenues and channels for economic prosperity. The spots of appalling poverty, hunger, starvation deaths, acute unemployment and malnutrition dot the world map, especially in areas where the majority of its population live. This asymmetry and powerlessness, when combines with the larger world characterized by crass conspicuous consumption and hegemonic cultural onslaughts, creates a condition of anomie and unrest. Massive social, economic and technological transformations are under way with the speed which humanity had never experienced and the consequences of which are far beyond their comprehension. Faced with so much change and moments of flux, individuals, communities and societies are anxious and uncertain about their future in this new global world which some scholars have termed as "risk society" and its culture as "panic culture" (Beck, 1992).

Manufacturing identity umbrellas

The confusion and the element of uncertainty and fear are most palpable in the realm of culture. Globalization may have been driven and fuelled by the economic engine but its impact has been most felt in the interiors of human lives. One's music, food habits, traditions, norms, folkways and customs have been faced with constant interrogation and insistence for change and reconstitution by transnational forces. "Private" is no more innocent, static and non-negotiable. In short, "private" has become "public" and there is buying and selling going on in the name of celebrating diversity. Thus, identity becomes a product, a commodity in a world where everything is for sale as long as they are packaged well. Cultures which have the economic and political wherewithal to package its products well and glossy become predatory. The more the interrogation, the sharper and intense gets the reaction from the cultures at the receiving end.

In this clash of cultures market even commodifies the tools of protests. One doesn't assert one's identity, one pays to assert it, and one pays to observe others asserting it, and some people even sell our identity (Wallerstein, 2004: 91; also see Gilroy, 2000). The pertinent question here is why identity became such an issue to die for in contemporary times. There can be and are multiple explanations. But, the one which seems to be the most convincing is the cultural protest argument necessitated by the market forces which have created an acute sense of off-centredness in the lives of people. The beneficiaries of the process of globalization have amassed wealth and prosperity at the cost of a vast multitude of people who had nothing but their sense of belongingness to their cultural roots – be it religion, caste or ethnicity. The picture is however not as tidy and neat as it appears. The undercurrents of economic inequality have significant bearings but the reality is far more complex and its explanation certainly goes beyond mere "economism".

So, when Switzerland shows intolerance to minarets or France displays disapproval to turban or burqua, these responses trigger multiple counter-responses in the remotest corners of the world and in places and peoples separated by thousands of miles. Identity industry goes on an overdrive thanks to the global media networks.

And after a point the conflict grows beyond the rhetoric of rich versus poor. It then takes a form of all encompassing ideological outfit which merges all differences – rich and poor, literate and illiterate, have and have nots – into one homogeneous whole. As a result, a manufactured sense of identity umbrella is created, which promises a sense of security, belongingness, protection and not-alone feeling to its members. Interestingly, the fear and panic grips all – the rich and the poor and the developed and the developing. Vincent Geisser, a scholar of Islam and immigration at the French Centre for Scientific Research, has been quoted recently as saying, "the more Europe's Muslims establish themselves as a permanent part of the national scene, the more they frighten some who believe that their national identity could be altered forever."[4]

In the background of a new controversy on assimilation surrounding a proposed minaret of the grand mosque of Marseille in France which will be silent where no muezzin, live or recorded, will disturb the neighbourhoods with the call to prayer and instead the minaret will flash a beam of light for a couple of minutes, five times a day, Geisser comments:

> There is angst over identity in Europe. There is a feeling that Europe is becoming smaller and less important. Europe is like an old lady who whenever she hears a noise thinks it's a burglary. This generalized anxiety and fear is translated in to a specific one called Islam, a box in which everyone expresses their fears.

The reasons for this anxiety in Europe, however, involve a complex set of issues. This stems from economic crisis, the fear of globalization, the perceived increase in immigration as European birth rates fall and the subsuming of national states into an enlarged Europe. However, the fear of Islam crystallizes all other fears. For it is more visible and evokes xenophobic anxiety courtesy round the clock demonisation of a faith by global media networks. Similar reactions are being witnessed elsewhere. The transnational media channels, many a time inadvertently, transports these malignant and malafide hate products in the form of stereotypes, prejudices and more importantly visuals to the remotest societies of the globe. These supposedly global concerns and fears get replicated and xeroxed in various forms in different settings. That is, identity umbrellas take different shades in different contexts. The common themes however are the "longing for the roots", sometimes imagined sometimes real, and "fear of losing its sense of collective self" among the people across the world.

As a consequence, groups and communities everywhere have become hyperactive and combative in the face of some mysterious fear. The most visible are those formed on religious lines. With globalization making the interlinkages between the local and the global more strong, elaborate and easily mediated, identity-based clashes have shown phenomenal growth. India is no exception to this. As a multi-faith, multilingual and poly-religious society India harbours mind-boggling diversity. Globalization has transported some of its best to the world, at the same time, it has posed some challenges as well. India, like other nations, has benefited from its linkages with the world. It in fact re-branded itself in the world through its people and products. Indians settled abroad, of which a large chunk come from the state of Punjab and who are variously referred to as the non-resident Indians (NRIs) or the Diaspora, have contributed enormously to its homeland. The longing is still there among the people who had migrated to their adopted land many decades back.

However, sometimes, these linkages can pose and create highly volatile situation as it was witnessed recently in the state of Punjab. An incident, which took place in Vienna, the capital of Austria, threw an entire state back in India, in flames and total lawlessness for many days with far-reaching implications. This essay attempts to highlight in the next section the role of globalization in fomenting such identity articulations while dwelling upon the local socio-cultural context and history. The role of mass media and the de-territioriality of identities are amply on display in this case. An issue of local origin and history gets played out at a place separated by continents from its place of origin. Indeed, it also revealed the extent of globalization of an issue of local nature and the frightening potency of media networks in augmenting it.

Clash in Vienna, backlash in Punjab

In Vienna, Austria, on 24 May 2009, a Ravidassia[5] religious congregation was in progress. The congregation was special as it was being attended by the top two most revered saints of the sect, Sant Niranjan Das and Sant Ramanand, from its Dera Sachkhand Ballan in Jalandhar, Punjab, India. The meeting later turned into a seat of violent bloody clashes as some assailants entered the premises and grievously injured the *Sants*. While Sant Ramanand later succumbed to his injuries, Sant Niranjan Das, the chief of the Dera, survived but in precarious health. As the news of the attack in Vienna flashed across Punjab, and the district of Jalandhar in particular, the followers of the Dera and other Dalit bodies took to the streets and soon Punjab was in flames. As the print and the visual media broke the news of Sant Ramanand's demise and the live visuals of saints from the hospital of Vienna were repeatedly flashed across, the crowd went hostile, plunging the entire region into a state of lawlessness. Large-scale riots and arson followed within hours of the Vienna attack. The loss of private and public property to the tune of hundreds of crores of rupees was reported in a short span of a few days of unrest.[6] Instanteity of violent reactions and the scale was unprecedented.

Curfew was imposed in many parts of Punjab, especially in the Doaba region[7] of the state, which is the seat of the Dera and a large number of its followers come from this area. Incidentally, this region is also considered the "NRI zone" of Punjab. It is believed that almost all the households here, including the Ravidassia community, have at least one person settled abroad. After a few days of concerted efforts from politicians, community leaders and the law and order machinery, the region showed signs of recovery. However, as the reports from Vienna filtered through the media about the identity of those assailants who killed Sant Ramanand and injured others, rumour mongers had a field day. Many tried to give it a secessionist slant reviving the memory of hoary days of militancy in Punjab (see Gupta, 1997). Confusing and ambivalent reports regarding the identity of those who were involved in the Vienna incident kept appearing in the local newspapers to keep the atmosphere volatile and ominous looking. Interestingly, the six suspects whose names appeared in the Indian media courtesy the Austrian police had two common things about them. One, they were all either illegal emigrants or seeking asylum on flimsy grounds and second, none of them had any prior criminal record against them.[8]

Admittedly, the ruling political combine in the state showed exceptional political maturity and seriousness in dealing with the crisis in the aftermath of the incident in Vienna. The chief minister of the state, while on a visit to the Golden Temple in Amritsar to organize an Akhand Path – continuous reading of Guru Granth Sahib, the most sacred book of the Sikhs – at the temple complex for the early recovery of Dera head Niranjan Das was quoted as saying, "No individual or political party, but collective forces outside country are responsible for the attack. There are forces outside the state and country which are bent upon disturbing peace in the state. Punjab has undergone troubled times earlier. Such forces want to destabilize the hard earned peace".[9] He also offered to organize the cremation of Sant Ramanand with state honours, if the Dera organizers so demanded. Later, a special aircraft arranged by the Punjab government was sent to Austria to bring the body of Sant Ramanand. His funeral back home in Jalandhar was attended by the prominent leaders of all political parties across the board, including the representatives of the Shiromani Gurudwara Prabandhak Committee (SGPC) – the central governing body of the Sikh religion. This was unprecedented as so far these political parties have hobnobbed with Deras only clandestinely and never under full public gaze.

Understandably, the fact that Punjab happens to be a state with the largest concentration of the Dalits in the country with the census 2001 pegging it at 29 per cent did have its role in the way various political parties reacted to the incident in Vienna. Politicians of course understood that they better take these numbers seriously, for a large number of them happen to be the followers of these Deras with Doaba region alone comprising about 37 per cent of them. A brief background here of the history of these Deras and its strained engagement with Sikhism, the mainstream religion in Punjab, will help us in our understanding of the local contexts which was played out globally in Vienna.

Understanding the subaltern behind the sacred

Sikhism was founded by Guru Nanak Dev (1469–1539) against the repressive ethos of ritualism, idol worship, magic, miracles and preponderance of caste Brahminical orthodoxies prevalent in Hinduism (McLeod, 1968; Grewal, 1990). The new faith was premised on the principles and ideals which stressed on equality rather than hierarchy of caste system. Most importantly, Guru Nanak extolled the virtues of a life of religious obedience and devotion focused on an abstract conception of the divine power and affirming the same through *nam simran* (name remembrance), that is, chanting of hymns. He called for an alternative path, beyond Hindu or Muslim, comprising moral duty (*dharma*), human effort (*karma*), spiritual knowledge, truth and divine benevolence. Nanak represented the medieval Sant tradition of syncretic religious devotionalism and those who believed in his ideas became his followers or disciples (sikha, the word from which Sikhism originated) and came to be called Nanakpanthis. Simplicity and ethos of equality characterized and constituted the core of the new faith or panth.

In true Indic tradition disagreements, arguments and contestations also followed. Guru Nanak's son himself became a renouncer and some of his followers who did not follow all of his core teachings founded other sects as well. Changes over the next two centuries with many modifications, movements and routinization "blurred the distinction between Sikhism and caste Hinduism rendering the Sikh identity rather misty" (Madan, 2003). However, major "institutionalization" of Sikhism took place with the interventions of the tenth guru of the Sikhs, Guru Govind Singh (1666–1708), who gave the faith more stable structures and some rigidity with his insistence on five symbols. He also introduced *pahul* or the initiation through offering of *amrit* or nectar, the baptismal water, injunction to retain bodily hair unshorn and substitution of the last names with Singh (lion) and Kaur (lioness) for men and women believers, respectively. The obvious attempts at retaining its original anti-caste and equalitarian tenets while giving the faith some kind of uniformity and objective martial form are reflected in these processes.

Large-scale entry of the landed Jat peasantry into the Sikh fold and the armed conflicts with the Mughals marked by the sacrifices made by the Sikh gurus proved to be the most crucial moments in Sikh history as they had the most long-lasting impact on the larger image formation of the community later on. The dominance of Jat Sikhs, as "cultivator par excellence", in the religious and community affairs as also their assertion for separate community identity today and most critically their role in perpetuating caste-like formations leading to plethora of volatile inter-caste strife in contemporary times, emanate from these historical events. The exaltation and veneration of martyrdom in defence of faith also has its roots in its history (see Madan, 2004).

A study of the origin and the growth of Sikhism shows that reformist tendencies and movements were found to be at loggerheads with the orthodox elements who believed in true "Khalsa" faith (those believing and practising five Ks and other prescriptions) and the sanctity of the Akal Takht, the seat of temporal power of the panth. Most notable among them, the Nirankari and Namdhari, for instance, were sectarian in character and acknowledged gurus subsequent to Guru Gobind Singh, who had proclaimed closure of the life of personal gurus. While Nirankaris called for a return to the teachings of Guru Nanak, who had characterized the divinity as nirankar or formless, the Namdharis focused their attention on regenerating the Khalsa as introduced by Guru Gobind Singh. These tendencies with a guru-like figure at the centre have always been contested by the orthodox elements as they were considered antithetical to the true Khalsa faith. In fact, the militancy in Punjab, which later on took a dangerous fissiparous tone in the last century in the seventies and lasted till late eighties and early nineties, had its origin in the conflict between the Nirankaris and the Akalis (see Kapur, 1986; Jurgensmeyer, 1988; Gupta, 1997).

The Dera phenomenon

Deras are, theoretically, places or centres of religious congregation mostly formed around a revered person and engaged in community welfare works with accent on *sadachar* or good deeds and conducts of its believers. The followers of the Dera are dictated by the commands of the spiritual guru, who may subscribe to the tenets of Sikhism or may have evolved a syncretic tradition of its own. As per a recent estimate, there are more than 9,000 Sikhs as well as non-Sikh Deras in the 12,000 villages of Punjab (Tehna et al., 2007). In Sikh Deras, Sikh rahit (code of conduct) is observed strictly, whereas in non-Sikh Deras different ritual practices are followed.

In fact, the phenomenon of Dera is as old as the Sikh faith itself. During the period of the historic gurus, different Deras of Udasis, Minas, Dhirmalias, Ramraiyas, Massandis and others cropped up. All these earlier Deras primarily emerged as an outcome of the disgruntled and the unsuccessful attempt of the "fake" claimants to the title of guru (Marenco, 1976: 28–30; Bingley, 1970: 85–93). Many more Deras emerged at various points of time in the process of consolidation of Sikh religion. While in Sikh Deras only gurubani of the sacred text Guru Granth Sahib is recited, in the non-Sikh Deras, along with the gurubani of Guru Granth Sahib other sacred texts are also referred to. Idol worship and devotion towards a human guru is also quite common in these non-Sikh Deras. It is also perhaps because of this tendency to tamper with the Sikh panthic traditions that these non-Sikh Deras are viewed as potentially threatening by the main religion.

To understand the origin and mushrooming of Deras in Punjab, it would be germane to recollect some of the contradictions which emerged within the main religion. The first and the foremost is the fact that despite complete rejection of Brahmanical caste doctrine in theory Sikhism continued to retain the spirit of hierarchy in its praxis. The marginalization of the Dalits (the untouchable outer castes in the Hindu varna-fold), such as Mazhabis and Ramdassis within Sikhism, has been near complete. The Dalit Sikhs, who once had joined the panth in anticipation of an equal treatment and a dignified existence, found to their utter disillusionment the new set-up as unrelenting and unaccommodating as the Hindu social order. This seems to have pushed these marginalized low caste segment of the society towards these Deras which offered them alternative socio-cultural space (Ram, 2007: 4066).

Unequal treatment meted out to these Dalits and the marginal segments of the society in the hands of the dominant Jat Sikhs, who almost have a monopoly over matters, both religious and temporal, in the panth are backed by facts. For instance, all the Sikh organizations like gurudwaras (place of worship for the Sikhs), Sikh Deras, SGPC etc., are under the dominant control of the Jat Sikhs. In a recent empirical work done on the caste background of the members of the SGPC it has been found that 80 per cent of its administrative posts are under the control of the Jat Sikhs, 15 per cent under other castes and only 5 per cent with the Dalit Sikhs. All the three current secretaries of the Shiromani Committee are Jat Sikhs (Singh, 2007). This is besides increasing cases of social exclusion as reported in local newspapers about denials of Dalits to use the main cremation ground or gurudwara or marriage centres in the villages. This is also reflected in the way there has been mushrooming of separate Dalit gurudwaras in Punjab (Puri, 2003: 2700; Jodhka, 2004: 79).

At a more social and cultural level, especially in matters pertaining to marriage and commensality, even though it is much less rigid than the Hindu caste system, it has been found that the loosening of inter-caste marriage norms are more to be seen among the marginalized Jat Sikh peasants rather than the influential and the affluent strata. Even in these cases the Jats willingly accepted women from the lower castes, but showed no inclination to give their daughters to them (Judge, 2002: 180). It is however to be admitted that there is no element of "sacrilege" involved in these interactions between various caste-like groups, rather it is more often than not an issue pertaining to defilement of honour or prestige in the local sense and certainly nothing to do with the notion of pollution as it existed in the Hindu caste system. The "essence" notwithstanding, the "forms" these caste-like structures attained were to have serious implications.

The dominant caste status for the Jat Sikhs is a function of a composite set of conditions, which included their numerical strength (one-third of the total population of the state), ownership of land (more than 80% of the available agricultural land is owned by them) major stakeholding in agriculture, their historical martial race status etc. In contrast, however, the Dalits of Punjab, even though they have substantial numerical clout, but in terms of share in land they are terribly marginalized. This has rendered a large proportion of them as agricultural labourers working on the land of the landed Jat Sikhs. Also, while the Jat Sikhs are a homogenous category, more or less, the Dalits are a fragmented lot with all kinds of larger affiliations like religion and caste or occupational status to divide them. Hence, the Dalits in general, including the Mazhabis and Ramdassias within Sikhs, have been engaged with the dominant landed Jat Sikhs in a relationship historically based on asymmetry and exploitation with the former at the receiving end.

The Dalit consciousness, however, has shown steady growth and upswing among the Dalits in Punjab. Hosts of factors have contributed to the crystallization of the community identity. Post-green revolution, there has been steady decline in agriculture in Punjab. Large-scale immigration of labourers to Punjab from underdeveloped parts of the country contributed in pushing the Dalits further outside the village looking for all kinds of non-farm work, which actually helped them in liberating themselves from the repressive old arrangement by making the most of the new economic opportunities (Jodhka, 2004; Ram, 2004a). Emergence of a small but influential segment of Dalit diaspora, coupled with phenomenal political rise of Dalit leadership and political consciousness in the neighbouring state of Uttar Pradesh, have also significantly helped in homogenization of Dalits of Punjab. Rising cases of clashes with the dominant Jat Sikhs, other than the prominent ones which made headlines such as Talhan conflict in 2003 and then in Meham,[10] can be seen as symptomatic of this new found sense of self and identity awareness among the Dalits. A history of subjugation under Jat domination and simmering counter-currents as a result thereof, provided that necessary background for other forces to combine. Simultaneous large-scale exodus of the Dalits and other backward communities to these Deras as signs of articulation and assertion of their new identity can be fully understood in this backdrop.

The Deras therefore gradually emerged as strong sign posts of subaltern protests in the form of Dalit assertion in Punjab against the oppressive old socio-cultural arrangement including religion. Building on a rather sober and largely non-combative history, these

Deras have gradually started asserting themselves. For a long time the simultaneity of traditions was followed. Ravidassis have been worshipping the Guru Granth Sahib, holy book of the Sikhs, along with the images of Sant Ravidass. And, it is not difficult to comprehend this scenario, given the similarity of historical contexts of these traditions rooted in the 14th century bhakti movement. For instance, what binds the Ravidassis to the Sikhs is the fact that Sant Ravidass' *bani* or teachings have been enshrined in the Guru Granth Sahib, which has forty *shabads* and one *shloka* of Sant Ravidass included in it. In many Dalit gurudwaras photos of Ambedkar have also been found signalling the community's increasing political awareness about their identity. Instances of Dalit families solemnizing their marriages in front of a photo of Ambedkar or Bhagat Singh[11] in protest against the entry ban in gurudwaras by the local Jat Sikhs have been reported in local media. These trends, which have gathered momentum now, had first germinated in the 1920s under the leadership of Mangoo Ram and which gradually got crystallized as "Ad-Dharmis" in the census of 1931. This event marked a departure for the Dalits of the region in the form of a separate independent identity from both the Hindus and the Sikhs.

The century-old Dera Sachkhand Ballan, as it stands today, is the product and a symbol of a long history of exploitation and marginalization of the Dalits and of course their struggle. The Dera, which was founded by Baba Pipal Das, became a strong force in the sixties and presently it is considered the Mecca for Ravidassis all over the world. The Dera, it is believed, has been the central force behind opening of hundreds of Ravidass temples and "Guru Ka Ghar" (the abode of the saint) all over the world. A Dera source has been quoted as saying that there are about 20 such temples in UK, 15 in Canada, 20 each in USA, European countries and the Gulf.[12] Presently, it is considered the biggest Dera of the community in the world. The majority of the followers of the Deras belong to the "Ad-dharmi" sect and they have been mostly from the erstwhile untouchables or the Dalit segment of the Hindu society.

The diaspora connection of the Dera

One of the most prominent reasons behind the expansion and growth of the Dera Sachkhand Ballan has been its phenomenal overseas growth, courtesy its followers from the region having a long and successful history of such overseas migrations. During the British colonial rule small islands of Sikh populations appeared in a number of countries – first in the far eastern countries, then in East Africa, followed by the pacific states of North America. The post-1947, the year of India's independence, is marked by a large exodus of Sikhs from Punjab and their concentration in three western countries, the UK, the USA and Canada, as also generally across the world (see Dusenbery and Tatla, 2009, for a detailed account of Sikh diaspora philanthropy and their connection with the roots). The overseas migration trends from the region picked up with the onset of globalization era. The post-1947 period migration took place under the new Indian regime that coincided with rapid changes in transportation and communications: air travel, courier, faxes and then e-mails and satellite TV.

> In the 1910s it took three weeks from Calcutta to Vancouver and traveling via Hong Kong was the only mode of travel between India and Canada until the 1940s. Then the journey time was reduced to a day with the advent of air travel. Today passengers can land in Amritsar from Toronto in just eighteen hours. Moreover instead of sending a letter by surface mail, one may telephone or even better just e-mail one's relatives or business associates. These changes in communication also altered the way in which migrants could relate to their ex-homes (Dusenbery and Tatla, 2009: 35).

Other than the globalization juggernaut, the reasons for intensification in the trend towards overseas migration are rooted in region's economy and society. One of them being the decline of agriculture-based prospects in the region. Punjab, once the seat of India's green revolution experiments, which once boasted its "granary basket of India" epithet and took immense pride in being a place of "agriculturists par excellence", today, finds itself under serious economic crisis.

The young generation today is just not interested in agriculture anymore. According to 2007 census, from Punjab, nearly 2 lakh marginal and small farmers left the occupation between 1991 and

2001. Another report titled, "Status of farmers who left farming in Punjab-2007" and compiled by the Punjab State Farmers' Commission in collaboration with the Department of Economics of Punjab Agricultural University concludes that every ninth farmer in the state has quit agriculture over the past 25 years.

The mad rush to move abroad as it exists among the youths in particular of the region has a lot to do with the super success of its diaspora in the past. Their display of overseas success as reflected in the highly ostentatious marriages, marbled residential palaces and costly imported cars that they flaunt back home in their villages and towns in Punjab made them objects of neighbour's envy. Gradually, the diaspora or the Non-Resident Indians (NRIs) as they are often referred to emerged as a powerful reference group in the region. People try all possible options – if not through education or job, then through marriages to establish links with the land of opportunities and wealth in the west. Despite the fact that a large number of failed NRI marriages involving deceit, forgery, lies, blackmailing and torture have been reported in the local media, the urge for NRI connection refuses to die.

The era of globalization opened enormous opportunities and channels for migration abroad for jobs and education and ultimately for a permanent settlement there. The mushrooming of multi-crore coaching industry in Punjab for the preparation of the IELTS, the International English Language Testing System, a test in English language proficiency and one of the basic mandatory requirements for study visa abroad in the last decade reflects the impact of globalization.

The number of Punjabi youth seeking foreign pastures can be gauged from the manifold increase in the applicants for IELTS. This is a universally recognized proficiency test for English, made mandatory by most institutions of higher education across the world. About a decade ago, the British Council, which was then the sole agency authorized to conduct the test, had only one test centre in Chandigarh, with barely a handful of candidates from Punjab applying for their monthly test. They were generally high achievers in medicine or engineering, with at least a graduation degree under their belts.

However, within the span of a few years, the scenario has changed drastically. The Council now conducts tests at least twice a month in Amritsar, Jalandhar, Ludhiana and Patiala, to which hundreds of youngsters flock. About four years ago, IDP, the Australian IELTS partner, also started conducting the test. Last year, it was estimated that at least 50,000 students sat for this test in Punjab alone. The majority of these candidates are in their late teens, having just passed the plus 2 examination. Most of them are from the rural areas and can barely speak or understand English. Academics is not their concern; most of them have no idea of what they want to study, except for whatever course their "agent" has told them is easy to get admission into.

Significantly, most of them are not from the "gentry", but from the lower socio-economic strata; the families of many have sold off their meagre landholdings and livestock, and incurred huge loans simply to get a chance to jump on to the "Overseas Express", heading for Australia, Canada, New Zealand, England, USA, Cyprus, Turkey – or wherever a visa is obtainable.[13]

The Doaba region of the state has been in the forefront of this. Traditionally an NRI belt, it has expectedly benefited the most from the new environment. These developments also percolated down to the lower rungs of the society across the communities. Ravidassis and the other Dalit groups were no exceptions to this. It was therefore not a mere coincidence that the test centre for IELTS outside Chandigarh was first opened in Jalandhar, the epicentre of NRI base in the region and the seat of Ravidassis' political ascendance and concentration. Moreover, migration from Doaba – with a very high proportion of Ravidassis (as high as one-third in some districts) – has seen a number of Ravidassis become millionaires.

The NRI Sabha of Jalandhar puts the Dalit NRI figures to between 25 per cent and 30 per cent of the total 80 lakh diaspora from the region. Such is the affluence of these NRI Dalits that they have built their own gurudwaras in various countries.

The recent economic clout of the Dalits in the region, especially in Jalandhar, has a lot to do with their success in the local leather industry and their wealthy NRI base. This prosperity is being channelized for assertion in public domain mostly through symbolic and religious means. Better economic standing has also revived the centuries old sense of denial and marginal treatment meted out at the hands of the upper caste Jat Sikhs.

As a result, the region has become a hub of Dera activities with construction of majestic bhawans, expensive Deras and multistoreyed temples in the name of Sant Ravidass dotting the landscape. In the last couple of years, Dalit NRIs have raised nearly half a dozen shrines in the Doaba region with crores of rupees being spent on each structure. Over Rs 3 crore have already been spent on multistoreyed Sat Guru Ravidass Dham, a sprawling one-acre building in Dalit-dominated Buta Mandi locality in Jalandhar. According to its managing committee president, Surinder Mahey, who has been quoted as saying that, "it would be a completely white structure with golden domes and lots of craftsmanship. The complete project cost is expected to be somewhere around Rs 30 crore".[14]

Interestingly, most of these buildings and Deras have separate flats for NRI devotees, such as the one at Dera Sachkhand Ballan, within its premises in acknowledgement of diaspora's contribution and support. This also suggests that these Deras are fast emerging as centres for global-local interlinkages. The *sants* from these Deras visit their branches abroad on a regular basis to seek donations and to propagate their religious beliefs.

The Vienna visit may have ended in a tragedy but frequent trips to countries all over the world have been a matter of routine for its *sants* to garner support and financial help to run the Dera activities back home in India. In fact, the NRIs helped set up a hi-tech studio in the Dera premises in Ballan from where live telecast of the *satsung*, religious congregation, is beamed to several countries and a regular weekly programme is produced for the Doordarshan – the state run television network.

For the followers of Dera the loss of Sant Ramanand has come as a major setback at this crucial juncture for the community as the slain *sant* was believed to be the man responsible for the spread of Dera activities abroad and in organizing its NRI networks. He was actually second in command after Sant Niranjan Das in the Dera's organizational hierarchy.

Unlike the general trend of Sikh diaspora philanthropy in the region, which has made significant contributions in the area of education, health and other physical infrastructure in the villages and towns of Punjab, the focus of the Dalit diaspora so far has been on building of places of worship rather than on improvement of socio-economic conditions of its community back home. It is believed that they are shy of displaying their wealth unlike their upper caste counterparts, for fear of challenging and instigating the upper castes' pride locally.

As these subaltern sign posts of protest, assertion and identity articulations become more and more visible, brighter and multistoreyed, the hostility has also increased with the local mainline religion with the demands for separate religious identity by the Dalits becoming shriller. Instances of clashes between the Dalits and the Jat Sikhs are regularly reported in local newspapers. Events such as the Vienna attack and similar such moments of disputes as reported and hyped by the media add to the identity crystallization processes and polarization of communities.

Reports in the newspapers related to Vienna incident continued to appear for many months after the funeral of Sant Ramanand. The most prominent of them was about the removal of Guru Granth Sahib from the Ravidassia temple in Vienna. News of shifting of "Bir"[15] out of the Ravidass temples in Germany, Portugal and Italy and the proposals of similar action from other places were reported in the media threatening to disrupt the already fragile state of affairs in the region.[16] The signs of boundaries getting more rigid were evident even in India when Dera Ballan in Jalandhar had made a clear departure from the tradition during the *antim ardas* or the last rites of the slain Sant Ramanand by not organizing any *akhand path* during the religious function held on June 13. Similar acts of defiance and disrespect were reported from a few places in the region. For instance, tension prevailed in a village near Jalandhar when the "Bir" was found on the floor and the palanquin was replaced with a photograph of Sant Ramanand of Dera Ballan.[17]

It was an unsubstantiated belief till now that the Dalit NRIs were largely in favour of change in religious practices and rituals including shifting of Guru Granth Sahib. But, the events post-Vienna and the quickness with which temples after temples in various countries followed suit in shifting of holy books only gave credence to the argument. This also adds credibility to the theory that the diaspora looks at its roots or homelands from a vantage point which more often than not is premised on sentimental reasoning, nostalgia and memory without caring much about the real and practical considerations on the ground.

This applies to all people in exile, whether forced or voluntary. Expecting the Dalit diaspora to behave any differently would be unfair and in fact may be construed by some as politically motivated, if not incorrect. The Dalit NRIs have earned enough economic capital, now they want to earn some social capital in their home lands where lie their roots, enmeshed in a history soiled with oppression, social ostracisation and extreme denial.

After centuries of oscillation between Hinduism and Sikhism in quest of a rightful place of dignity and social honour, the Dalit NRIs today naturally want to first settle it out within the religious domain. Perhaps they have lived on the margins in uncertain corridors of the sacred for far too long. They want to declare that "they have arrived" through the pomp and heavy decoration of these places of worship.

This also partly explains why the Dalits of the region could not forge any significant political base for themselves despite having a substantial numerical strength. Their fixation with the "religious" sidesteps the "political". This in turn limits the issue of identity articulation almost exclusively to the realm of the symbolic and the sacred. This is clearly in contrast to what happened in say Uttar Pradesh, one of Punjab's neighbouring state, where identity politics as represented by the Bahujan Samaj Party (BSP) revolved around secular (as opposed to sacred) and was negotiated principally through caste ideology.

Religion did not create any mist around the process of the consolidation of caste consciousness in Uttar Pradesh. In Punjab, however, various religious alternatives as represented through these Deras do create hurdles in their complete polarization. Ironically, Kanshi Ram, the man who founded the BSP, which has emerged as a formidable political front of the Dalits in Uttar Pradesh in particular and other northern states in general, was from Punjab. While the NRIs sponsored identity articulation may give the Dalits back home some episodic moments of euphoria, to create any real significant alternative the Dalits of the region will have to generate their own resource pool, not necessarily economic, based on internal sources that are guided by local agenda.

In other words, if the Dalits of the region really aim to grab the social space, political channels in a democratic set-up have to be utilized. The fight for social honour and dignity will prove to be effective only when they emerge as a force to reckon with politically. The large-scale violence and arsoning that followed the Vienna incident may have given a momentary psychic sense of hijacking of the public space but it is not going to be lasting and certainly not going to be of any real consequence for the vast number of Dalits of the region for whom education, health and income generating avenues are needs of the hour. The NRIs connection can be also utilized in creating these basic infrastructures if the Dalit politics in Punjab has to become a formidable force. That is, the transcendence from the symbolic and sacred to the political is extremely crucial for the Dalits of the region.

The road ahead

The era of globalization, as we have seen, has created a vast network of both human and non-human channels linking the local with the global in an unprecedented way. This also has the dreadful potential of setting the "local" up in flames in a span of barely some minutes as happened in the case of Vienna incident. The bottled up simmering discontent and historical hostility between two communities back home was played out in a bloody clash at a global location.

As globalization and its paraphernalia of message vending machines penetrate the remotest parts of the world and the more the linkages are established, the identity umbrella industry will grow at an unheard pace and scale. With the scattering of more and more people and products of different origins and roots across the globe, there will be scattering of cultures also, leading to possibilities of integration as well as dissonance. The challenge of our time will be in managing the "others". The key to success lies in first accepting that complete assimilation of two cultures is never ever possible on the ground. Assimilation is a theoretical proposition which sadly was taken literally by the believers of modernity.

As things stand in Punjab (India), there are silver linings on the issue of Dera amidst zones of stalemate and conflicts as represented by sporadic instances of violence reported from across the region involving the Sikhs and the Dera believers.[18] Perhaps, for the first time, there have been serious efforts to engage in a dialogue with the Deras by the political parties as well as the SGPC. This was amply evident in the way various political parties and various Sikh organizations were unambiguous in condemning the Vienna incident. Deras also represent the failure of the mainstream to accommodate and integrate the seekers in to its fold with equality and dignity. In the true Indic tradition, argumentation and differences are integral to our common religious heritage. And, dialogue is the only option. The way forward is to accept each other with dignity and respect each others' autonomy. Annihilation and intimidation only prove to be counter-productive. We know it from our history. Let us learn from it so that it does not repeat itself.

NOTES

1. "Spirituality gives a boost to trade", *The Times of Chandigarh*, the local supplement of the *Times of India*, 30 October 2007. The general secretary of the Chandigarh Beopar Mandal has been reported as saying, "The market for spiritual goods in Chandigarh has reached about Rs 25 crore and it is still growing. The sale of idols depicting Indian gods alone increased by 30 per cent this year".
2. "India's billionaire list nearly doubles", *The Indian Express*, Delhi/Chandigarh, 20 November 2009.
3. "5,000 kids under 5 die in India daily", *The Indian Express*, Delhi/Chandigarh, 21 November 2009.
4. "The symbolism of Mosque", *The Indian Express*, Chandigarh/Delhi, December 2009.
5. Ravidassi is a tradition based on the teachings of Ravidass who is considered the sat guru. Ravidassi tradition itself is not a part of Sikhism but is part of the larger Sikh ethnic group; other teachings of Ravidass are part of the holy Sikh scriptures, the Guru Granth Sahib. In 14th

century India, Ravidass, a Dalit by birth, taught spirituality and tried to bring forward the equality message of Guru Nanak Dev based on emancipation from the oppression of the Indian caste system. He was born in an oppressed community known as Chamars, who were considered "untouchable". Ravidass attracted the lowest strata of Hindu society according to the caste system. A member of the Ravidassi sect is called a "Ravidassi" or "Ravidassia". The sect is also known as the "Ravidassi sampradaya".

6. "Crores lost in two days of violence", *The Indian Express*, Delhi/Chandigarh, 28 May 2009.
7. The state of Punjab in India is divided into three main regions, namely Doaba, Majha and Malwa. The Doaba literally means "Land of two rivers". The Doaba region is surrounded by two rivers, Beas and Sutlej, and considered one of the most prosperous regions.
8. "Vienna attack suspects identified", *The Times of India*, Chandigarh/Delhi, 29 May 2009.
9. "Outside forces behind turmoil in Punjab", *The Indian Express*, Chandigarh/Delhi, 28 May 2009.
10. Talhan is a place in Punjab where in the year 2003, the dalits of the area protested against the Jat Sikh domination in the management committee of a smadh-turned gurudwara named after a local carpenter from backward caste. The dalits of Talhan village despite being the majority in the village (72%) were kept out of the membership on the gurudwara management committee because of their lowly caste status. Other than an act of local assertion of their socio-economic and political status in the area by the Jat Sikhs, one of the motives behind the conversion of a smadh or a small prayer room in reverence of a martyr who sacrificed his life for the community as in this case when Nihal Singh, a local backward caste carpenter died while laying a wooden wheel at the base of a well in Talhan village into a gurudwara was widely seen as an effort to grab the large amount of money, approximately $1.1 million offered at its altar by the devotees (Philip, 2003). Similarly, Meham also witnessed Jat Sikh-Dalit clash when a Dera of Khazan Singh Udasi that was being looked after by the Ad-Dahrmis, another dalit caste, for the last six decades was forcibly taken over by the Jat Sikhs. They replaced all Udasi symbols and placed with that of the Khalsa and objected to the offering of liquor as sacramental food among the devotees of Dera (Ram, 2007: 4072). Many other cases of violence of this nature in the region as reported in local newspapers also indicate the motives of appropriation of land and money attached with the places of worship as crucial factors behind such mobilizations.

11. Both Ambedkar and Bhagat Singh fought against the British colonial rule for India's independence. Ambedkar, who belonged to lower caste untouchable community, is considered the architect of India's constitution and today after many years of his death he remains the most prominent Dalit icon. Bhagat Singh, a young freedom fighter from Punjab, was hanged by the British for his anti-Raj activities. He is revered all over India as Shaheed-e-Aaazam, a secular youth icon who represents the ultimate martyrdom for the motherland.
12. "Dera Ballan a Mecca for Ravidassis", *The Indian Express*, Chandigarh/Delhi, 28 May 2009.
13. These facts are based on my personal interview with an examiner associated with the British Council who has been conducting these tests for the last over a decade and has seen the trends from a very close quarter.
14. "Grand structures mark Dalit Identity", *The Times of India*, Chandigarh/Delhi, 28 May 2009.
15. "Bir" is a Punjabi word meaning the holy book.
16. "Birs shifted out from 6 Ravidass temples" and "Bir shifted out from Vienna temple", *The Times of India*, Chandigarh/Delhi, 11 July and 16 July 2009.
17. "Village tense after Bir replaced with photo", *The Times of India*, Chandigarh/Delhi, 14 September 2009.
18. Instances of violent clashes are reported regularly from remote villages and towns, especially involving the Dera Sachha Sauda and the Sikhs (see Baixas, 2007).

REFERENCES

Baixas, Lionel. "The Dera Sacha Sauda Controversy and Beyond". *Economic and Political Weekly*. October 6, 2007.

Bauman, Zygmunt. *Globalisation: The Human Consequences*. Cambridge: Polity Press, 1998.

Beck, Ulrich. *Risk Society: Towards a New Modernity*. London: Sage, 1992.

Bingley, A.H. *Sikhs* (2nd ed.). Patiala: Department of Languages, 1970.

Dasgupta, Samir (ed.). *The Changing Face of Globalization*. Delhi: Sage, 2004.

Duesenbery, Verne A. and D.S. Tatla (eds.). *Sikh Diaspora Philanthropy in Punjab*. New Delhi: Oxford University Press, 2009.

Friedman, Thomas L. *The Lexus and the Olive Tree: Understanding Globalisation*. New York: Farrar, Strauss and Giroux. 1999.

——. *The World is Flat: A Brief History of the Tewnty-First Century*. New York: Farrar, Strauss and Giroux. 2005.

Giddens, Anthony. *Runaway World: How Globalization is Reshaping Our Lives*. New York: Routledge, 2000.

Gilroy, Paul. *Against Race: Imagining Political Culture beyond the Color Lines*. Cambridge: Harvard University Press, 2000.

Grewal, J.S. *The Sikhs of the Punjab*. Cambridge: Cambridge University Press, 1990.

Gupta, Dipankar. *The Context of Ethnicity: Sikh Identity in a Comparative Perspective*. Delhi: Oxford University Press, 1997.

Huizer, Gerrit. *Globalisation from Above and from Below: A Dialectical Process*. Inhoud, 2003.

Huntington, Samuel. *The Clash of Civilizations and the Making of World Order*. New Delhi: Penguin Books India, 1997.

Jodhka, Surinder S. "Dissociation, Distancing and Autonomy: Caste and Untouchability in Rural Punjab", in *Dalits in Regional Context*, edited by Harish K. Puri. New Delhi: Rawat Publications, 2004.

Judge, P.S. "Religion, Caste and Communalism in Punjab". *Sociological Bulletin*, Vol. 51, No. 2, September (2002).

Jurgensmeyer, Mark. *Religious Rebels in the Punjab: The Social Vision of Untouchable*. Delhi: Ajanta, 1988.

——. *Radhasoami Reality: The Logic of a Modern Faith*. Princeton: Princeton University Press, 1991.

Kapur, Rajiv. *Sikh Separatism: The Politics of Faith*. London: Allen and Unwin, 1986.

Madan, T.N. (ed.). *Religion in India*. Delhi: Oxford University Press, 1997.

——. "Religions of India, Plurality and Pluralism", in *The Oxford Companion to Sociology and Social Anthropology*, edited by Veena Das. New Delhi: Oxford University Press, 2003.

——. (ed.). *India's Religions: Perspectives from Sociology and History*, New Delhi: Oxford University Press, 2004.

——. "India's Religions: Plurality and Pluralism. Religious Pluralism as Ideology", *International Journal on Humanistic Ideology*, Vol. 1, No. 1 (2008): 15–24.

Marenco, Ethne K. *The Transformation of Sikh Society*. New Delhi: Heritage Publisher, 1976.

McLeod, W.H. *Guru Nanak and the Sikh Religion*. Delhi: Oxford University Press, 1968.

McLuhan, Marshall. *Understanding Media*. London: Routledge, 1964.

Meeta and Rajivlochan. "Caste and Religion in Punjab: The Case of Bhaniarawala Phenomenon". *Economic and Political Weekly*, Vol. XLII, No. 21, May 26, 2007.

Philip, A.J. "All in the Name of Almighty: The Caste Divide at Talhan". *The Tribune*, Chandigarh, June 16, 2003.

Pinch, William R. *Peasants and Monks in British India*. Berkeley: University of California Press, 1996.

Puri, Harish K. "Scheduled Castes in Sikh Community: A Historical Perspective". *Economic and Political Weekly*, Vol. 38, No. 26, June 28–July 4, 2003.

Ram, Ronki. "Untouchability, Dalit Consciousness and the Ad-Dharm Movement in Punjab". *Contributions to Indian Sociology (NS)*, Vol. 38, No. 3, September-December, 2004.

——. "The Dalit Sikhs". *Dalit International Newsletter*, Vol. 9, No. 3, October, 2004a.

——. "Social Exclusion, Resistance and Deras: Exploring the Myth of Casteless Sikh Society in Punjab". *Economic and Political Weekly,* October 6, 2007.

Ritzer, George. *Explorations in the Sociology of Consumption*. New York: Sage, 2001.

Singer, M. *When a Great Tradition Modernizes*. London: Pall Mall, 1972.

Singh, N. "Shiromani Committee and Caste". *Desh Sewak*, a Chandigarh Punjabi daily. Sunday magazine, July 1, 2007.

Tehna, Avtar Singh et al. "Kyon Bandey hann Dera? (Why Deras come into existence)". *Desh Sewak*, June 3, 2007.

UNDP. *Human Development Reports*. New York: Oxford University Press, 1992–1999.

Wallerstein, Immanuel. "Cultures in Conflict: Who are we? Who are the others?", in *The Changing Face of Globalization*, edited by Samir Dasgupta. Delhi: Sage, 2004.

Weigel, George. "Religion and Peace: An Argument Complexified". *Washington Quarterly*, 1991 Spring.

CHAPTER 4

Illud tempus in Greek Myth and Ritual*

RADEK CHLUP

Few theories of myth and ritual can equal in fame the one proposed by Mircea Eliade. According to him, archaic societies generally refuse to put up with the profane time of history, feeling the need to relate to the time of origins when the world was still fresh and strong, "as it came from the Creator's hands" (Eliade, 1959: 92). The time of origins is a time out of time, an *illud tempus*, "which is always the same, which belongs to eternity; [...] the time that 'floweth not' because it does not participate in profane temporal duration, because it is composed of an *eternal present*" (Eliade, 1959: 88). Archaic societies attempt to evoke the fullness of primordial time in rituals that repeat the archetypal events which took place in the mythical era. By "indefinitely reproducing the same paradigmatic acts and gestures" religious man manages "*to live close to his gods*" (Eliade, 1959: 91).

In the course of the last fifty years, Eliade's theory of myth and ritual has often been the subject of criticism. Its reception has been particularly lukewarm with the anthropologists, most of whom have failed to recognize in his idealized image of the "archaic man" any of the natives that they spent many months with during their field research. Eliade is often regarded by them as an armchair scholar in the Frazerian mould, trying to squeeze all primitive societies into his

*First published in *Religion* © 2008 published by Elsevier Ltd., Volume 38, Issue 4, December 2008, pp. 355–365, on the occasion of The Centennial of Mircea Eliade. Reprinted in this volume with Radek Chlup's permission and free permission of Elsevier Limited. http://www.sciencedirect.com/science/journal/0048721X.

sweeping artificial patterns (see e.g., Leach, 1966; La Fontaine, 1985; Wallace, 1966; for a neutral appraisal of anthropological critique cf. Saliba, 1978). All of these rebukes are certainly justified: it is obvious that Eliade's conception is unbearably idealizing and indiscriminate, and we would hardly find a "primitive: that would conform to it fully. Despite this, I would deem it rash to turn it down completely. As a religious studies scholar I consider the formulation of general, simplifying schemata indispensable for capturing religious phenomena, no comprehensive science of religion being possible without them. Eliade may not be a reliable guide to the world of primitive cultures, but the question remains whether at least he offers an interesting model for making sense of myths and rituals in general.[1]

To answer this question, I shall try to apply Eliade's theory to some of the myths and rituals of the ancient Greeks.[2] I hope to show that his basic notion of ritual as an attempt at periodically re-actualizing the primordial era is in harmony with them, though it needs to be modified and further elaborated. However, while largely agreeing with Eliade at the level of phenomenological description, my own interpretative position will be entirely different.

Where Eliade only aims at interpreting the religious worldview in its own terms (though not necessarily emic ones), I shall also strive for its non-religious explanation. It was recognized by Edmund Leach already that some of Eliade's ideas are strikingly parallel to the French structuralist tradition, whether in its Durkheimian form or the Lévi-Straussian one (Leach, 1966: 29–30; cf. Dudley, 1977: 144–160). Following this suggestion, I shall transplant the scheme of ritual repetition into a different methodological framework, reading it from the perspective of the Paris school of Jean-Pierre Vernant and his followers.

Ritual repetition: playing the bear for artemis

At first sight Greek rituals appear well suited for an Eliadean type of interpretation. Most of them had one or more aetiological myths associated with them, explaining how the ritual had come to be instituted in ancient times and giving the "reason" (Gr. aition, pl. aitia) of its performance. Aetiological myths were no dogmas and could apparently be altered and created freely, needing no official sanction. Often there were several ones in circulation, whether covering different aspects of the festival, or giving alternative explanations. Most of them were probably later than the rituals themselves, but that does not make them any less authentic. No matter how recent they were, they reflected adequately the meanings assigned to rituals by their participants and must have been of considerable import to them (Redfield, 1990: 118–119, 123–124; Parker, 2005: 374–383).

The existence of aetiological myths is in accord with Eliade's conception of ritual as repetition of mythical events. Primordial happenings indeed count here as timeless archetypes to be imitated forever. At closer inspection, however, the pattern of repetition turns out to be slightly different from any of those described by Eliade. In his best known examples what we have is a straightforward imitation of ancient events: "for the traditional societies, all the important facts of life were revealed ab origine by gods or heroes. Men only repeat these exemplary and paradigmatic gestures ad infinitum" (Eliade, 1954: 32). In Greek rituals such a simple imitative pattern is less common and often we find a more complicated model. A significant number of Greek aitia do not tell of glamorous deeds of ancient gods and heroes that people would repeat over and again. Much more typically they tell of an offence committed in primordial times, angering the gods and causing a plague, famine or some other disaster. In their despair people consult the oracle to find out how to end the crisis. The oracle explains what has gone wrong and suggests a religious remedy: to placate the powers offended, men have to institute a ritual that repeats the original transgression but in doing so corrects the mistake and makes everything end well.

A typical example is a ritual performed in honour of Artemis Mounichia at the Athenian port of Piraeus. Its aition[3] tells of a she-bear who in ancient times came to frequent that place and grew tame. One day a young girl teased the animal and was scratched. The girl's brothers killed the bear; but Artemis, the protectress of wild animals, became offended and caused a famine or plague. On consulting the Delphic oracle the Athenians learnt that the plague would only stop when someone sacrificed his daughter to Artemis. Nobody was willing to do so, until a man named Embarus offered to fulfil the task, on condition that he and his descendants should become lifelong priests at the sanctuary; people agreed. Embarus embellished his daughter and led her to the innermost part of the temple. There, however, he played a trick: hiding the daughter, he adorned and sacrificed a goat instead whom he had given the name of Daughter. The famine ceased but people became suspicious and went to ask Apollo again. The god ensured them that everything was alright: from then on they should sacrifice just as Embarus had done. Since then all the girls of Athens have been required to "play the bear" (arkteuein) for the goddess. The ritual itself can only be reconstructed fragmentarily, but we may safely suppose that it was meant to imitate the ancient events: a girl was presumably adorned for sacrifice, but then a goat was killed instead (for a goat sacrifice at the allied Artemis Sanctuary of Brauron see Hesychius, s.v. Brauroniois). "Playing the bear" probably means that the earlier part of the aition was also enacted and the girls were chased by some men playing the "brothers" (thus e.g., Redfield, 2003: 102).

An interpretation of this remarkable ritual would be well beyond the scope of this article.[4] What is important for us is the basic pattern that we find here and that is by no means exceptional. At the beginning we have an idyllic state of primal harmony: the bear, normally wild and dangerous, is tame and playing with a girl. Yet the idyll soon turns out to be illusory and untenable: the animal is incapable of playing safely with humans and the girl gets scratched. The break-up of primal harmony is further accentuated by the brothers' revenge. The gods consider it an offence but by sending a famine they only highlight the crisis. The good old idyllic world is in ruins. The solution suggested by Apollo is hardly encouraging: the sacrifice of a daughter may well end the famine, but its cruelty just confirms the disintegration. It is only through the deceit of Embarus that a true solution is found. Order is restored, but it is not a copy of the original idyll. Far from it, the god orders the original misdeed and the ensuing deceit to be repeated forever. The ritual is meant to corroborate the change that has taken place. Through it a new order of things has been established, sharply separated from the old one. The founding of the ritual means the end of primordial time and the beginning of history.

The myth and ritual can be analyzed into three stages: (1) The starting point is a state of primal harmony. It is pleasant, but being unnatural – or rather all too natural – it cannot last long. Men seem equal to animals at this stage and they live like them: enjoyably but wildly. Unlike them, however, they are not adjusted to this kind of existence, and sooner or later their maladjustment must come out. It is symptomatic that the dissolution of primal unity is more or less spontaneous and is not really anyone's fault. The bear could hardly guess that her claws would prove too sharp for the girl; and conversely, the brothers can hardly be blamed for having revenged their sister. (2) The misdeed generates a schism in the primal world and reduces it to chaos. Yet the schism has a positive potential: it becomes the germ of a borderline between humans and animals, between culture and nature. (3) Accordingly, its ritual repetition is prescribed by Apollo and his oracle. The task of the ritual is to cultivate and institutionalize the boundary that so far has only emerged wildly and spontaneously. The result is a clear division of reality into the orderly world of men and the savage, chaotic area beyond it:

Figure 1

1. 2. 3.

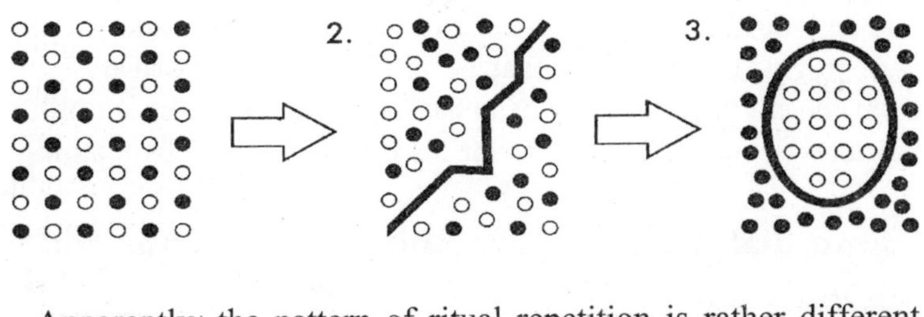

Apparently, the pattern of ritual repetition is rather different here from the one Eliade usually speaks of. The Athenians do repeat mythical events indeed, but in an indirect way. The middle term between their ritual acts and the original mythical events is the first ritual devised by Embarus and confirmed by the oracle. No doubt Embarus can be seen as a primordial cultural hero defeating the powers of darkness, and in this sense his action would fit into Eliade's scheme of ritual repetition.[5] Yet such an interpretation would overshadow what I find most interesting about the ritual, namely the fact that while still a part of the mythical era, the accomplishment of Embarus means the end of it. The first ritual staged at the end of the aition is already a part of history and is meant to be identical to that performed in the Classical period. There is in fact a double repetition involved: the Athenians repeat the first mythical ritual, which in turn repeats the previous events. It does so in a non-literal way, however, thereby changing their meaning. The ritual repeats the original misdeed to amend and cultivate it. Its performance does not bring the participants into the heart of primordial time, but is just an excursion to its borders. It is a powerful reminder of *illud tempus*, but one that is strongly negative. The Sacred Time that is evoked is not a glorious era of meaning that the Greeks would nostalgically long for. It is rather a period of indeterminacy and ambivalence, a period that does have certain paradisiacal aspects indeed, but that is fraught with danger and unsuitable for a civilized human existence.

The Greeks certainly found their *illud tempus* fascinating and saw it as a sacred source of power – otherwise they would not keep returning to it during their festivals. Yet in the course of their returns they took care to set up a clear dividing line between themselves and the primordial era, guaranteeing that the mythical events would never repeat in their original form. Embarus is not a cultural hero in that he would follow in the wake of mythical beings and partake of their might, but rather in that he proved able to extricate himself from the mythical pattern of behaviour and acted like an ordinary mortal who must compensate for his lack of strength by cunning.

Primordial time and its ambivalence: cronus and the cronia

Greek aetiological myths throw interesting light on the concept of primordial time, one of the cornerstones of Eliade's thought. In his view, ritual repetition is driven by the desire of homo religiosus to become "contemporary with the gods", "to reintegrate a primordial situation" (Eliade, 1959: 91):

> Man desires to recover the active presence of the gods; he also desires to live in the world as it came from the Creator's hands, fresh, pure, and strong. It is nostalgia for the *perfection of beginnings* that chiefly explains the periodical return *in illo tempore*. In Christian terms, it could be called nostalgia for paradise. (Eliade, 1959: 92)

In their rituals, the Greeks indeed kept returning to the mythical era of famous founding heroes who were still able to meet the gods face to face. This era undoubtedly does resemble the Judaeo-Christian paradise in many respects. In a classic passage of his *Works and Days* Hesiod calls it the Golden Age, the time when "Cronus ruled the heaven" and "men lived like the gods, free of care in their hearts, [...] rejoicing and having fun, unburdened by evil of any kind" (111–115). By contrast, men of Hesiod's time live in the Age of Iron, ever toiling and suffering, living a life full of troubles (176–178).

At first sight, Hesiod confirms the words of Eliade. On closer inspection, however, the notion of a Golden Age becomes more complicated. Its true nature is epitomized in the figure of Cronus, its divine patron. The Greeks were unanimous in regarding him as the just ruler of the Golden Age, but they also knew his darker side: in the *Theogony* of Hesiod he is depicted as a cruel king who has seized power by castrating his father Uranus, eating his own children in a desperate effort to safeguard his position. It is only when Rhea manages to hide Zeus, their youngest son, that after a long battle Cronus' regime can be overthrown and the Olympians set up a true cosmos. Accordingly, Cronus appears as a two-faced divinity: cruel and kind, beastly and idyllic. Both aspects are present in stories of his final fate: he was supposed to have ended up imprisoned in Tartarus, but it was sometimes added that he was eventually freed by Zeus and transported the Islands of the Blessed. He has become their ruler, but even there he still retains some measure of his beastliness and has to exercise his function in fetters or even in sleep (for sources cf. Versnel, 1994: 90–99).

Similar inconsistencies can be found in Cronus' rituals. Cronus was very much a *deus otiosus*. In terms of cult he was marginal and was not regarded as an active power to be worshipped. Nevertheless, throughout Greece one festival at least was celebrated in his honour: the Cronia, a counterpart to the Roman Saturnalia. These, too, were full of striking contradictions (Versnel, 1994: 99–105). On the one hand, they included bloodless offerings of cakes and bread, i.e., of idyllic foodstuffs typical of the Golden Age when men were vegetarians and refrained from killing animals. Primordial harmony is strongly evoked by the best-known feature of the festival: servants dined together with their masters, recalling thus the ancient era of universal equality. On the other hand, the Cronia were associated with cannibalism and human sacrifices. These were not actually performed, of course, and were projected into the mythical era[6]; nonetheless, stories about them showed clearly that the age of Cronus was far from idyllic.

As has been shown by H.S. Versnel (1994: 106–135), the best modern interpreter of Cronus, both images of the god are really complementary, contradictory as they may seem to be. They both present a picture of the Other, of a world turned upside down. Every otherness has a double face, being both utopian and scaring. It is liberating, removing the strains of our present world order and presenting other possibilities of being. Yet it is dangerous, threatening to destroy the cosmos altogether.[7] When masters dined with their servants during the festival, they were re-installing the Golden Age for a moment – not because they would long to return to it, but in order to remind themselves how problematic such a return would be. It would mean harmonious co-existence, but one achieved at the expense of abandoning the rules of civilization. The Greeks did not desire to merge with their origins and took care to remind themselves of both faces of Kronus. They knew how difficult origins can be and were grateful enough for their Iron Age, despite bemoaning its hardships once in a while.

While scarcely pointing to a "nostalgia for paradise", the Greek attitude is not in conflict with Eliade's wider conception as such, of course. Eliade knows well that the mythical period need not just resemble a paradise but may equally well turn into a chaos. In one of his late essays (Eliade, 1969: 87) he makes a distinction between two kinds of primordiality: (1) "a precosmic, unhistorical primordiality", in which the mythical era is understood as primal perfection while the creation amounts to a fall, and (2) "a cosmogonic or historical one", in which the creation is seen as an act of ordering the chaos that prevailed at the beginning. To these correspond "two species of *religious nostalgias*: (1) the longing to reintegrate the primordial totality that existed before the creation, [...] and (2) the longing to recover the primordial epoch that began immediately *after* the creation". A good example of the second type are rituals of the New Year, guaranteeing the continuity of life by dissolving the old year in primordial chaos and letting a new one arise fresh and strong by repeating the mythical creation (Eliade, 1954: 51–77). It is interesting that in Eliade's view "the New Year scenarios in which the Creation is repeated are particularly explicit among the historical peoples, those with whom history, properly speaking begins" (Eliade, 1954: 74). Apparently, these peoples start to be able to appreciate their historical existence more, striving for a *regeneration* of history rather than its complete abolition.[8]

A similar approach may well be applied to the ancient Greeks. As an example we can take the Cronia again. In Athens they took place shortly after harvest in the month of Hekatombaion, the first month of the year. Hence, while not being a New Year festival in the strict sense of the term, typologically they may be classified as one (Versnel, 1994: 119–121). The Otherness evoked in them is certainly a kind of chaos, dissolving the usual order of things to make it rise anew. The creative stage is missing from the Cronia as such (they only echo the rule of Cronus, not his subsequent overthrow by Zeus), but as Walter Burkert has shown (1985: 227–234), in Greece the transition between the old year and the new one was really realized by a sequence of several rituals, of which the Cronia only formed the first stage. In Athens, the Synoikia took place shortly after them, recalling the unification of Attica by Theseus, and thus the establishment of the city of Athens in its historical form. Then at the end of the month came the Panathenaia, the greatest Athenian festival (for details see Parke, 1977: 33–50).

Its main event was a bombastic procession to the Acropolis, bringing a new robe for Athena – a huge *peplos* for the colossal statue of the goddess woven by a special team of maidens and embroidered with scenes from the battle of gods and Giants.[9] In the procession all classes of inhabitants were hierarchically represented, including deputies from around 400 other cities that in the 5th century formed the Athenian empire. In many cases the procession resembled the modern May Parades of former communist regimes and there can be little doubt that its function was very similar: it reconfirmed the present political order and manifested its strength. Thanks to this the Panathenaia can be seen as a creative stage of a ritual sequence whose chaotic stage was played by the Cronia. It is significant that one of the aetiological myths claimed the festival to have been established in commemoration of Athena's victory over Aster in the battle of gods and Giants, which was the last step in establishing the orderly rule of Zeus. It was precisely this victory that was most frequently woven into the *peplos*.

In this respect the Cronia correspond to Eliade's New Year pattern and we can see them as a festival of chaos in which the old, worn-out order is dissolved to be re-created by a repetition of primordial cosmogony – represented here by the victory over the Giants periodically re-actualized on Athena's *peplos*. Nevertheless, this model only captures one side of the picture. From a different perspective, the chaos evoked in the Cronia can be seen as a Golden Age, bearing features of primal harmony. On this reading the end of Cronus' rule would amount to a fall, and would thus agree with the other type of primordiality sketched by Eliade. This is highlighted by a number of *aitia* in which the end of primordial harmony results from a human offence. Moreover, we have seen (and will see further) that Greek rituals can easily imply both models at once, presenting the end of the mythical era as both a fall and a creation. The Greek concept of primordial time thus implies a more complicated relation of chaos and order and can never be squeezed into a simple linear model in which primal chaos is followed by a period of creation, producing the ideal mythical Cosmos in its strong and "golden" form.

Setting up the boundaries: the rite of animal sacrifice

While not seriously contradicting Eliade's scheme, Greek myths and rituals seem to represent a rather intricate subtype of it. Unlike most cases discussed by Eliade, the Greek examples analyzed so far are characterized by an essential ambivalence that is connected with mythical events in all their stages. Eliade generally tends to depict the mythical world in an idealistic light. He knows that chaos is a regular part of it and that myths can be full of crises and primordial schisms, but on the whole he is inclined to see things in a more or less black-and-white way and prefers instances in which negative aspects are outweighed by glorious creative actions of gods and heroes. The Greek version of the Sacred Time theme is interesting in that it makes such a simplified polarisation impossible, inviting us to reconsider the meaning of the whole conception.

What seems particularly conspicuous is the crucial part played by the boundaries that in most aetiological myths are carefully being set up between our world and the primordial one. To illuminate their importance, we can have a look at what is generally considered the most important Greek ritual – the rite of animal sacrifice. The classic aition is given by Hesiod (Theogony: 535–616; Works and Days: 45–105). It takes place in ancient times before the birth of culture when the relations between gods and men were unclear and were a subject of negotiation. Prometheus tried to improve the lot of mankind by suggesting a division of sacrificial animals that is most advantageous for men. Killing an ox, he separated the flesh and entrails from the bones. Enclosing the former in the stomach and covering the latter with fat, he gave Zeus to choose. Zeus understood his deception all too well (Theogony: 550–552), but planning to impose hardships on mankind anyway, he pretended not to know and chose the inviting-looking parcel of fat – only to get furious on discovering that he had got nothing but bones. Hence it is that men burn fat and bones for the gods but eat all the meat themselves.

The myth recalls a familiar pattern. Its starting point is a state of primal harmony, which from the very first is depicted as problematic. It is felt to be confusing and gods and men are negotiating to find a way out of it and establish proper distinctions. These are established by deceit, i.e., there is something unnatural about them. Prometheus' cunning trick initiates a mythical crisis – but one that is seen as correct, being in concord with the plans of Zeus. A retaliation follows, taking place in three stages: (1) Zeus takes away from men the celestial fire that they had so far been able to use; Prometheus steals it back. (2) In revenge, Zeus strikes even harder and produces the first woman, the source of all evil. (3) To make things even worse, a third catastrophe follows: in his anger Zeus hides from men their livelihood, so that they have to start working. What this punishment implies is that hitherto men had no need to work, living in a Golden Age in which the earth produced everything by itself. From now on, they will have to practice agriculture and toil hard for their living.

What does this mythical scenario tell us about the meaning of sacrifice? A classic answer has been given by Jean-Pierre Vernant (1982: 135–140, 168–185), who shows the institution of animal sacrifice as highly ambivalent. On the one hand, it marked the end of a Golden Age, a separation of gods and men, the beginning of toil and suffering. On the other hand, it meant the beginning of culture in three regards: (1) It amounted to the rise of agriculture, which was not only seen as hard work but even more importantly as the foundation of human civilization. The Greeks valued agriculture highly and regarded it as a sign of cultivated life. (2) Nor did the advent of the first woman have negative consequences only: it made the crucial civilizing institution of marriage possible. While animals mate at random, human procreation is subject to strict cultural rules. The Greeks considered marriage as parallel to agriculture and the association of both figured even in the marriage ritual (Detienne, 1994: 116–117). (3) Last but not least, the theft of fire was a fundamental achievement too. Previously, men had had fire at their disposal as a matter of course, i.e., as something natural. After having been deprived of it, they had to obtain it again and henceforth guard it anxiously. In this way, fire has passed from the realm of nature into the sphere of culture, and Prometheus could justly be regarded as a civilization hero who had wrested mankind from its primitive bestiality. For the same reason fire plays a prominent part in the sacrificial ritual: while animals eat meat in its raw state, men cook it and roast it, turning food consumption into a cultural act.

The institution of animal sacrifice has created a gap between gods and men but it has elevated mankind from the level of animals to that of cultural beings. We may thus say with Vernant that the sacrificial ritual has situated mankind firmly "between the beasts and the gods" (1982: 183). Interestingly enough, however, the two extreme poles of this system are strikingly close to each other. By separating themselves from the gods, men lost their animal features too. The Golden Age bears remarkable bestial characteristics and it is only after breaking loose from it that men attain their proper cultural state. One cannot help but regarding the Golden Age as analogous to the realm of Nature which is both bestial and divine, both wild and idyllic. For this reason it is only right that the primal era has ended. To return to it would mean to abandon one's civilized humanity, which the Greeks refused to do. In the long run, Prometheus' deceit has proved appropriate for mankind, just as Zeus had foreseen. Animal sacrifice kept reminding the Greeks of their cultural state, setting up a clear dividing line between culture and nature. The sacrificial act as such stands at the boundary between these two spheres and is liminal in many respects: it resulted from Prometheus' cheating and has something dark and terrifying about it, being an act of killing. Paradoxically, however, it is through this very act of killing that cultural order can be defined and upheld.

Clearly, the sacrificial scheme corresponds to the pattern we have traced in the Mounichian myth and ritual, being but an amplification of its third stage. At the same time, it bears strong resemblance to a pattern that Eliade discusses in connection with sacred space:

Figure 2

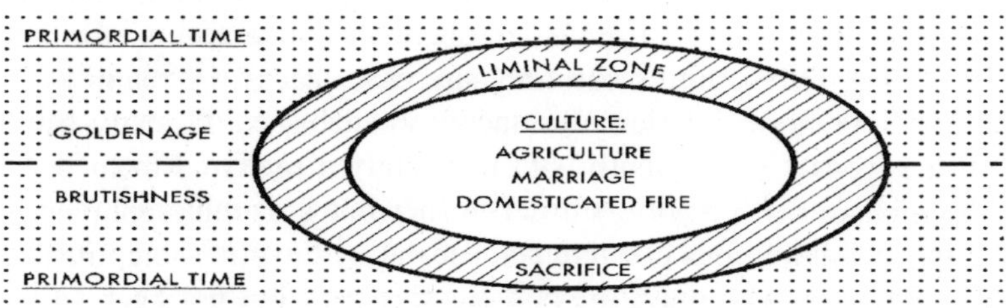

> One of the outstanding characteristics of traditional societies is the opposition that they assume between their inhabited territory and the unknown and indeterminate space that surrounds it. The former is the world (more precisely, our world), the cosmos; everything outside it is no longer a cosmos but a sort of "other world", a foreign, chaotic space, peopled by ghosts, demons, "foreigners". [...] At first sight this cleavage in space appears to be due to the opposition between an inhabited and organized – hence cosmicized – territory and the unknown space that extends beyond its frontiers; on one side there is a cosmos, on the other a chaos. But we shall see that if every inhabited territory is a cosmos, this is precisely because it was first consecrated, because, in one way or another, it is the work of the gods or is in communication with the world of the gods. The world (that is, our world) is a universe within which the sacred has already manifested itself, in which, consequently, the break-through from plane to plane has become possible and repeatable (Eliade, 1959: 29–30).

The model that Eliade sketches in these lines is analogous to the three stages of myth and ritual at Mounichia. The "chaos" of uninhabited territory corresponds to the untenable "natural" state in stage one. Stage two coincides with what Eliade later in the same book terms an "irruption of the sacred" (1959: 97), causing a schism that in stage three will become the basis of a boundary between cosmos and chaos. The same structure is apparent in the myth of the institution of sacrifice, the manifestation of the sacred taking the form of the first sacrifice followed by a struggle between Zeus and Prometheus.

The question is in what sense the "irruption of the sacred" serves as a foundation of the world. Eliade mostly takes it for granted that it does so by means of a positive creative act of some sort. He sees its manifestation primarily "as an irruption of creative energy into the world" that "*establishes* the world as a reality" (Eliade, 1959: 97). Often this is certainly the case, yet in Greek *aitia* the situation is more complex. The sacred as such (i.e., the intervention of the gods) is frequently of a strongly negative kind. In the Mounichian myth Apollo's order to sacrifice a daughter can hardly count as a glamorous creative act, escalating the crisis even further. It is Embarus who plays the constructive part, but not even he is a prototype of the founding hero. His heroic deed consists not so much in having defeated the powers of darkness and set things in order, but rather in "neutralizing" the conflict, in having deprived it of its destructive power and turning it into a source of life and strength. Following in his footsteps, the Athenians forever repeat his achievement, recalling the ancient crisis in a ritual manner that makes it harmless and sets clear boundaries to it. By doing this they reconfirm the present order of the world that was introduced after the crisis had been warded off. Yet the crisis as such – i.e., the "irruption of the sacred" – is purely negative. To the Athenians it indicated the limits of their cosmos, without providing a positive foundation for it. Indeed, most of them probably had no idea what crucial cultural values those ancient events were supposed to have established.

The myth of first animal sacrifice is more explicit in this regard, referring the institutions of marriage and agriculture. These were undoubtedly among the cornerstones of the Greek "cosmos" and were connected by an intricate network of relations to a number of crucial cultural values (Detienne, 1994; Vernant, 1982: 130–167). It is symptomatic, however, that in myth even these are only present negatively: the creation of the first woman and the necessity to work the earth are depicted as Zeus' punishments, not as magnificent culture-founding acts. The positive establishment of both of these institutions was of course the topic of other myths. The gift of farming, for instance, was frequently attributed to Demeter. Yet even in this case the central subject of the cult – such as the Eleusinian mysteries or the Thesmophoria – was rather the crisis that had preceded the spread of agriculture (see the *Homeric Hymn to Demeter*). It was caused by the goddess herself, who made the earth infertile as a protest against the abduction of her daughter by Hades. From the Greek perspective justice was on Hades' side, for he took Persephone for a bride after having obtained the consent of Zeus, her father, i.e., in accordance with standard Greek marriage customs. Nevertheless, Demeter refused to admit the marriage and against all cultural rules insisted on keeping her daughter to herself. After long negotiations all the parties reached agreement, the goddess restored fertility and with the help of Triptolemus spread agriculture all over the world. The constructive ending of the myth conforms to Eliade's classic pattern. It is noticeable, though, that in myth and cult the spread of agriculture was more of a postscript, the main topic being Demeter's anger and its seeming inappeasability. At its basic level the cult of Demeter looks not so much as a celebration of the gift of farming but rather as a powerful reminder of how fragile and precarious human agriculture is.[10]

Eliade is convinced that a cosmos can only by established by a manifestation of the sacred, nothing else being able to "project a fixed point into the formless fluidity of profane space" (Eliade, 1959: 63). A similar conclusion was much earlier reached by Émile Durkheim (1915: 9–20, 427–447) and Greek myths and rituals seem to support it. Nonetheless, they also show that the "irruption of the sacred" need not just consist in a positive act of creation. In Greece it is more commonly described as a mythical crisis and a source of danger. The aim of rituals is to turn the danger into a blessing. A good example of an "irruption of the sacred" is the most important of all Greek ritual acts – animal sacrifice. The killing of the victim – normally accompanied by a shrill scream of female participants – as an extreme act at the border of life and death was a perfect way of re-actualizing that flash of Otherness with which the sacred breaks into the world. The sacrificial act recalled the ancient strife between gods and men and reconfirmed it. The deceit of Prometheus was constantly repeated: over and over again the gods were receiving nothing but worthless bones. At the same time, however, the ritual was able to repair the ancient crisis, for it was seen as a way of approaching the gods and paying tribute to them.[11] Animal sacrifice thus functioned as a landmark, keeping the sacred at a safe distance while making communication with it possible.

Nature and culture: the bouphonia

Why do the gods in Greek aetiological myths call basic social institution into question so often rather than positively founding them? Why is cultural order based on a crisis occasioned by the gods and human deceit reacting to it? Eliade provides no answer and prefers other mythical patterns in which similar problems do not appear. In the second half of my article I am going to attempt an answer of my own, though one heavily inspired by contemporary anthropological approaches to the study of Greek myths and rituals. My interpretation shall digress from that of Eliade not only by laying stress on the ambivalence of mythical events but even more importantly by being set in a different methodological framework.

As a convenient starting point of our discussion we may once again take the subject of animal sacrifice. An alternative view of it was offered by a remarkable Athenian rite called Bouphonia, "Ox-Slaying". It was a part of the Dipolieia, a festival of Zeus Polieus (Protector of the City) which took place at the summit of the Acropolis. Its detailed description was given by Theophrastus at the turn of the 4th century B.C., and it is worth quoting in full (as preserved by Porphyry, On Abstinence 2.29–30):

> In antiquity […] humans sacrificed grain to the gods, not animals, and they did not use them for their own nourishment. At a public sacrifice in Athens, one of the oxen coming in from the fields is said to have eaten some of the meal in honeyed oil and the incense and to have trampled all over the rest. A certain Diomos or Sopatros, not a native but someone farming in Attica, became enraged at what had happened. He seized an ax that was being sharpened nearby and struck the ox. The ox died. When the man recovered from his anger and realized what he had done, he buried the ox and went of his own accord into exile in Crete as one who had committed impiety. Then the rain stopped falling, and the grain no longer grew. Delegates were sent by the state to Delphi to inquire of Apollo. The Pythia responded that the exile in Crete would redeem these conditions: avenge the murder and resurrect the dead in the same sacrifice in which it died, and things would be better for those who tasted the dead and did not hold back. A search was undertaken, and the man responsible for the deed was discovered. Sopatros reckoned that he would be released from the unpleasantness of being polluted if they all did these measures in common. He told those who came to him that the ox must be slain by the city. Since they were at wit's end over who would be the slayer, he offered them this possibility: if they made him a citizen, they would share the murder with him. Agreement was reached on those terms. When they came back to the city, they arranged the affair in the way in which it remains today.

> They chose girls to bring the water. They fetched the water used for sharpening the ax and knife. After sharpening, one man administered the ax, another struck the ox, and a third cut its throat. They next skinned it, and everyone tasted the ox. Afterwards, having sewn up the hide of the ox and stuffed it with hay, they set it up again with the same stance as when it was alive and yoked it to the plow as if ready for work. Assembling a trial for murder, they summoned all who had participated in the deed to defend themselves. The water fetchers charged that the sharpeners were more to blame than they. The sharpeners said the same about the ax-administrator, and this one of the throat-cutter, and this one of the knife which, being without a voice, was condemned to murder. From that time to the present always during the festival of Zeus Polieus on the Acropolis at Athens those mentioned above perform the sacrifice of the ox in the same way. Having placed meal in a honeyed oil and cakes of ground barley on a bronze table, they drive around it selected oxen. Whichever takes a taste is struck. The families of those who perform these rites exist today. Those descended from Sopatros, who struck the ox, are all called Ox-Smiters. Those descended from the one who drove the ox around are called Prodders. Those descended from the slaughterer they named Carvers because the feast came from the distribution of the meat. They filled up the hide, whenever they were brought to court, and threw the knife into the sea.[12]

Plainly, the Bouphonia are to be read as a defence of animal sacrifice and a justification of the awkward fact that innocent domesticated animals were daily being slain to the gods, despite being useful members of the household. In case of the working ox the paradox stands out particularly well – no wonder that normally its sacrifice was forbidden and was only reserved for this one extreme occasion (Parker, 2005: 190–191). On closer inspection we discover that in fact the Bouphonia merely underscored some standard features of the sacrificial rite (for its description see e.g., Burkert, 1985: 55–57). Its participants typically tried to preserve the feeling of innocence till the very last moment. The knife that was soon to cut the artery of the animal was carefully hidden in a basket beneath grains of barley. Moreover, like most cultures the Greeks took great care to make the impression that the animal approached its death willingly, considering it as a privilege. To this end the beast was sprinkled with water and its consequent shiver was taken as a sign of assent.

Several modern scholars have interpreted these measures as symptoms of guilt that the Greeks were supposed to feel for the killing. The Bouphonia have been regarded by them as a "comedy of innocence" performed by the Athenians in order to appease their guilt feeling and persuade themselves that everything was in order (Meuli, 1946: 275–277; Burkert, 1983: 16–22). Such a view, however, is entirely unlikely. In the Classical period the Greeks considered the rite a farce themselves (see Aristophanes, *Clouds:* 984–985), and it is barely imaginable that even in earlier times the absurd lawsuit staged during the festival could have disguised the cruelty of sacrificial killing in any way. Indeed, the actual effect of the Bouphonia must have been exactly opposite: rather than camouflaging the problematical nature of animal sacrifice, the ceremony brought it to light. If the Athenians really wished to hide from themselves the obvious fact that innocent domesticated animals got killed during sacrificial rites, they would have done better not to mention it at all and stress the positive side of animal sacrifice only (as they frequently did). If instead they periodically reminded themselves that the first sacrifice had been a crime, they must have had more interesting reasons for such a curious activity.

It is more promising to look at the Bouphonia from the perspective of the aetiological pattern sketched above. We have seen that in many cases rituals imitate an ancient mythical misdeed in order to correct it. As a consequence rituals constantly evoke the danger that would threaten if we failed to perform them (Redfield, 2003: 91). This is just what happens at the Bouphonia, which follow this pattern step by step: an ancient transgression (more or less inadvertent) is followed by divine punishment; an oracle commands the offence to be repeated. The ritual instituted by Sopatros manages to atone for the crime by being non-literal. The primordial crisis is forever evoked only to be averted and turned into a triumph. The result is the foundation of culture, i.e., in this case of the sacrifical ritual that was the cornerstone of Greek religion. The comic lawsuit staged at the Bouphonia is no less bizarre than the substitutional goat sacrifice for Artemis Mounichia. In the eyes of the Greeks it no doubt corroborated the victory of culture over nature. The slaying of a working ox was essentially a crime but ritual was able to provide a cultural justification for it (Vernant, 1991: 299–301).

From this point of view the subject of the Bouphonia is the passage from nature to culture. This passage frequently entails crime and deceit, because the separation of culture from nature is always partly deceptive. Culture is opposed to nature and in many respects needs to present itself as its adversary. But it also grows out of nature and needs to stay in touch with it. Human identity is cultural. Man differs from animals in that he needs to identify with a social group, its cosmology, its rules and principles. Despite this, however, he remains a biological being. He may tame and cultivate natural processes, he may classify them and impose cultural order on them – yet he continues to be subject to them himself and at a certain level the difference between him and animals is slight. It is hardly accidental that rituals deal with biological processes so often (such as food consumption or sexuality). It is in them that the overlap of culture and nature is most conspicuous, and great pains have thus to be taken to keep the two spheres separate without blocking their contact altogether.

Greek animal sacrifice is a good instance of this problem. Its subject is the slaying of animals, which is biologically indispensable. Let us recall that the main part of the sacrificial ritual was the feast that followed the killing, and that sacrifices were the main occasion for meat eating (Detienne, 1989: 3, 11). Sacrifice is thus at heart a biological event with a nutritive function. Yet it is subject to strict rules that strive to separate the realm of nature and culture as clearly as possible. By killing animals in an institutionalized way, man rises above them and demonstrates his superiority.

But how to discriminate what at bottom is blended? How to make one and the same act both cultural and natural without losing the distinction between the two? To a paradoxical problem there can only be a paradoxical solution. If we are to separate two terms without preventing their communication, we need a third term that contains elements of both while standing outside them. The middle term has to represent a liminal zone "betwixt and between" (Turner, 1969: 95) in which everything is possible. Greek rituals evoke precisely such a liminal zone. The whole process strongly resembles van Gennep's three stages of rituals of passage. The starting point is a mythical offence, corresponding to the phase of segregation. The offence is inevitable and often accidental (Sopatros can hardly be blamed for punishing the ox). Yet it is perceived as a crime, for it amounts to a suppression of nature, which must always be unnatural. Stage two follows, throwing things into a state of liminal chaos – in our case taking the form of famine and the pollution and exile of Sopatros (vaguely reminiscent of the temporary expulsion of initiands that frequently takes place during rites of passage). A solution is discovered in stage three, which is symmetrical to stage one, imitating the original misdeed, yet leading to a new, cultural state. Accordingly, the form of imitating is cultural as well (Vernant, 1991: 300–301): it is based on a *deceit* that enables the participants to have their ox and eat it too. The deceit is still a part of liminal chaos – in everyday life the ludicrous lawsuit would have been unacceptable. But it is already halfway towards being cultural, demonstrating human cleverness that all culture is based on. Equally cultural are the particular measures taken by Sopatros: the guilt is erased in a lawsuit and the ox is symbolically resurrected in a cultural position – harnessed to a cart. The *rite de passage* pattern is well illustrated by the fate of Sopatros: originally he was a stranger, i.e., a person standing outside the cultural order of Athens; at the end of the story he becomes a citizen, i.e., is integrated into the order.

By symbolically resurrecting the ox, Sopatros has sealed the passage from nature to culture. By repeating the archetypal ritual periodically, the Athenians re-confirm the passage, but they also ensure that their cultural order is in touch with something that transcends it and that due to its liminal nature is capable of mediating between cultural order and its opposite. The killing of the sacrificial animal embodies precisely this mediating element (Endsjø, 2003: 335–336). Normally, killing has its place outside the realm of culture: it is animals that eat one another at random, not civilized human beings. Yet killing is indispensable even within culture. The act of killing thus needs to be transformed: stripped of its natural, beastly aspect, it is turned into a cultural act with clear rules. It is no wonder that on standard occasions the victims could only be domesticated animals, i.e., those incorporated into culture. Significantly, however, the killing is done for and in the name of the gods – despite the fact that most of the animal is eaten by humans. The gods stand outside the polarity of nature and culture, being thus able to connect them without blurring the borderline between them.

Figure 3

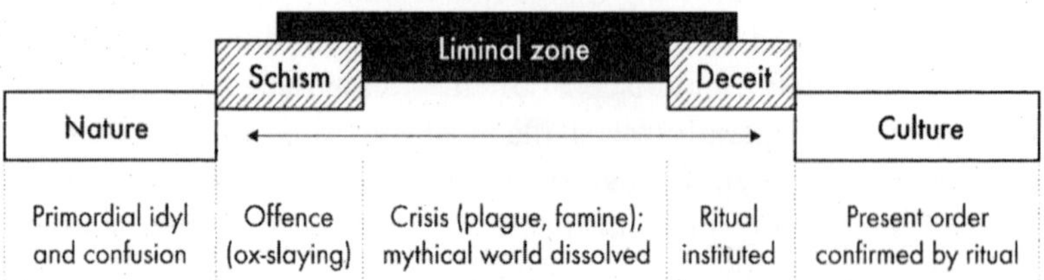

Socio-political implications: the arrhephoria

The relation between nature and culture is not only to be negotiated in case of biological conditions of human life, but even more urgently in connection with the status of all socio-political arrangements as such. This is fittingly illustrated by the last ritual that I have chosen for my discussion – the Arrhephoria, a mysterious Athenian festival in honour of Athena Polias (Protectress of the City). Its brief description is given by Pausanias (*Description of Greece* 1.27.3, tr. by J. Frazer):

> Two maidens dwell not far from the temple of the Polias: the Athenians call them Arrhephoroi. These are lodged for a time with the goddess; but when the festival comes round they perform the following ceremony by night. They put on their heads the things which the priestess of Athena gives them to carry, but what it is she gives is known neither to her who gives nor to them who carry. Now there is in the city an enclosure not far from the sanctuary of Aphrodite called Aphrodite in the Gardens, and there is a natural underground descent through it. Down this way the maidens go. Below they leave their burdens, and getting something else, which is wrapt up, they bring it back. These maidens are then discharged, and others are brought to the Acropolis in their stead.

As we know from other sources, the ritual was performed every summer (*Etymologicum Magnum* 149.14). Since the new maidens were brought in immediately after the old ones had been discharged, it follows they had to serve to the goddess for a full year. They were between seven and eleven years old and were chosen for their task by the Archon Basileus, one of the highest officials of Athens (*Etymologicum Magnum* 149.14, 362.39). Throughout the year they had other services to fulfil, such as assisting in the weaving of the sacred *peplos* that was to be presented to Athena at the Panathenaia (Harpocration, *s.v. arrhephorein*).

In themselves the Arrhephoria are hard to make sense of, but modern scholars have noticed that they relate to the myth of Athenian origins (for its classic account see Apollodorus *The Library* 3.14). In the myth we find two interesting personages. The first one is Cecrops, the first king of Athens who was born from the earth and was snake-formed where his legs should have been. The second one is Erichthonios, whose birth was even more remarkable. His father was the god Hephaestus, who once fell into a passion for Athena and tried to get hold of her. Athena would not submit and he only managed to ejaculate on her thigh. Athena wiped the sperm off with wool and threw it to the ground, thus impregnating it. After some time Erichthonios was born from the earth. Athena put him in a chest and gave it to the three daughters of Cecrops to guard, strictly forbidding to open it. But two of the girls opened it out of curiosity, beholding a dreadful spectacle that various authors describe differently: they may have found a snake coiled around the baby, or even two snakes or perhaps it was Erichthonios himself who was partly a snake like Cecrops. The girls were driven mad by the sight and leaped from the Acropolis.

Plainly, the myth is a mythical model for the Arrhephoria and we may read it as their *aition*, though an incomplete one. By comparing the myth with the ritual we find the familiar pattern once again. At the beginning there is an offence taking place in primordial time. We do not know how the ritual was instituted but it is obvious that it is meant to repeat the original tragic story in a non-literal way, trying to amend what had gone wrong in the myth. The mythical maidens die, but the ritual ones overcome their curiosity and keep the chest closed. The ritual does not imitate the mythical archetype out of nostalgia but in order to correct it and prevent its repetition.

What is the meaning of the Arrhephoria? There is no unanimous answer to this question, of course, for rituals are essentially polyvalent and one of their chief achievements is precisely their ability to connect various levels of meaning that would otherwise seem incompatible and contradictory (Turner, 1967). One possible interpretation is suggested by the myth, which is generally read as dealing with the problem of Athenian *autochthony* (see e.g., Csapo, 2005: 238–244; Redfield, 2003: 118–127; Loraux, 1993, *passim*). The Athenians were among the few Greek cities that claimed to have been born out of their own earth. While other cities told myths of how their ancestors had conquered their territory, the Athenians insisted on having lived in Attica since time immemorial and being linked to their land in a natural way through the half-chthonic figures of Cecrops and Erichthonios. The ideological import of this was enormous: in the 5th century B.C. it made the Athenians feel much superior to other Greek communities, a true mother city of them all (Loraux, 2000: 47–64).

The idea of autochthony was crucial for the Athenians, yet it was highly unnatural:

> In actuality, people occupy territory; they secure it by military organization, and by the application of technique they cultivate it and turn it to the purposes of culture. By the myth of autochthony, however, the people, and (more important) their cultural organization (since the autochthon is a founder-king), are represented as natural products of the soil. Thus a historically contingent fact – the location of a culture – is represented as a natural kingship; an event is transformed into a structure. (Redfield, 2003: 123–124)

The Greeks recognized the problem themselves and at a certain level of their thought were aware of the historical contingence of all territorial claims.[13] Despite this, the Athenians pretended to have a natural claim to their land, having grown out of it in the manner of vegetables. Why is this so? The answer is connected with the status of all socio-political arrangements (of which the possession of land is just one aspect). Not even these can ever be "natural", as the Greeks knew all too well, priding themselves on their cultural institutions and feeling above all natural conditions.

Nonetheless, the Greeks also knew that if socio-political forms are to persist throughout the never-ending debates of conflicting individuals, they must make a claim to being more than a contingent product of history or the result of rational agreement.[14] In other words, they must present themselves as at once cultural and natural.

What we have here is a paradox similar to that we have detected in the Bouphonia: just as man is both a biological and a cultural creature, and thus needs to keep both of these aspects together without losing the distinction between them, the same holds for the *polis* as a whole. The *polis* is a creation of culture, but to survive it has to be depicted as equally a product of nature.[15] The solution of this paradox is the same we have seen in the previous section: we need to find a mediating term that would connect the two realms while separating them clearly. Once again, myth is an ideal mediator, referring to a plane of reality that transcends standard human categories, including the law of contradiction. The myth of Erichthonios illustrates this well (Peradotto, 1977; Csapo, 2005: 238–240). Being a founder of the cultural order of Athens, Erichthonios is neither a being of nature, nor that of culture. His birth is both sexual and asexual: there is an ejaculation, but no intercourse. Equally asexual was the birth of his parents: Athena was born from Zeus' head, Hephaestus was conceived by Hera without a male partner. There is something monstrous about Erichthonios and it is no wonder that the sight of him scarred the daughters of Cecrops to death. The snake-motif suggests that the monstrosity has to do with mixing up the human and the animal, the civilized and the chthonic. Erichthonios is a liminal creature – which is why he is able to bridge the unbridgeable.

The sphere of nature is represented in the myth by the daughters of Cecrops. From the Greek perspective, girls from their first menstruation to the point of their wedding belonged to Artemis, the goddess of wild, "virgin" landscape. Free of work and adult responsibility, these innocent maidens personified the Golden Age, and the Greeks let them dance in choruses during religious festivals

(Calame, 2001: 90; Redfield, 2003: 113–114). Yet they also had a share of the savagery of nature – this being the point of their association with bears in the Mounichion ritual (Vernant, 1991: 200). In myths the followers of Artemis mostly end tragically: they wish to preserve their purity but inevitably at the bloom of their youth they are pursued by male seducers, choosing to die rather than succumb to their sexuality. In practice this mythical motif was associated with the passage of girls into the "cultural" state of marriage (Vernant, 1991: 198–201). Once at its threshold, the girls had to let die their "natural", virginal identity to become women and mothers. The death of a maiden ripe for marriage was a powerful image helping to articulate the boundary line between nature and culture. In real life girls were able to cross this boundary, of course, avoiding the sad fate of their mythical forebears. But the myths reminded them that the passage was substantial and not to be taken lightly (Redfield, 2003: 111–118).

In this light we may understand the death of the daughters of Cecrops as a necessary end of the natural and "virginal" stage of the history of Athens. The Arrhephoria imitate this crucial event, but do so from the perspective of culture, trying to amend what in ancient times had gone wrong. In myth the daughters of Cecrops are adolescent,[16] pertaining to Artemis (who is virginal but sexual); in the rite they are between seven and eleven years, i.e., at an age when their sexuality is still dormant and they are the servants of Athena (who is virginal but asexual). Their mysterious chests, on the other hand, associated sexual content in antiquity already,[17] and it is perhaps not accidental that the girls pass close to the precinct of Aphrodite. "In this way they represent the ambiguity of the myth, which tell us that the origin of the Athenian people is both sexual and asexual" (Redfield, 2003: 125). Unlike their mythical predecessors, however, they manage to curb their curiosity, performing thus the victory of culture over nature.

> Their service is a sacrifice in that it requires them the suppression of an impulse – in this case, the impulse of curiosity, which plays such a large role in the sexuality of children. They have learned their lesson from the daughters of Cecrops; they will not inquire

> too closely into the origins of Athens, into that primal scene that generated the Athenian state. (Redfield, 2003: 126; cf. Zeitlin, 1982: 152)

The Arrhephoria call our attention to a crucial dimension of myth and ritual. Myths tell of roots and origins – not in a temporal sense, but in a metaphysical one. Myths talk about what is beyond the horizon of our world but what this world rests upon. Why do all worlds need to be anchored in myth? Because every socio-cultural system is an arbitrary construct that is unnatural and yet cannot do without a connection to nature. As a result, every socio-cultural arrangement is based on a paradox. Myth is one of the few cultural media that can absorb the paradox and work with it constructively. The myth of Ahtnian autochthony is but one of many examples of this, reflecting the general truth that the ultimate roots of social and political arrangements are always monstrous and mysterious (Redfield, 2003: 126). The Athenians acknowledge this, but while admitting the monstrous foundations of their own identity, they make the decisive step of not tampering with it, leaving it behind the borders of their world. The Arrhephoroi carry the arcane source of Athenian power in their chests, but they resist the temptation and do not open them. The secret of primordiality can remain concealed and keep its strength. The same maidens help to weave the *peplos* which is an epitome of the socio-political order of Athens. In this way they embody a link between the dark primordial origins of the *polis* and its present arrangement as celebrated by the Panatheaia and their *peplos*.

Conclusion

My discussion has not been meant as an exhausting analysis of all the patterns that we can find in Greek myths and rituals, and still less as a model valid for all religions in general. My aim has been more modest: to compare the Greek concept of primordial time with that of Eliade, showing that the former emphasizes certain interesting features not quite evident in the latter. The Greeks were acutely aware of the ambivalence of the mythical era, and their rituals were not just meant to evoke it but to keep it off as well, protecting the cosmos from it and making sure that it does not flow into it freely. A particular part was played by mythical heroes, who tended to use tricks and deceits as their main weapon. In the eyes of Eliade none of these differences would probably be disturbing. He admitted that particular conceptions of primordiality differ from culture to culture[18] and the Greek model would no doubt seem to him as one of the variants of the need of archaic peoples to relate to the world of myth and draw strength from it. Its peculiarities might be explained by the fact that the Greeks were already a highly developed society with a sense of history, their attitude towards mythical beginnings being more complicated than in traditional ahistorical societies (Eliade, 1963: 110–112; cf. Allen, 2002: 200–203).

It is questionable, though, whether the Greeks really were that specific. Their ritual patterns might have been more complex than those of more primitive societies, but the essential ambiguity that we have seen to pervade them seems to be a fundamental feature of myths in general. The mythical era is sacred, thus sharing a basic property of the sacred that was already indicated by Durkheim: its ambivalence. The sacred is both attractive and repulsive, both *tremendum* and *fascinans*. Accordingly, the task of rituals is not just to bring the profane world in touch with the sacred (as Eliade keeps emphasizing) but also "to prevent undue mixings and to keep one of these domains from encroaching upon the other" (Durkheim, 1915: 299). Eliade is aware of the ambivalence of the sacred (see e.g., Eliade, 1958: 14–19), but he tends to marginalize it in his discussions, preferring to picture the time of origins as a magnificent epoch to be longed for with nostalgia. The Greek examples make it possible to correct his account and give more depth to it.

At the same time, the Greek vision of primordial time is highly interesting in that it offers an opportunity for setting the whole problem of ritual repetition in a different methodological perspective. This is important, for it is precisely Eliade's methodology that has often been a subject of critique. He has commonly been blamed for being "crypto-theological" and presenting an original religious vision of the world rather than a neutral scholarly analysis.[19] Penetrating as some of his analyses may be, in most cases they only satisfy those who see the world religiously themselves.

Secular readers are rightly puzzled by the idea of the sacred "irrupting" into the world, and they would like to know how the archaic peoples arrived at their worldview in the first place. Eliade provides no answer and does not even feel the need to ask the question. Being a religious person himself, he found the archaic vision natural and meaningful enough. Indeed, he refused to take seriously all explanations of religion that would take their starting point from elsewhere than the sphere of religious ideas. No wonder that a number of secular scholars refuse to take him seriously.

My own interpretation has the advantage of being able to keep a number of Eliade's descriptive categories while placing them in a different explanatory framework which is not religious itself but is not reductionist either – for it does not deny mythical entities their transcendence. In my account the mysterious power of primordial time has to do with the nature of order, its boundaries and its relation to what transcends it – to chaos and disorder. The point is well put by Mary Douglas in *Purity and Danger*:

> Granted that disorder spoils pattern, it also provides material of pattern. Order implies restriction; from all possible materials, a limited selection has been made and from all possible relations a limited set has been used. So disorder is by implication unlimited, no pattern has been realised in it, but its potential for patterning is indefinite. This is why, though we seek to create order, we do not simply condemn disorder. We recognise that it is destructive to existing patterns; also that it has potentiality. It symbolises both danger and power. Ritual recognizes the potency of disorder. (Douglas, 2002: 117)

On this interpretation, chaos is not a nihilistic negation of order but corresponds to what Eliade calls "a plenitude of being" (1959: 97). It contains all possible arrangements of reality, every particular ordering of the world being but a segment of it. Consequently, while being a source of threat for every cultural arrangement by pointing to its limits, it remains its ultimate foundation. Every cosmos is dependent on chaos and needs to come to terms with it. It needs to face the possibility of alternative orderings of things. It needs to take into account that no ordering is able to contain all of reality; there will always be situations that do not fit. Moreover, no cultural arrangement can avoid internal contradictions, "since in the endless variety of real situations, norms considered equally valid in abstraction are frequently found to be inconsistent with one another, and even mutually to conflict" (Turner, 1967: 40). Finally and most importantly, every cultural arrangement is in danger of ossifying. If it is to avoid this danger and keep its dynamics and capacity for change, it needs to have some sort of meta-order at its disposal that makes modulation possible (Redfield, 1990: 121–123, 132–133).

For all these reasons most traditional societies need myths – for myths deal precisely with the "orderly disorder" (Redfield, 1990: 122) that all order is rooted in. Myths embody the Other; they present alternative possibilities of being, but do so in a way that in the end legitimizes the present status quo. Myths provide a means of bridging the contradictions that no ordering can escape (the nature-culture relation analyzed above being but one particular example). They offer a flexible, transcendent framework that cultural order can have recourse to when in danger of suffocating by its own rules. Myths are fundamentally polyvalent and their holistic images are susceptible to an infinite number of interpretations. Owing to this they can support various mutually exclusive claims that are raised by different members of the society at different times. Myth thus enables social and cultural change – for every new form of ordering can be understood as a legitimate reinterpretation of the same set of myths (Leach, 1954: 264–278).

The bottomless world of myth and the present socio-cultural arrangement are bridged by ritual. With the help of ritual cultural order can return into the mythical era regularly and purify itself of all that has become stale or subversive. Ritual is a part of cultural order but in its heart it opens up to the world of chaos, imitating mythical events that stand beyond the horizon. It does so in a controlled way, however, being bound by strict ritual rules, constructively absorbing chaos into the present world-order (Turner, 1982: 79–85). This is why Greek rituals attempted to correct so often what in mythical times had gone wrong. They enabled the Greeks to draw power and reality from primordial times, and yet leave them safely detached behind the boundaries of their world.

It is not likely that Eliade would have accepted all of these synthetic conclusions, but he would no doubt have been familiar with most of the building blocks of which they are composed. It has been my aim to show that while the basic patterns I have traced in Greek myths and rituals would have been familiar to him (despite not being identical to any of those explicitly discussed by him), they can also be put together and made sense of in a different way than he would have preferred. Thanks to this Eliade's ideas can continue to be fruitful even for scholars who do not share his overall approach to religion. In my view, it is precisely in such cases that a scholar's legacy can be shown to be truly abiding.

NOTES

1. In my approach I partly follow Guilford Dudley, in whose view the generative power of a theory system "lies in its capacity to make intelligible what had been unintelligible or less intelligible before" (Dudley, 1977: 159) and it is from this point of view that Eliade should be judged. According to Dudley, though Eliade's theory "is one flawed by inconsistency and ambiguity" (159), it is still one that deserves to be treated seriously. Its future, however, depends "on its capacity to make adaptations" (160). For Dudley, the "creative shift needed for Eliade's program is one that will align it straightforwardly with a major research tradition, that of French deductive, systemic analysis" (160; cf. 144–156). This is basically what I mean to do in my article.
2. The choice might seem surprising, for the Greeks can scarcely count as a typical specimen of those "archaic societies" that are the main focus of Eliade's attention. Eliade himself took little interest in them, seeing them as too imbued with history already and claiming even that in Greece true archaic ontology was no longer practised in the sphere of myth but in that of philosophy (Eliade, 1963: 111–112; Eliade, 1954: 34–35; Eliade, 1969: 72–73). Yet "archaic mentality" need not be incompatible with history. In my view, Eliade's claims concerning the "archaic mentality" should be read as *typological* statements, i.e., as referring not to a historical stage in the development of humankind but to a timeless pattern which runs across various societies and which can

easily combine with that of "historical mentality". It is only on this reading that Eliade's reflections on the traces of the archaic mentality in modern times can be made sense of. Cf. Allen, 2002: 236–242.

3. The story is told by a number of late encyclopedias. See e.g., *Anecdota Graeca* 1.144 (ed. L. Bachmann); *Suda, s.v. Embaros eimi.*
4. Modern scholars mostly assume that the rite was a kind of initiation for girls. Cf. Vernant, 1991: 198–203, 217–219; Redfield, 2003: 102–110; Parker, 2005: 242–248.
5. The whole pattern might be compared e.g., to that of the healing ritual of the Na-khi in south-eastern China that Eliade discusses several times (see e.g., Eliade, 1963: 26–28); the ritual repeats the ancient mythical fight that the First Shaman Dto-mba fought with evil spirits bringing sickness; by recapitulating the Creation of the World, the rise of sickness and the emergence of the First Shaman, the real shamans are able to draw from his strength and repeat his victory. In a similar way we might claim that the Athenians rehearse a primordial crisis only to stage its mythical solution once again.
6. On Rhodus, for instance, they were supposed to have been performed in ancient times, but later a symbolic substitution was discovered and a criminal sentenced to death that would have been killed anyway started to be executed instead (Porphyry, *On Abstinence* 2.54). What we have here is a shift from the literalness of myth to the symbolicalness of ritual similar to that we have seen in the Mounichia ritual. In most cases, however, human sacrifices were projected not into the past but outside the borders of the Greek world (cf. e.g., Sophocles, fr. 126 Radt); structurally this amounts to very much the same thing, the boundaries of time and space being often symbolically identical.
7. Cf. the role of the "savage" peoples in modern European thought: often idealized in the manner of Rousseau, their image could easily switch to that of beastly cannibals. By way of analogy, the Greeks imagined the first people as having fruits in plenty from the trees and having no need for clothing or bedding due to the mild climate (Plato, *Statesman* 272a), yet the same natural simplicity in other contexts could appear as primitiveness and brutishness (see the *Homeric Hymn to Hephaestus* 4: "in earlier times men used to live in caves in the mountains, just like wild beasts").
8. It needs to be remarked, though, that Eliade does not distinguish clearly between these two approaches and claims repeatedly that even in these cases a desire to *abolish* all creation is implied; cf. Eliade, 1958: 399–400, 402; Eliade, 1963: 50–51.

9. The huge *peplos* was only prepared for the greater Panathenaia, celebrated every four years. Whether a smaller *peplos* was offered to the goddess during the lesser Panathenaia is disputed; against this view cf. Parker, 2005: 268–269.

10. Indeed, Demeter is not a patroness of agriculture as such but rather of *fertility* as an unpredictable power that cannot be secured by technological means only, being perceived as transcending the reliable structures of man's world (Chlup, 2007).

11. As a matter of fact, the Greeks took it for granted that the gods regarded sacrifices as a tribute (*geras*) and ignored their material aspect, living sufficiently well on nectar and ambrosia. See already Homer, *Illiad* 4.48–49.

12. I am using the translation given in Vernant, 1991: 301–302, signed as 'T. Taylor (Oxford, 1913)', a source I have not been able to trace (it is not the classic translation of Thomas Taylor published in 1823).

13. A good example of this is given by Thucydides, *Peloponnesian War* 4.97–98: When in 424 BC the Athenians took over Delion, a Boeotian sanctuary of Apollo, and fortified the temple, they were accused of impiety by the Boeotians. The Athenians replied that they had done no harm to the sanctuary; they occupied it, no doubt, but there was nothing wrong about that – it is only natural that land and sanctuaries are sometimes conquered by others: "The Boeotians themselves now hold as a rightful possession sanctuaries that they had originally entered as usurpers – just like most other people who had conquered a territory, having driven out its inhabitants by force".

14. This is well reflected by Plato, who knows that not even the most perfect constitution could ever inspire confidence without being legitimated by myths. Thus, after the lawgiver has brought up the first generation of citizens according to his rules, he must next persuade them that they received from him all their education and training in appearance only: "in reality during all that time they were being formed and fed in the womb of the earth; … when they were completed, the earth, their mother, sent them up; and so, their country being their mother and also their nurse, they are bound to advise for her good, and to defend her against attacks, and her citizens they are to regard as children of the earth and their own brothers" (*Republic* 414d–e, tr. by B. Jowett). A page later Plato asks himself if the citizens can ever believe this, answering that those of the first generation probably not, but their sons and further descendants yes (415c–d).

15. Similarly, it is widely held even in our own Western civilization that its founding principles – such as the equality of all human beings or the existence of universal human rights – are "natural" and thus valid for non-Western countries too.
16. We can see this not just from numerous vase paintings but also from the fact that Euripides in *Ion* (495–502) lets them dance in a chorus; see Redfield, 2003: 120.
17. According to the Lucian scholiast (p. 276.13, ed. Rabe) they contained models of snakes and genitals made of dough. There is no reason to take his information seriously (Pausanias stresses that not even the priestess knew what the objects were), but they illustrate how the rite was understood at the level of popular imagination
18. See particularly Eliade, 1963: 42, 93. In his earlier works Eliade often underestimated cultural distinctions and tended towards sweeping generalizations, but he seems to have become more careful in the 1960s.
19. The debate is too extensive ad sufficiently well known to be summarized here. Among the best known representatives of the critical approach are Donald Wiebe or Robert Segal. Interestingly enough, Eliade is sometimes condemned by the adherents of phenomenology themselves. Dan Merkur, for instance, contrasts his approach to the sacred with that of Rudolf Otto, accusing him of practising "idealism [...] under the name of phenomenology" (Merkur, 1996: 112).

SELECT REFERENCES

Allen, D. *Myth and Religion in Mircea Eliade*. New York and London: Routledge, 2002.

Burkert, W. *Homo Necans*. Trans. by P. Bing. Berkeley and Los Angeles: University of California Press, 1983.

——. *Greek Religion*. Trans. by J. Raffan. Cambridge, Mass.: Harvard University Press, 1985.

Calame, C. *Choruses of Young Women in Ancient Greece*. New and revised ed. Trans. by D. Collins and J. Orion. Lanham: Rowman & Littlefield Publishers, 2001.

Chlup, R. "The Semantics of Fertility: Levels of Meaning in the Thesmophoria". *Kernos* 20 (2007): 69–95.

Csapo, E. *Theories of Mythology*. Malden: Blackwell, 2005.

Detienne, M. *The Gardens of Adonis: Spices in Greek Mythology*. Trans. by Janet Lloyd. Princeton: Princeton University Press, 1994.

——. "Culinary Practices and the Spirit of Sacrifice", in *The Cuisine of Sacrifice among the Greeks*, edited by M. Detienne and J.P. Vernant. Trans. by P. Wissing. Chicago and London: The University of Chicago Press, 1989, pp. 1–20.

Douglas, M. *Purity and Danger: An Analysis of Concept of Pollution and Taboo*. With a new preface by the author. London and New York: Routledge, 2002 [1st ed. 1966].

Dudley III, G. *Religion on Trial: Mircea Eliade and his Critics.* Philadelphia: Temple University Press, 1977.

Durkheim, Émile. *The Elementary Forms of the Religious Life*. Trans. by J.W. Swain. London: Allen & Unwin, 1915.

Eliade, M. *The Myth of the Eternal Return: or, Cosmos and History*. Trans. by Willard R. Trask. London: Routledge & Kegan Paul, 1954.

——. *Patterns in Comparative Religion*. Trans. by R. Sheed. London: Sheed & Ward, 1958.

——. *The Sacred and the Profane: The Nature of Religion*. Trans. by Willard R. Trask. New York: Harcourt Brace Jovanovich, 1959.

——. *Myth and Reality*. Trans. by Willard R. Trask. New York: Harper & Row, 1963.

——. *The Quest: History and Meaning in Religion*. Chicago: The University of Chicago Press, 1969.

Endsjø, D.Ø. "To Control Death: Sacrifice and Space in Classical Greece". *Religion* 33 (2003): 323–340.

La Fontaine, J. *Initiation: Ritual Drama and Secret Knowledge across the World.* Harmondsworth: Penguin Books, 1985.

Leach, E. *Political Systems of Highland Burma*. Cambridge, Mass.: Harvard University Press, 1954.

——. "Sermons by a Man on a Ladder". *The New York Review of Books* 7/6 (1966): 28–31.

Loraux, N. *The Children of Athena: Athenian Ideas about Citizenship and the Division between the Sexes*. Trans. by C. Levine. Princeton: Princeton University Press, 1993.

——. *Born of the Earth: Myth and Politics in Athens.* Trans. by S. Stewart. Ithaca and London: Cornell University Press, 2000.

Merkur, D. "The Numinous as a Category of Value", in *The Sacred and its Scholars*, edited by T. Idinopulos and E.A. Yonan. Leiden: E.J. Brill, 1996, pp. 104–123.

Meuli, K. "Griechische Opferbräuche", in *Phyllobolia für Peter von den Mühll*, edited by Olof Gigon. Basel: Schwabe, 1946, pp. 185–288.

Parke, H.W. *Festivals of the Athenians*. Ithaca and New York: Cornell University Press, 1977.

Parker, R. *Polytheism and Society at Athens*. Oxford and New York: Oxford University Press, 2005.

Peradotto, J. "Oedipus and Erichthonius: Some Observations on Paradigmatic and Syntagmatic Order". *Arethusa* 10 (1977): 85–101.

Redfield, J. "From Sex to Politics: The Rites of Artemis Triklaria and Dionysos Aisymnetes at Patras", in *Before Sexuality: The Construction of Erotic Experience in the Ancient Greek World*, edited by D.M. Halperin, J.J. Winkler and F.I. Zeitlin. Princeton: Princeton University Press, 1990, pp. 115–134.

——. *The Locrian Maidens: Love and Death in Greek Italy*. Princeton: Princeton University Press, 2003.

Saliba, J.A. "Homo Religiosus", in *Mircea Eliade: An Anthropological Evaluation*. Leiden: Brill, 1978.

Turner, V. *The Ritual Process: Structure and Antistructure*. New York and Chicago: Aldine, 1969.

——. "Symbols in Ndembu Ritual", in *The Forest of Symbols: Aspects of Ndembu Ritual*. Ithaca and London: Cornell University Press, 1967, 19–47.

——. *From Ritual to Theatre: The Human Seriousness of Play*. New York: PAJ Publications, 1982.

Vernant, J.P. *Myth and Society in Ancient Greece*. Trans. by Janet Lloyd. London: Methuen, 1982.

——. "Mortals and Immortals", in *Collected Essays*, edited by F.I. Zeitlin. Princeton: Princeton University Press, 1991.

Versnel, H.S. "Kronos and the Kronia", in *Inconsistencies in Greek and Roman Religion II: Transition and Reversal in Myth and Ritual*. Leiden: Brill, 1994, pp. 89–135.

Wallace, A.F.C. *Religion: An Anthropological View*. New York: Random House, 1966.

Zeitlin, F. "Cultic Models of the Female: Rites of Dionysus and Demeter", *Arethusa* 15 (1982): 129–157.

CHAPTER 5

Eliade's History of Religions

A reaction against historicity and historicism

SANJUKTA BHATTACHARYYA

Mircea Eliade's attitude towards history is one of the most crucial components of his thoughts. As a historian of religion, Eliade believed that any historical study implies certain familiarity with universal history. He pointed out that the historical study of religion should be illustrating the continuous emerging changes and modifications of idea of the sacred and how around those sacred objects, myths and rituals grow up. As for Eliade, human beings are not only *homo sapiens* but are also *homo religiosus*.

Therefore, he conceived the study of history of the *homo religiosus* as the study of history of the "total person"[1], which not only includes the conscious mind but also encompasses the unconscious and the trans-conscious mind. Eliade's history of religion is the history of the *homo religiosus* that includes not only the study of the pre-reflective and non-rational but also of the rational beings. At the same time, his history of religions also includes the study of the non-temporal, non-historical and even temporal historical ideas. Eliade's history of religions in effect is a methodology to understand the significance and meanings of the sacred and mythic events in human life and also to explore how traditional, archaic man tolerated the sufferings and "terror of history" with the help of trans-historical history. He rejected the idea of "historicity" and "historicism" on the ground that by denying the basic sacred, mythic foundation of the human nature and reducing them to certain economic, social or materialistic plane, they fail to solve the most fundamental and existential crisis – "the terror of history"– on man.

Eliade's "history of religion" therefore could be considered as a reaction against "historicity" and "historicism". The conventional historians and historicists have severally criticized Eliade for his "different" interpretation of history of religions as an approach or as a method and considered his historical approach as "non-historical" and even "anti-historical". The aim of this paper is to elucidate Eliade's approach towards history and its meaning in religion, with the notion that his "history of religions" could be considered as a reaction against historicity and historicism. The paper also focuses on the Eliade's grounds for rejecting the historicist theories and historicism for which he was relentlessly criticized. The paper attempts to bring out a critical analysis of Eliade's historical approach in this regard.

Eliade's history of religion

In his book titled *The Myth of the Eternal Return*,[2] Eliade shared his view towards interpretation of history and its significance in human life. He also analyzes historicism and historicist theories on history and their loopholes to solve the basic crisis of human life, that is, the "terror of history". In his analysis, he consciously differentiated between religious and non-religious humanity.

Eliade contented that the perceptions of time and history, as homogeneous, linear and unrepeatable medium, are a peculiarity of "modern" non-religious humanity. According to Eliade, the archaic religious men that he called *homo religiosus* apprehend time as being heterogeneous – divided between, linear profane time and cyclical reactualizable sacred time. Myths and rituals give access to this sacred time and protect religious humanity against the "terror of history" – a form of existential anxiety in which the absolute "givenness" of historical time causes helplessness.

Eliade, however, tended to undermine this distinction insisting that non-religious humanity in any pure sense is non-existent and that religiousness understood in this way is omnipresent. Myths and *illud tempus* – the temporal continuum of mythic events – still exist, although concealed, in the world of "non-religious" humanity and there is no "[...] solution of continuity between archaic mind and scientific ideologies of the nineteenth century".[3]

Eliade had often used the terms "history", "time", "historicity" and "temporality" interchangeably. He had analyzed the sacred-profane relationship and the dialectics of the sacred as one disclosing universal structures in terms of which a natural, temporal, historical phenomenon is transformed and burst open to reveal supernatural dimensions of reality.[4] Eliade had analyzed "sacred" as being a permanent structure of the consciousness that expresses a trans-historical structure of transcendence. According to him, a meaningful world is the result of a dialectical process that may be called the manifestation of the "sacred". Human life becomes meaningful by imitating the paradigmatic models revealed by the supernatural beings. Eliade asserted that one of the most archaic levels of culture – living as a human being – is in itself a religious act.[5]

According to Eliade, traditional men also believed that there is a history of the cosmos and it exists because it is the creation of the God. It was also held to have been organized by supernatural beings and mythical heroes. In Eliade's opinion, the history of the cosmos is a "sacred history" that has been preserved and transmitted through myths. Moreover, he also asserted that this history could be repeated indefinitely in the sense that the myths serve as models for ceremonies that periodically reactualized the tremendous events that occurred at the beginning of time.[6]

Eliade believed that the primitive or the traditional men have been able to endure the sufferings and pressures of history because they were either regarded as the punishments given by God or as symptoms for the end or fall of an age. These beliefs made the archaic men to accept the sufferings and tolerate the terror of history. They believed in the sacred events and the associated myths because they had a meta-historical meaning. Eliade also asserted that for the greater part of humanity, which still believe in the traditional viewpoint, history did not have and could not have value in itself.

A history primarily meant where every hero repeated the archetypal gestures, every war rehearsed the struggle between the good and the evil, every fresh social injustice was identified with the sufferings of the saviour, and where each new massacre repeated the glorious end of the martyrs. Eliade believed that it is not our role to decide that whether refusal of such history would always prove to be effacious. However, he highlighted that the endurance and tolerance of such sufferings, and tolerance of history by millions of peoples for centuries, were by the sheer virtue of their trans-historical view – a virtue that allowed for the endurance and the tolerance without despairs, without committing suicide or falling into the spiritual aridity.

According to Eliade, these sufferings always brought with it a relativistic or a nihilistic view of history.[7] In his opinion, the man of the archaic and traditional cultures had at his dispositions all the myths, rites, rituals and customs to defend himself from the terror of history. Moreover, the idea of God and religious experiences that they implied existed from the most distant ages. Later on they could have been and were replaced at time by other different religious forms like totemism, cult of ancestor worship, great God and Goddesses and so on, which also answered the religious needs for the primitive humanity.[8] As stated by Eliade, the desire of the traditional *homo religiosus* to refuse history, to give up "memory", to have temporal events unrecorded, to endure temporality only as a dimension of his existence without "interiorising" it, without transforming it into consciousness – proves his thirst for "ontic" dimensions, thereby allowing the insignificance of profane existence to invade him. The "archaic ontology" is based on the belief in an "absolute reality" as opposed to the profane world of "unrealities". It is translated practically in the endless imitation of the archetypes of an original hedonic state that saved man from the non-existent and from nothingness.[9]

Eliade maintains that *homo religiosus* represents the "total man". Therefore, the history or science of religion must become a total discipline in the sense that it must use, integrate and articulate the results of various methods of approaching religious phenomena. Eliade believed that to understand and grasp the meaning of any religious phenomenon it is necessary to study their history. This history not only unravels its changes and modifications but also helps to elucidate the contributions of the religious phenomena to the entire culture where it exists.

Eliade is also of the view that there are no "pure" religious data outside history. Every religious experience is expressed and transmitted in a particular historical context. Eliade insisted that a new theoretical approach, new hermeneutics is necessary to interpret the meaning of the sacred, mythic and other religious phenomena. He claimed that by using an empirical approach it is possible to recognize the historical nature of the sacred and mythic data.

In his book *Myths, Dreams and Mysteries*[10], Eliade stated that in order to grasp the meaning of religious phenomena like myth, one must make "an effort to understand them in their own plane of reference".[11]

Eliade, at the same time, emphasized the need for phenomenological and empirical method to study the sacred and mythic events, and advocated modern scholars to realize that for studying sacred events they should work exclusively with historical documents, as reflected in his article "Methodological Remarks on the Study of Religious Symbolism" in the book *The History of Religions: Essays in Mythology*, where he said that, "Historian of religions uses an empirical method of approach. He is concerned with religio-historical facts which he seeks to understand and to make intelligible to other".[12]

Eliade criticized historicity and historicism, and the reductionist approaches, on the ground that they denied the basic foundation of the sacred and mythic beliefs. As an alternative, he propounded his methodological theory of "anti-reductionism" in terms of irreducibility of the sacred. He had criticized earlier rationalists and positivists for forcing their data into an unlinear and evolutionary scheme assuming certain norms. Though he agreed that twentieth century anthropologists, sociologists, psychologists and historians did open up new dimensions of the "sacred", at the same time, he criticized them for reducing the meaning of "being religious" only to its anthropological, sociological, psychological or historical analytics.

The reductionism's interpretation did not do justice to the "complexity", "totality", "ambiguity" and "unaccountability" of the sacred, but instead reduced the mythic narratives to some partial, oversimplified, one-sided, or otherwise incomplete perspectives.[13] He said that "the historicity of religious experiences does not imply that they are reducible to non-religious forms of behaviours – for example to an economic, social or political history. We must never lose sight of one of the fundamental principle of modern science: the scale creates the phenomenon".[14] Thus, his history of religion as a methodology and his historical approach towards sacred and mythic events have an "anti-reductionist" orientation to analyze the meanings and significance of the trans-historical events in human life and culture.

Against historicity and historicism

As stated at the outset, Eliade's history of religion is a reaction against "historicity" and "historicism". As an approach and methodology, it has also been a prescription for modern man to deal, endure and tolerate the sufferings and terror of history. Historicism that was once considered a glory in the nineteenth century, and whose hue still remains in the twenty-first century, bases its understanding on facts and on documents.

The great revolution that the historicists declared to have accomplished in the judgement of reality is in effect in establishing the primacy of the document. It is in this primacy of the document that the justifications are found for critics to make both of "abstract history" and "romantic history". The critics did not believe in anything not confirmed by documents or unless and until it has been subjected to "textual criticism". For them, the modern man, who believes in a kind of historicity and historicism, is of the view that he is the creator of "history". The modern man values the historical event and therefore seeks to preserve it.

According to historicism man makes himself through history and there is no mode where time irrespective man made himself that is to be. Hence, everything that has happened in history is meaningful because man makes it. However, Eliade asserted that even this non-religious man, who pretends that he made himself in history, is still a descendent of the *homo religiosus*.

Eliade argued that if this modern man claims that he is only a historical being, then he also must accept that historically he is the product of his forefathers. Thus, Eliade pointed out even if the non-religious man claims that he has emptied himself of all religious values, he is still somehow related to them historically.[15] At the other end of the spectrum, the secular historicists did not abolish the "sacred" but have given it a different orientation; and this orientation could be clearly discerned through a hermeneutical analysis performed with the help of a phenomenological history of religions.[16]

In his concluding critique of "historicity and historicism" in his article "The Quest for the 'Origin' of Religion" reprinted as the book *The Quest: History and Meaning in Religion*[17], Eliade asserted that for the historicists in its trace for the origins of religions, "history" primarily meant where all religious phenomena were conditioned or have taken place in historical time. According to him, modern scholars, who were impressed by the discovery of the importance of history, were carried away in their way – and therefore a tendency to explain everything on a historical plane of reference and in forms of historical conditionings.

According to historicists, religion is exclusively a historical fact without any trans-historical meaning or value and simply seeks "essences" for falling back to the old Dark Age. Eliade distinguished his conception of history from historicity and historicism by saying that "we must not confuse the historical circumstances which make a human existence what it actually is with the fact that there is such a thing as a human existence".[18] For the historians of religion the fact that myths or rituals were always historically conditioned does not explain away the very existence of such myths or rituals.

In other words, the historicity of a religious experience does not tell us what a religious experience ultimately is. Having known that the "sacred" could be only grasped through its manifestations that are always historically conditioned, Eliade felt that the historicists themselves knew about their shortcomings. They are therefore condemned to work exclusively with historical documents in order to find out something more than the simple fact that reflect historical situations. Though, according to Eliade, the historicist "feels somehow that they reveal to him important truths about man and man's relation to the sacred".[19]

According to Eliade, the justification of a historical event by the simple fact that it was a historical event, or in other words "it happened that way", given by historicism and historicist theories, would not free humanity from the terror that the event usually brings with it. In the modern times, archaic history, that is, the sacred history of myths and supernatural beings has been rejected as being meaningless and on the ground that such trans-historical meanings have got no justifications.

Reacting to such observations, Eliade said that the historicists from Hegel to Marx were not able to solve the crisis of man. From Hegel, every effort was directed towards saving and conferring value on the historical events as such, the event in itself and for itself. From Marx, all transcendental significance of history was cast off which was attached with Hegel in terms of the "universal spirit". History was no longer more than an epiphany of the class struggle. However, both Hegel and Marx were unable to solve the problem of "terror of history" for man. Terror of history became more and more intolerable within historicism where historical events can find their full and only meaning in their realization alone.

Along with significant ontological claims about reality, time and history, Eliade also made claims about the true human mode of being in the world and the human condition as such. Having made these various claims, he was able to conclude that history should be such that would help man to tolerate the terror of history. For Eliade, it was more authentic to live one's life in terms of the transcendent, exemplary, mythic and religious models, non-temporal, non-historical structures, than to identify oneself fully with the temporal and historical dimensions of existence. According to him, historical persons who refuse any "religious solutions" would not be able to solve their most fundamental existential crisis. As there is something fundamentally inhuman, even anti-human, about modern historicism and materialism that denies the basic sacred and mythic foundations of human nature and human conditions as such.[20]

Eliade, therefore, having evaluated, rejected the interpretations of the existentialists, historicists, materialists and others as they have identified that temporal and historical dimensions of existence as being only truly human and denied non-temporal and non-historical or trans-historical existence of man. For Eliade, this denial is to deny the "total person" as such, who according to him is fully and authentically human. He continues to say that "whatever be the truth in respect to the freedom and creative virtualities of historical man, it is certain that none of the historicist philosophers is able to defend him from the terror of history".[21]

Eliade also said that these theories in modern times do not help either to escape or tolerate the catastrophes and horrors of history starting from collective dispositions and massacres to atomic bombings – "beyond them he can glimpses no sign, no trans-historical meaning. If they are reduced to the blind play of some economic, social or political forces or even worse – the only result of the liberties that a minority takes and exercise directly on the stage of universal history?"[22]

According to Eliade, for a historian to offer a mere objective description of events in some casual nexus, however thorough and accurate rendering it may be, was nothing but to increase the futility and hopelessness that has infused the consciousness of modern, historicized man. It must be said at this juncture that Eliade was so metaphysically entrenched against, not simply because of the empiricism in the methodologies, but because of the proposition that it is also the consciousness of history as a reality, which determined man's existence.

In his book *The Myth of Eternal Return*, Eliade opines that "the consciousness of history" determining man's existence as being a mere surrender to what is ultimately the sheer terror that the very historical existence generates. According to him, Hegel – the modern man – has tried to valourize history as purposefully and historical truths as being meaningful. However, this valourization of history and its supposedly transparent events have only incarnated man in a terror-ridden existence lending irreducibility to death.[23]

Historicity and historicism boasted of freedom for modern man from all sorts of angelic, mythical bindings, trans-historical dependence and idealism. It also claimed of him being creative as he creates his own history – a quality that the traditional man did not have. Against such criticisms, Eliade said that if the modern man insists on being exclusively historical then actually either he becomes a "man" of historicism, or a "man" of Marxism, or a "man" of existentialism and without the defence against the terror of history.

For history either then becomes a result of the seeds sown by acts that occurred in the past, several ages ago. Or it tends to be made by a populace that increasingly prohibit the majority of their contemporaries from directly or indirectly intervening in the making of history. However, on the contrary, in addition to have sufficient means at their disposal to free each individual for enduring his part of the consequences of this history which according to Eliade is to live immediately and continuously in the dread of history.[24]

Against this boasting of the modern man about freedom, Eliade opined that the kind of "freedom" which historical existence implies was possible only at the beginning of modern period that too within certain limits. It became impossible as the period became more historical, i.e., more alien from any trans-historical model. Eliade cited, "for example, Marxism and Fascism must lead to two types of historical, existence: that of the leader (the only really 'free' man) and that of the followers, who find in the historical existence of the leader, not an archetype of their own existence but the law giver of the gestures that are provisionally permitted to them".[25]

Eliade pointed out the self-contradiction of historicism that denies the reality of the occult, mythical, mystical and "supernatural" phenomena, recorded in folkloric documents. He therefore said:

> Here we see the contradiction of the historicist spirit because a historian, who declares himself to be the slave of the document, does not have the right to reject a text or for rational, philosophical reasons; this implies an *a priori* theory of the real which cannot prevail over an historicist one without renouncing his point of departure, the *primacy of the document.*[26]

Eliade drew attention to the assertion of the historical manifestation of the "universal spirit" in Hegel's philosophy of history. According to him, it therefore meant that Hegel might also have believed in the destiny of the people still preserving a trans-historical significance, because all history reveals a new and more perfect manifestation of the "universal spirit".

Eliade also pointed out that even for Marxists who uphold historicism, events of history are not mere successions of arbitrary accidents. The events exhibit a coherent structure and above all, they lead to a definite end of "salvation" – final elimination of the terror of history. He opined that in effect the most exact precedence, to the consequent disappearance of historical tensions in Marx's classless society, could be found in the myth of the Golden Age, which according to a number of traditions lies at the beginning and end of history. Hence, according to Eliade, Marx had in effect enriched this venerable myth with an ideology that is truly messianic Judaeo-Christian ideology. This was brought about by the prophetic and soteriological function that Marx ascribed to the proletariat, on the one hand, and on the other hand, by the final struggle between the good and the evil that might as well could be compared with the apocalptic conflict between Christ and Antichrist, ending in the decisive victory of the former. Eliade therefore concluded that:

> It is indeed significant that Marx turned to his own account of an Judaeo-Christian eschatological hope of an absolute (end to) History; in that he parts company with other historical philosophers (Croce, for instance, and Ortega, Y. Gasset), for whom the tensions of history are implicit in human conditions, and therefore can never be completely abolished.[27]

At the end of Marxist history lies the Age of Gold of the archaic eschatologist. According to Eliade, Marx therefore re-confirmed upon exclusivity of the human level – the value of a primitive myth of the Golden Age. Here, as argued by Eliade, lies the secret of the remedy for the terror of history for the militant Marxist. Thus, Eliade tried to establish that both Hegel and Marx having rejected any trans-historical existence they themselves took the help of trans-historical events to establish their own theories of historicism. Arguably, this was more apparent in their rejection of trans-historical existence – the self-contradiction lays here.

Eliade felt that mere justifications of a historical event by the simple fact that it is a historical event would not go far towards freeing humanity from the terror that the events inspire. He pointed out that there are a large number of documents that the historical science does not take into account. Not because the authenticity of these documents were in doubt, or because textual criticism had demonstrated their uncertainty, but simply because they dealt with miracles and with impossible things. Reference here again could be drawn to where Eliade cited the hagiographic documents that refer to the "miracles" of the saints, where Eliade points out the contradictions of the historicist spirit. Because a historian, though having declared himself the slave of the documents, does not have the right to reject a text for rational, philosophical reasons, which results in an aprioristic theory of the real that cannot prevail over a historicist without renouncement of his point of departure from the primacy of the document.[28]

Eliade had settled himself against "the historicistic position, in all its varieties and shape – from Nietzsche's 'destiny' to Heiddeger's 'temporality'".[29] He regarded the attempt to "real" time exclusively to historical time as an unacceptable reduction.[30]

He was suspicious of demystification, empiricization and reduction to "anthropologism" of all trans-historical reality – the realm of the sacred, by the categories of human sciences. He termed this as "the fallacy of demystification".[31]

Eliade was indeed deeply disturbed by the efforts on the part of historicists, sociologists and psychologists to demystify reality. He was also perturbed by the tendency to treat things as objects for interrogation in the language of man's finitude. According to Eliade, a language that enthrones empiricism and discounts all that is outside the "episteme" of man's finite reality.

Critical evaluation of Eliade's historical approach

It also needs to be said that many scholars have either completely ignored or vigorously attacked Eliade's approach towards history and religion and his methodology. One of the most frequent expressions of general criticism has been of Eliade being methodologically uncritical and anti-historical. And also that he did not do justice to the historical nature of the religious phenomena. Some even claimed that his whole historical approach is non-empirical, non-historical and at times even anti-historical. One of such critics John A. Saliba, claimed that "Eliade, like Frazer, lumps religious beliefs and practices together in a comparative way which ignores differences and the cultural and historical situation".[32]

Eliade had asserted that a "self-contradictory attitude" occurs in all religions. On the one hand, while there is the desire to secure and strengthen one's own reality in the "sacred", on the other hand, there is the fear that individuality may be lost if one is absorbed completely in the "sacred". This became the reason for Eliade's own ambivalence towards history.

Therefore, though Eliade had recognized profane historical condition to be necessary for revealing the "sacred", nonetheless he concluded that for full experience of the "sacred" one should abolish the profane existence. Hence, it could be said that his attitude towards history includes both rejection and affirmation.

Seymour Cain had asserted that this rejecting and affirming of history has been a result of Eliade's own methodology, where the historical-cultural gave way to "trans-historical intentionality".[33] Similarly, Bryan Rennie further argued that, however, its not Eliade's focus on the trans-historical intentionality itself which reflected the ambivalence, it was in the way he interpreted this intentionality. As in the Eliade's world, in his history of religions, trans-historical intentionality has been displayed in both positive and negative attitudes towards the unfolding of time and history.[34]

Cain also asserted that Eliade's own worldview was implicit in his interpretation of history. In fact, according to Cain, Eliade's understanding of Hebrew history bears that out.

As for Eliade, the historical events for the Hebrews became a theophany, where the sacred was revealed through history and the revelations themselves became the very dimensions of the sacred. And, Eliade thought each historical event to be a further and irreversible revelation of God.

Further, human beings were able to advance their knowledge and experience only through history. However, this positive and linear view of history was momentary for Eliade. At the same time, he also felt that the Hebrew people were not entirely successful in transcending the cyclical pattern. They too longed for the end of history while tolerating it at the same time because it was known that history would one day cease to exist. As their "paradise state" was at the beginning, therefore the end of historical period has begun.[35] Eliade's understanding of the Hebrew viewpoint represents two sides of the paradox. Where history becomes a means to the sacred and yet it is also to be abolished. Because, history could be distracting as well – when the peace and prosperity in history often cause people to turn away from God.

The same paradox also surfaced in Eliade's interpretation of Christianity also. In spite of Christianity's more positive emphasis on history, Eliade's ambivalence towards it indicates his more than often uncomfortable feelings with history. Eliade opined that while history provides the possibility for further and further revelations of the sacred or coinciding of opposites in time and history, he viewed further historical unfolding as a threat to the struggle for a sanctified mode of being.[36]

Eliade, even with respect to the so-called historical religions, while not denying the historical innovations, interpreted "historical" mythic, religious phenomena as being essentially non-historical and even anti-historical. His emphasis, in their respect, had been solely on archaic myth and religion.

According to the historically-oriented empiricist, Robert D. Baird, Eliade assumed this a-historical archaic model for all religious experiences. Baird expressed that Eliade's method with its search for structures is not historically falsifiable and has become a barrier to the attainment of authentic religio-historical understanding. For him, Eliade's phenomenology is "as normative as theology because it is based on assumed ontology, which is neither historically derived nor descriptively verifiable".[37]

According to Ivan Strenski, Eliade's history of religions was based on *a priori* truths that stand in an *apriori* relationship to historical data both logically and chronologically. These "truths" may sometimes be confirmed "in historical materials, but falsification from these materials seems ruled out".[38]

Another critic of Eliade, Carl Olson, claimed that Eliade's approach was based on an anti-historical theological orientation. He argued that Eliade's anti-historical theology advocates abolishing time and history. This Eliade sought to achieve through an eternal return to a primordial sacred history that are embodied in myths. Olson criticized Eliade for rejecting the positive attitude of historicity and historicism – its role in historical progress, and also for failing to see the need for integrating history and nature.[39]

After noting Eliade's frequent claim that he used an empirical and historical approach, Guilford Dudley III showed the continuous criticism and dismissal of Eliade by empiricists only. He agreed with the critics that Eliade could not meet their minimal empirical historical inductive criteria for a "scientific" approach, such as the criteria for empirical verification or falsification.[40]

Although Dudley criticized Eliade's approach, he also expressed conformity with Eliade's proposal of an anti-historical theory of religion as the leading candidate to bring some sense of unity among the contending methodologies and for the future of development of history of religion as a discipline.

Eliade's position perhaps has been most clearly stated in his book *The Myth of the Eternal Return*. He held that the modern evaluations of historical realities, which were the only source of significance, meaning, truth and power, is in itself an attribution of a religious nature brought about by the developments in the history of religion. Thus, according to Eliade, even the modern historicists who limit all effective causality to historical realities could be classed as religious in this way and such religiousness were omnipresent.

David Cave, on the other hand, attempted to establish that critics and even supporters of Eliade had misinterpreted him as being emphasizing on the "ahistorical" or on the "non-historical". For Cave, Eliade was obsessed by history – his method was ruled by history and his morphology was "limited to its governing paradigm [...] unconcerned with history or that he is 'anti-history'".[41] History – existential, chronological, sacred or secular – was important to him, either in a positive or in a negative way.

Indeed, it could be said that Eliade's "new humanism" may be limited because it is too historical. As Cave said, "in a sense, if the new humanism is to be more universal, it is not more historical consciousness that is needed, but less".[42] Cave might also be correct in saying that Eliade maintained the actual religious experiences or the "sacred" being manifested in history. Where those sacred structures were incarnated in relatively imperfect forms that were limited by historical conditionings. Cave also opined that Eliade, in his personal life and in his scholarship, was obsessed with the "problems of history" as well.

But this obsession took the form of his desire and need to overcome or escape from the conditionings and terror of history. Nevertheless, this perhaps in no way negates the lofty methodological, phenomenological and ontological status that Eliade granted to his non-historical, non-temporal sacred structures and meanings.[43]

Bryan Rennie, examining Eliade's historical approach, argued that Eliade had a personal idiosyncratic meaning of "history". Eliade equated this meaning of "history" with personal experiences, personal events, and actual or lived experiences. For Rennie, Eliade also used "history" to refer recorded past events or the history of antecedent events. And, it is here that he did not distinguish this common usage from his idiosyncratic meaning of "history", as being a personally experienced actuality.

However, according to Rennie, scholars have misinterpreted Eliade's religious approach as being anti-historical. For him, Eliade had been anti-historicist and not anti-historical. As what Eliade opposed were narrow, modern, reductionist, and historicist's explanations. The explanations that attempted to reduce the whole meaning and significance of the sacred ideals, norms, the imaginations, and dreams etc., to physical determinants within a narrowly defined historical, temporal and spatial reality.[44]

Thus, in spite of all such criticisms, Eliade maintained, "a religious phenomenon will only be recognized as such if it is grasped at its own level, that is to say, if it is studied as something religious".[45] Eliade provides such an anti-historical proposal to interpret archaic religious data in the hope of the cultural and spiritual renewal of modern human beings, in order to fight against the terror of history. Eliade's personal attitude, time and history greatly influenced his generally unsympathetic formulations of non-religious historical approaches.

Eliade's approach towards history perhaps could be best described in Mac Linscott Ricketts' words: "He tends to 'lump together', ignoring their differences, and vaguely labels as 'positivism', 'historicism', 'existentialism' and 'materialism'".[46]

But we must acknowledge that Eliade's history of religion reveals a much broader and more radical anti-historical orientation than just the label of critic of historicism only. For this very reason, even many scholars who are critical of extreme historicism and historicist explanations find valuable ideas in various modern interpretations and explanations that Eliade himself either devalued or more than often dismissed.

Conclusion

It could be summarized that Eliade advocated the primacy of the phenomenological, hermeneutical interpretation of meanings of religious phenomena to stand for as the "history" of religion. He acknowledged the importance of the historical conditionings also and went on to make the controversial claim that the interpretation of the meanings is completely different from just providing historical explanations.

Thereby, Eliade got into a deeper level of meanings of mythic and sacred religious history. Moreover, he attempted to go beyond historical explanations. He did it through his ontological move on the basis of primordial, non-temporal, non-historical mythic and religious structures and meanings. This enabled Eliade to make significant claims about reality, time and history, about the true human mode of being in the world and also about the human condition as such. In short, Eliade's history of religion has been a dynamic interaction between historical and non-historical interpretations.

These dynamic interactions are essential for the sacralization process in order to have the universal religious experience as

Douglas Allen had pointed out in his book *Mircea Eliade on Myth and Religion*. For Eliade, actual religious experience, therefore, always entails the dynamic interaction between the historical particular and the non-historical universal structure.[47]

Thus, we can say that Eliade not only interpreted and presented the archaic anti-historical conception and significance of the trans-historical reality, but also endorsed the archaic man's history. In this endorsement of the significance of trans-historical reality, he rejected the idea of historicity and historicism, because they fail to cope with the terror of history.

Eliade's history of religion has been the history of the trans-historical, non-temporal or non-historical conceptions, which, according to him, acts as an instrument for enduring and overcoming the terror of history. At the same time, Eliade's history of religion also revealed essential truths about human condition, historical existence and reality as such. His own conception about his mission was that of a historian of religions who seeks to "awaken" the world to its entire forgotten religious heritage.

This is evident most clearly in those places where Eliade compared the man of the traditional societies with that of the "modern" man and where the difference between the religious and non-religious man could be reduced to the difference in the consciousness and unconsciousness of religious realities. For Eliade modern man has either forgotten or has suppressed into the unconsciousness what the traditional societies knew and celebrated consciously.

In Eliade's approach towards or in his interpretation of history of religion, historicity and historicism neither give modern man the status of a free being nor of a creator of his own history. On the contrary, Eliade's history of religion enables the traditional man, the man who believes in his sacred history, to be free and creative. Man is free to be no longer what he was earlier. Man is also free to repeat his own history through periodic abolition and collective regeneration of time. Moreover, Eliade offered a prescription for modern man to cope and tolerate the sufferings and terror of history.

In his study of "Symbolism of the Centre", in *Images and Symbols: Studies in Religious Symbolism*, Eliade discussed how the history of religion could lead to a modern awakening. In this context, he said that since non-historical symbolic structures already exist in modern human beings, it is only necessary to reactivate them and bring them to the level of consciousness. This could be done by regaining awareness of his anthropocosmic symbolism.

According to Eliade, by regaining such awareness of just only one variety of archaic symbolism, modern man would obtain a new existential dimension. The existential dimension, which Eliade opined, has been totally unknown to the present-day existentialism and historicism. It would be an authentic and major mode of being, which would defend man from the nihilistic and historical relativism without thereby taking him out of history. An argument which made Eliade concludes that "for history for itself will one day be able to find its true meaning: that of the epiphany of a glorious and absolute human condition".[48]

Therefore, from the above discussion, it would perhaps be not wrong to conclude that Eliade's history of religion has been something quite different from "history" as it is commonly perceived. Eliade was not a conventional historian; he was rather a philosopher, a phenomenologist, who attempted to interpret history from a philosophical angle. His historical approach has been different from the other approaches towards history that seeks for an accurate reclamation and reconstruction of past events and their present entailments.

On the contrary, when put together, Eliade's historical and ethnographical references were to bring out and exemplify a pre-envisioned system or paradigm. But, at the same time, Eliade's history of religion was not a theological or ontological explanation of an ultimate truth in a given religious tradition. It was a systematic, synchronic, radical way of "knowing" everything. To us it is an epistemological system ascribed generically to the trans-consciousness of human mind to *homo religiosus*. Thus, Eliade's history of religion has a philosophical orientation and it would not be a mistake to call his historical approach a philosophy of history, which Eliade himself also insisted in the foreword of his *The Myth of Eternal Return*. Eliade's viewpoint regarding history of religion as a discipline has been that it is a cultural and trans-formative discipline.

Eliade through his phenomenological approach attempted to decipher the empirical, historical and mythic data in order to describe the phenomenon that constitutes the mythic world and interpret their religious meanings. On the one hand, his methodology with an anti-reductionist orientation provides irreducibility to religious interpretations of specific mythic and other religious data. While, on the other hand, it also has a special role of integrating and synthesizing the contributions of other specialized approaches within a broad, meaningful and irreducible religious framework.

As for Eliade, history of religion's mission is to "integrate the result of ethnology, psychology, sociology, yet in doing so it will not renounce its own method of investigation or the viewpoint that specifically defines it".[49]

NOTES

1. Mircea Eliade, *Cosmos and History: The Myth of the Eternal Return*, trans. Willard R. Trask (New York: Harper and Row, 1959), 8.
2. Eliade, *Cosmos and History.*
3. Mircea Eliade, *The Quest: History and Meaning in Religion* (Chicago: The University of Chicago Press, 1970), 41.
4. Douglas Allen, *Myth and Religion in Mircea Eliade* (New York: Routledge, 2002), 211.
5. Eliade, "Preface" to *The Quest*, ii.
6. Eliade, "Preface" to *Cosmos and History*, xiii-iv.
7. Eliade, *Cosmos and History*, 151–152.
8. Eliade, *Cosmos and History*, 161.
9. Mircea Eliade, "*Eseuri*", translation of *Cosmos and History: The Myth of the Eternal Return*, trans. M. Ivanescu and Cezar Ivanescu (Bucharest: Editura Stintifica, 1991), 72–73, cited from Mihaela Gligor and Mac Linscott Ricketts (eds.), *Professor Mircea Eliade: Reminiscences* (Kolkata: Codex Publishers and Book Sellers, 2008), 46.
10. Mircea Eliade, *Myths, Dreams and Mysteries*, trans. Philip Mariet (New York: Harper & Row, 1967).

11. Eliade, *Myths*, 13–14.
12. Mircea Eliade, "Methodological Remarks on the Study of Religious Symbolism", in *The History of Religions: Essays in Mythology*, edited by Mircea Eliade and Joseph M. Kitagawa (Chicago: The University of Chicago Press, 1959), 88.
13. Douglas Allen, *Myth and Religion in Mircea Eliade* (New York: Routledge, 2002).
14. Eliade, *The Quest*, 7.
15. Mircea Eliade, "The Sacred and the Secular", *Cultural Hermeneutics* 1, ed. Christopher J. Arthur (1973): 101–103, quoted in Bryan Rennie (ed.), *Mircea Eliade: A Critical Reader* (London: Equinox Publishing Ltd., 2006), 65.
16. Eliade, "The Sacred and the Secular", 67.
17. Mircea Eliade, "The Quest for the Origin of Religion", *History of Religions*, Vol. 4 (1964): 154–169; reprinted as "Historicity and Historicism", in *The Quest*, 50–53.
18. Eliade, *The Quest*, 53.
19. Eliade, *The Quest*, 53.
20. Allen, *Myth and Religion*, 254–255.
21. Eliade, *Cosmos and History*, 159–62.
22. Bryan Rennie, "Terror of History", in Bryan Rennie (ed.), *Mircea Eliade: A Critical Reader* (London: Equinox Publishing Ltd., 2006), 319.
23. Eliade, *Cosmos and History*, 150–151.
24. Eliade, *Cosmos and History*, 156.
25. Eliade, *Cosmos and History*, 157.
26. Mircea Eliade, "Folclorul ca instrument de cunoastere", *Revista Fundatiilor Regale*, Vol. IV, No. 4 (Bucharest: April 1937) 137–152, quoted in "Time, History and Soteriology concerning Eliade's Philosophy of History and Indian Philosophy of Transcendency", by Liviu Bordas, in *Professor Mircea Eliade: Reminiscences*, edited by Mihaela Gligor and Mac Linscott Ricketts (Kolkata: Codex Publishers and Book Sellers, 2008), 47.
27. Eliade, *Cosmos and History*, 198.
28. Mircea Eliade, "Folklore as an Instrument of Knowledge", trans. Mac Linscott Ricketts, quoted in Bryan Rennie (ed.), *Mircea Eliade: A Critical Reader* (London: Equinox Publishing Ltd., 2006) 32.
29. Eliade, *Cosmos and History*, 152.

30. Bryan Rennie (ed.), *Mircea Eliade: A Critical Reader* (London: Equinox Publishing Ltd., 2006), 12.
31. Eliade, *The Quest*, 70.
32. John A. Saliba, "Homo Religiosus", in *Mircea Eliade: An Anthropological Evaluation* (Leiden: Brill, 1976), 111.
33. Seymour Cain, "Mircea Eliade: Attitudes towards History", *Religious Studies Review*, Vol. 6, No. 1 (1980), 14.
34. Rennie (ed.), *Mircea Eliade: A Critical Reader*, 181.
35. Eliade, *Cosmos and History*, 102–107.
36. Rennie (ed.), *Mircea Eliade: A Critical Reader*, 182–183.
37. Robert D. Baird, *Category Formation and the History of Religions* (The Hague: Mouton, 1971), 86–87, 152–53.
38. Ivan Strenski, "Mircea Eliade: Some Theoretical Problems", in *The Theory of Myth: Six Studies*, edited by Adrian Cunningham (London: Sheed and Ward, 1973), 151–52.
39. Carl Olson, *The Theology and Philosophy of Eliade* (New York: St Martin's Press, 1992), 55–59, 153, 156, 167–170.
40. Guilford Dudley III, Chapter 1 of *Religions on Trial: Mircea Eliade and His Critics* (Philadelphia: Temple University Press, 1977).
41. David Cave, *Mircea Eliade's Vision for New Humanism* (New York: Oxford University Press, 1993), 36.
42. Cave, *Mircea Eliade's Vision*, 195.
43. Allen, *Myth and Religion,* 230.
44. Bryan Rennie, *Reconstructing Eliade: Making Sense of Religion* (Albany, New York: State University of New York Press, 1996), 89–108, 110–111.
45. Mircea Eliade, *Patterns in Comparative Religion*, trans. Rosemary Sheed (New York: World Publishing Co., Meridian Books, 1963), XIII.
46. Mac Linscott Ricketts, "In Defence of Eliade: Towards Bridging the Communication Gap between Anthropology and History of Religion", *Religion*, Vol. 3 (1973), 28.
47. Allen, *Myth and Religion*, 260.
48. Mircea Eliade, "Symbolism of the Centre", in Mircea Eliade, *Images and Symbols: Studies in Religious Symbolism*, trans. Philip Mariet (London: Harvill Press, 1961), 35–36.
49. Mircea Eliade, *Shamanism: Archaic Techniques of Ecstasy*, trans. Williard R. Trask (New York: Pantheon Books, 1964), XIII.

REFERENCES

Allen, Douglas. *Myth and Religion in Mircea Eliade*. New York: Routledge, 2002.

Baird, D. Robert. *Category Formation and the History of Religions*. The Hague: Mouton, 1971.

Cave, David. *Mircea Eliade's Vision for New Humanism*. New York: Oxford University Press, 1993.

Cain, Seymour. "Mircea Eliade: Attitudes towards History". *Religious Studies Review*, Vol. 6, No. 1 (1980): 14.

Cunningham, Adrian (ed.). *The Theory of Myth: Six Studies*. London: Sheed and Ward, 1973.

Dudley III, Guilford. *Religions on Trial: Mircea Eliade and His Critics*. Philadelphia: Temple University Press, 1977.

Eliade, Mircea. *A History of Religious Ideas, Vol. 1: From the Stone Age to the Eleusinian Mysteries*. Trans. Willard R. Trask. Chicago: The University of Chicago Press, 1978.

——. *A History of Religious Ideas, Vol. 2: From Gautama Buddha to the Triumph of Christianity*. Trans. Willard R. Trask. Chicago: The University of Chicago Press, 1985.

——. *A History of Religious Ideas, Vol. 3: From Muhammad to the Age of Reforms*. Trans. Alf Hiltebeitel and Diane Apostolos-Cappadona. Chicago: The University of Chicago Press, 1988.

——. *Cosmos and History: The Myth of the Eternal Return*. Trans. Willard R. Trask. New York: Harper and Row, 1959.

——. *Images and Symbols: Studies in Religious Symbolism*. Trans. Philip Mairet. New York: Sheed and Ward, 1961.

——. *Myth and Reality (World Perspectives)*. Trans. Willard R. Trask. New York: Harper and Row, 1963.

——. *Myths, Dreams and Mysteries: The Encounter between Contemporary Faiths and Archaic Realities*. Trans. Philip Mariet. New York: Harper Collins College Div., 1960.

——. *No. Souvenirs: Journal, (1957–1969)*. Trans. Fred H. Johnson, Jr. New York: Harper and Row, 1977.

——. *Patterns in Comparative Religion*. Trans. Rosemary Sheed. New York: Meridian Books, World Publishing Company, 1966.

——. *Rites and Symbols of Initiations: The Mysteries of Birth and Rebirth*. Trans. Willard R. Trask. New York: Harper and Row and Torch Books, 1965.

——. *Shamanism: Archaic Techniques of Ecstasy*. Trans. Willard R. Trask. New York: Pantheon Books, 1964.

——. *The Quest: History and Meaning in Religion*. Chicago: The University of Chicago Press, 1969; 1970 and 1980 editions.

——. "The Quest for the Origin of Religion". *History of Religions*. Vol. 4 (1964): 154–169.

——. *The Sacred and the Profane: The Nature of Religion*. Trans. by Willard R. Trask. New York: Harcourt, Brace, 1959.

——. "The Symbolism of Shadows in Archaic Religions", in *Symbolism, the Sacred and the Arts*, edited by Diane Apostolos Cappadona. New York: Pantheon Books, 1964.

——. *Two Tales of the Occult*. Trans. William Ames Coates. New York: Herder and Herder, 1970.

——. Ed. in Chief. *The Encyclopaedia of Religion*. 16 vols. New York: Macmillan, 1987.

Eliade, Mircea and Joseph M. Kitagawa (eds.). *The History of Religions: Essays in Methodology*. Chicago: The University of Chicago Press, 1959.

Gligor, Mihaela and Mac Linscott Ricketts (eds.). *Professor Mircea Eliade: Reminiscences*. Kolkata: Codex Publishers and Book Sellers, 2008.

Olson, Carl. *The Theology and Philosophy of Eliade*. New York: St Martin's Press, 1992.

Rennie, Bryan (ed.). *Mircea Eliade: A Critical Reader*. London: Equinox Publishing Ltd., 2006.

——. *Reconstructing Eliade: Making Sense of Religion*. Albany, New York: State University of New York Press, 1996.

Ricketts, Linscott Mac. "In Defence of Eliade: Towards Bridging the Communication Gap between Anthropology and History of Religion". *Religion*. Vol. 3 (1973): 28.

——. "Mircea Eliade and the Terror of History: Anti-Historicism and History of Religions". *International Journal on Humanistic Ideology*. Vol. 1, No. 2 (2008): 15– 35.

Saliba, A. John. "Homo Religiosus", in *Mircea Eliade: An Anthropological Evaluation*. Leiden: Brill, 1976.

CHAPTER 6

Rationality, Relativism and Religion

A reinterpretation of Peter Winch

KEVIN SCHILBRACK

Peter Winch's *The Idea of a Social Science and its Relation to Philosophy*, first published in 1958, has been credited with initiating the debate whether criteria of rationality are universal.[1] In this work, and in its application to cultural material in "Understanding a Primitive Society",[2] Winch argues that the criteria of rationality can vary from one cultural context to another. Winch's position has been widely considered relativist – indeed, one often finds it treated as the paradigmatic example of cultural relativism in which there are no universal criteria and cross-cultural evaluation is not possible – but in my judgment Winch's relationship to relativism is widely misinterpreted.

I argue in the first part of this essay that despite his pluralistic understanding of rationality, Winch does allow for universal features of culture in virtue of which cross-cultural understanding and even critique is possible. I argue in the second part that given the kind of cultural universals that Winch produces, he still must struggle to avoid relativism, but that he fails. These issues become clear in Winch's work (as with many others in the debates about rationality and culture) when one gives attention to his interpretation of religions. Minimally, then, this essay argues for a reinterpretation of Winch's position. More importantly, it suggests that a lesson can be drawn from this reinterpretation: that in order to provide the standards without which relativism ensues, one requires a certain kind of criteria of rationality, namely, criteria which are not only universal but also substantive.

Winch and relativism

Winch argues that the criteria of rationality vary from one language game to another. The term "language game" has proved to be a notoriously shifty label, and I will not argue that it can be made trouble-free. Nevertheless, one should note that for Winch one language game is distinguished from another by its "point", which is to say, by the meaning and activities that it makes possible. Winch's treatment thus resembles the distinction of types of discourse according to their cognitive interests in the works of Jurgen Habermas and Karl-Otto Apel, though for Winch the types are innumerable and not limited to three.[3] Winch further claims that the break between language games sometimes falls between cultures.[4] That is, one culture may in its institutions and general public life predominantly appeal to one set of criteria of rationality, and another culture may appeal to another set. This is not to deny that (i) each culture may include other language games – neither is monolithic – and (ii) there may be overlaps, such as cases of supernatural or magical thinking among a predominantly instrumental or scientific culture, or vice versa. Winch's position, then, is that rationality is relative to the point of a social practice, and that sometimes this will mean that rationality is relative to a culture.

It follows from this claim that there are no standards of rationality independent of a social context, no neutral criteria of rationality. For the empiricist understanding of rationality against which Winch is primarily reacting, neutral criteria were provided both by the senses – or one could say, by the world itself, which the sense reveal – and by the principles of logic. Winch rejects both of these. Winch argues that the world cannot provide neutral criteria of what is rational, because all experience is influenced by the concepts involved in our modes of living. "Our idea of what belongs to the realm of reality is given for us in the language we use. The world is for us what is presented through those concepts."[5] And he argues that logic cannot provide neutral criteria, because what constitutes the proper application of logical principles also depends on social context and convention. "[C]riteria of logic are not a direct gift of God, but arise out of and are only intelligible in the context of, ways of living or modes of social life. It follows that one cannot apply criteria of logic to modes of social life as such."[6]

These negative claims have been widely taken to entail cognitive relativism. Typically, this has been for one of the following three reasons:[7] First, some charge that Winch's claim that all experience is concept-dependent reduces reality to a way of speaking or a social convention. These critics often point to Winch's statement that "[w]hat is real and what is unreal shows itself in the sense that language has" as well as the above quote that "[t]he world is for us what is presented through those concepts".[8] Second, Winch's claim that logic is intelligible only within a given social context has been similarly understood as asserting the possibility of rival logics, in which not even the principle of non-contradiction is held in common. Winch apparently puts this reasoning to use in "Understanding a Primitive Society", arguing that if the Azande are not interested in the fact their claims are self-contradictory, then to push this fact as a criticism involves a category-mistake.[9] Third, some charge that Winch's culturally-bounded understanding of rationality denies the possibility of explaining or criticizing alien social practices. Some hold that this denial is improbable, since it flies in the face of the practice of anthropologists, and others that it is self-contradictory, since it is refuted by Winch's own programme, and since the criticism of one social practice from the perspective of another is so pervasive that it can itself be treated as a social practice and so be immune to Winch's ban. In my opinion, none of these three criticisms – that for Winch reality is relative, logic is relative, and criticism across cultural practices is impossible – does justice to Winch's treatment of rationality. Let me respond to each in turn.

In response to the first criticism, one ought to consider Winch's statement that "reality is always given for us in the language we use" in its context in "Understanding a Primitive Society". Far from reducing reality to a social convention, Winch introduces the concept of reality right at the beginning of the essay expressly in order to avoid the relativism which follows when rationality is identified solely with what people say or think: "we should not lose sight of the fact that the idea that men's ideas and beliefs must be checkable by reference to something independent – some reality – is an important one. To abandon it is to plunge straight into an extreme Protagorean relativism, with all the paradoxes that involves".[10] Thus, Winch rejects as relativist and incoherent the idea that social agreement exhausts what is involved in a claim being rational. For Winch, to speak about the world is always to speak about the world in a language, but it does not follow that one can only speak about language. Just because there is no experience that is not theory-laden does not mean that theory-laden experiences are not of something. As he puts it, "To assume at the outset that one can make a sharp distinction between 'the world' and 'the language in which we try to describe the world,' to the extent of saying that the problems of philosophy do not arise at all out of the former but only out of the latter, is to beg the whole question of philosophy".[11] To speak of "agreement with reality" as Winch does here emphasizes that many uses of language are intentional, referring beyond themselves to affairs, which exist independently.

Since Winch contends that "reality" is never given except linguistically, however, one might ask whether he can avoid reducing it to language. On the disagreement between realism and conventionalism – that is, between the view that what is described within a form of discourse really exists and the view that such objects are merely heuristic and there is "reality" and "existence" only within the discourse – Winch appears to be a conventionalist. In my judgment, Winch avoids charges of reductionism and conventionalism by making a distinction between a statement's meaning and its truth. This distinction is implicit in Winch's repeated insistence that the world is both dependent and independent of what people say,[12] but it becomes explicit in his example of measuring a mountain. Although the goals of measuring depend upon social needs, and for this reason the meaning of "height" may be conventional, the truth or falsity of a statement like "the height of Ben Nevis is 4,406 feet" does not.

> What we need in order to determine the truth or falsity of this statement is geological, not anthropological or linguistic,

> information. [This is so because] the reality of Ben Nevis' height is extra-linguistic. [W]hat makes true any statement you like to mention about the height of a mountain (or anything else) has nothing to do with the ideas or wishes of any man or group of men you like to mention.[13]

Reality may not be what gives a statement its sense, for sense or meaning depends ultimately on how the statement is used, but reality does determine a statement's truth, for truth simply is agreement with reality.[14] Given this distinction between meaning and truth, Winch is able to affirm both that all knowledge is language-dependent without denying that existential claims are corrigible by the world.

If he is not a conventionalist, should one conclude therefore that Winch is a realist? It is instructive to compare Winch's statement that "reality is certainly independent of what any man may care to think, but what that reality amounts to can only be seen from the [...] tradition in which that concept [...] is used"[15] to an explicitly realist theory of science like that of Roy Bhaskar. Bhaskar calls theories "the transitive objects of science", which are created by communities to describe "the intransitive objects of science", the entities and structures of reality. Stating what I take to be precisely Winch's point, Bhaskar writes, that "[t]hings exist and act independently of our descriptions, but we can only know them under particular descriptions".[16] Winch has said that this quote from Bhaskar "coincides perfectly well with the position I have tried to develop".[17] Nevertheless, Winch would not call himself a realist, for he seeks to move beyond the distinction between realism and relativism. For Winch, the purpose of language is not to describe one world any more than it is to describe alternative worlds – for language does not have a purpose. Winch does not make the assumption that leads to either position, the assumption that all language is supposed to correspond to the world.

The second source of Winch's reputed relativism is his rejection of logic as a standard by which social practices as wholes can be judged.[18] Winch argues that logic is contextual in the sense that logical principles are always applied for a particular purpose, in a particular situation. It is the use of logic – "the actual process of drawing an inference" and of "grasp[ing] the connection" – that depends upon social convention or rules.[19] This is not to deny that one can also speak of logic as a formal system independent of any application, an abstraction from its uses.[20] Winch's point is that before one can identify a logical relation, say, a contradiction between A and B, one must judge that A and B concern the same thing. But two things must be judged "the same" in some respect: one can compare apples and oranges as fruit, but in other respects, they are still like apples and oranges. Bringing two things into logical relation with each other always presupposes an interpretive rule on the part of the observer, and an interpretive rule will depend upon contextually given concepts and purposes.[21]

It is this reasoning that Winch puts to use in his approach to Zande witchcraft. Evans-Pritchard had charged that Zande beliefs about the inheritance of witchcraft and the biological relations of all members of a clan "involve the whole notion of witchcraft in contradiction".[22] As Winch explains, "Contradiction would presumably arise because a few positive results of post-mortem examinations [for evidence of witchcraft], scattered among all the clans, would very soon prove that everybody was a witch, and a few negative results, scattered among the same clans, would prove that nobody was a witch".[23] This contradiction – which is, after all, internal to Zande beliefs – seems to show the illogic of labeling anyone a witch. But, what rule, Winch asks, does this judgment of contradiction presuppose? As what kinds of belief are witchcraft beliefs being interpreted Winch argues that to see a contradiction here assumes that Zande notions of witchcraft constitute a theoretical system, designed to identify and combat the causes of misfortunes, designed in short as "a quasi-scientific understanding of the world".[24] Zande witchcraft beliefs lead to a contradiction, then, only when interpreted as a medical or scientific theory. Winch suggests that this interpretation of Zande is suspect, since the Azande show no interest in the contradiction when it is brought to their attention (as Evans-Pritchard admits). For Winch, the question that the interpreter should ask is whether there is an interpretation in which the contradiction would not arise.[25] Winch suggests that Zande witchcraft can be interpreted as a form of religion, which for Winch means a form of reflection on the significance of life. In such an interpretation, witchcraft is seen not as a quasi-scientific means to control events but rather as a "drama of resentments, evil-doing, revenge [and] expiation", the rituals of which express an understanding of the fundamental features of life.[26] The point of Zande rituals is therefore not to bring about one specific end rather than another, but to come to terms with the contingencies of life, whatever one does. The logical contradiction does not arise, therefore, because an accusation of witchcraft is not a hypothesis in need of evidence, but rather a statement of how misfortune should be looked upon and dealt with.

To return to the accusation of relativism, then, logic is contextual for Winch only in the sense that logical principles alone are not sufficient to determine whether a set of beliefs and activities are consistent or inconsistent. Whether the Azande proceed logically or illogically depends not only on logical principles but also on what the Azande are trying to do, on the rule under which the activity is described. It should be clear that on this interpretation Winch's treatment of Zande magical claims does not imply that they are immune from logic nor that they might function according to some alternative logic. As Winch says,

> I never of course denied that Zande witchcraft practices involve appeals to what can be understood as standards of rationality. Such appeals also involve behavior that we can identify as "the recognition of a contradiction". What I was urging, though, is that we should be cautious in how we identify the contradiction, which may not be what it would appear to be if we approach it with "scientific" preconceptions.[27]

On the contrary, Winch insists that in abstraction from its various applications, logic is a formal aspect of any language. Logic is for Winch a universal feature of all language games, and necessarily so. I return to this claim in the next section.

The third critique of Winch as a relativist – that explanation and criticism of one social practice by another are impossible – can now easily be dealt with. Winch does not deny cross-cultural evaluations: "The question is not whether we can do this, but what sort of comparison is involved."[28]

According to Winch, two conditions must be met for genuine critique to be possible. The first is that the activity to be explained or criticized must be understood in terms intelligible to its participants. "[A]ny more reflective understanding must necessarily presuppose, if it is to count as genuine understanding at all, the participants' unreflective understanding."[29] Winch sometimes writes as if this condition precludes what might be called "external" explanations or critiques of a social practice,[30] but his own discussion of psychological and economic explanations of cultural practices shows that he does not reject this possibility, even when they use concepts not available to the actors, as long as they begin from the participants' understanding of the activity.[31] The second condition of genuine critique is that, as we have seen, one cannot compare the claims found in one practice to reality or logic directly, and therefore one must instead compare the claims found in one practice to those in another. Criticism is thus an elliptical process, in the sense that it always presupposes two sets of criteria of rationality, those of the participants and those brought by the observer.

As I see them, the possibilities for critique under such circumstances can be quite broad. For example, an observer might come to the conclusion that although a religious belief is rational in its own terms, it has no explanatory power. Or one might come to the opinion that although a business practice is efficient according to economic criteria, it is not ethical. In this way, one can criticize one social practice from the perspective of another, and one can even reveal aspects of the practice not appreciated by its participants. More radical criticisms, criticisms of the rationality of the practice as a whole, are also not impossible. Winch has argued that because logical principles must always be applied in a particular context, one cannot judge a priori that a practice is irrational. But it does not follow that the practice a priori is rational. Although Winch does not develop this point, he alludes to it when he writes that "somebody may want to raise doubts about the whole institution [of witchcraft];

… I do not deny the possibility of mounting such an argument" and again when he writes that the argument of "Understanding a Primitive Society" "is not, absurdly, that the ways in which men live together can never be criticized, nor even that a way of living can never be characterized as in any sense 'irrational'."[32] Once an observer understands a practice in terms intelligible to its participants, the observer may come to the conclusion that there are basic conflicts between the fundamental beliefs or between that beliefs and the activities involved in the practice. On Winch's principles, then, one may criticize a practice both "externally", from the perspective of another practice, or "internally", as logically inconsistent in its own terms.

If the former arguments are sound, then Winch's pluralistic understanding of rationality does not entail that reality is relative, that logic is relative, nor that criticism and explanation across language games is impossible. Winch is not a cultural relativist in any of these ways.

Winch and the interpretation of religions

Given the above conclusions, what tools does Winch have for making sense of religions across cultures? Let me return now to Winch's claim that logic is a universal feature of language games. According to Winch, the logical dimension of rationality not only happens to be common to different language games, the concept of rationality in this sense is analytic to communication, a condition of any meaningful use of language. "Rationality is not just a concept in a language like any other. […] It is a concept necessary to the existence of any language."[33]

> Where there is language it must make a difference what is said and this is only possible where the saying of one thing rules out, on pain of failure to communicate, the saying of something else. […] [Consequently,] the possibilities of our grasping forms of rationality different from ours in an alien culture […] are limited by certain formal requirements centering on the demand for consistency.[34]

In order to be successful, any attempt to communicate must include logical consistency as an abstract or formal feature. Rationality according to Winch therefore has at least one universal aspect: the principles of logical consistency. These principles presumably include at least the principle of non-contradiction, since a "set of beliefs and practices cannot make sense insofar as they involve contradictions".[35] Even if a culture has not become reflective about its use of language to the extent that it has made these principles explicit, their speech and behaviour must follow them, simply to be meaningful.[36] For this reason, Winch criticizes as relativist those who assume that the formal criteria of rationality are "ours". Winch argues that the appearance that the logical principles that represent the norms of consistency are Western or scientific is an optical illusion that can be dispelled if we try to imagine the norms by which an alien culture would translate our beliefs.[37]

What is the status of these cultural universals? That all cultures are subject to the requirements of logical consistency is not, Winch argues, an empirical discovery or hypothesis. Rather, it is the result of an analysis of the *concept* of social life, and in particular, the concept of communication as a dimension of social life. The universals are therefore a priori. Although Winch does not use the term, he implies that logic or logical consistency is a *transcendental* feature of communication, in the sense that it represents a condition for the possibility of meaningful speech and action. Logical consistency represents the bounds of sense. Precisely because they are a priori, however, these universals are purely formal. They are regulative and not substantive principles. They require that if one is to communicate at all, one must be consistent. "But they tell us nothing about what in particular is to *count* as consistency, just as the rules of calculus limit, but do not themselves determine what are to be proper values of *p*, *q*, etc."[38] In this sense, logical principles are empty, and this explains why Winch is adamant that one cannot use them to resolve differences between language games. Insofar as the claims made within a language game are logically consistent, they have already met the formal criteria of rationality.

Winch's position on rationality can therefore be clarified by seeing that he recognizes two levels of criteria. On the one hand, there are substantive, "local" criteria, which follow from the point of the discourse and are matters of convention. These one cannot know independently of context. On the other hand, there are formal criteria of rationality that require that whatever is said be consistent. These formal criteria are universal and context-invariant, the abstract features of meaningful communication as such. Steven Lukes and Martin Hollis later expounded this notion of double criteria of rationality in a series of articles.[39] Hollis and Lukes believed that they were defending universal criteria of rationality against the relativism of Winch, but on my reading the difference between them on this issue is merely one of emphasis.[40] The real difference between these two positions is that Hollis and Lukes argue that a shared world is a necessary assumption of interpretation, and that therefore descriptions of perceptions can serve as a "bridgehead" from one language game to another, whereas, as we have seen, Winch insists that the referent of "the world" is systematically ambiguous. According to Winch, perception statements may serve as a bridgehead when two language games are interested in describing empirical facts (and Winch does not deny that this interest is common), but they do not necessarily provide a bridgehead to every social practice.[41] The purposes people have – the points of their language games – are just too various.

If simple perceptual descriptions are not always a reliable bridgehead, however, what access does one have to language games that do not focus on the empirical? If the claims made within one language game share nothing in common with those made in another save the formal requirements of consistency, and if they may even be referring to the world in substantively different ways, how can one ever learn what the other is saying? To Winch's credit he recognizes this problem. His solution (admittedly "tentative"[42]) is that the concept of human social life includes a second set of cultural universals.

> [T]he very conception of human life involves certain fundamental notions – which I shall call "limiting notions" – [such as] birth, death, [and] sexual relations. The significance here is that they are

> inescapably involved in the life of all known human societies in a way which gives us a clue where to look if we are puzzled about the point of an alien system of institutions.[43]

What it means to be alive, what it means to die, what it means to be a sexual being. No matter how different cultures are, Winch proposes that their differences are limited by a common need to come to terms with these features of life, features we might call existential universals. They are not conventional but a human "constant". Therefore, if an interpreter is puzzled by a system of practices – say, if someone refers to his brother as a parrot or he claims to carry his soul around in a box, to take two famous examples – the interpreter can ask whether these activities are made intelligible when they are seen as attempts to deal with these existential issues.

Like the first set of universals, this set is known *a priori*. According to Winch, it is part of what is meant by human life that people interpret themselves in these ways. Also, like the first set of universals, this set is purely formal. "The specific forms which these concepts take, the particular institutions in which they are expressed, vary very considerably from one society to another."[44] For this reason, like the principles of logic, these existential universals do not provide a norm or standard that one can use to assess a social practice. There are innumerable rational ways to think of birth, death and sex.

If my reading of Winch is correct – that is, if his position includes universals but only formal ones – then I believe that a problem arises for his position. If both the logical and the existential universals are purely formal, then it seems that there might be social practices that are internally consistent and yet mutually contradictory. If both the logical and the existential universals are purely formal, then it seems that Winch has not really moved his position away from relativism. In such cases, the participants will disagree about what is right and true but will be unable to settle their dispute according to any rational criteria. This seems especially true in those language games that deal explicitly with the limiting notions: ethics, the arts and religion.

Winch not only admits this, he insists upon it. Between such language games, there not only *may be*, but *necessarily will be* such insuperable differences. Winch gives the example of Mohandas Gandhi, who believed that one's personal quest for perfection ought to take precedence over friendships, and George Orwell, who believed that friendship ought to take precedence over one's personal quest for perfection. Winch concludes that "the very nature of the issues which are at stake in the sort of discussion I have described presupposes a diversity of opinion", and "I feel like saying that such a background of sometimes irresolvable diversity of outlook and judgement makes an essential contribution to our understanding of what such judgements *are*".[45] As long as two language games are both internally consistent, universals cannot provide the terms with which the decision between them can be assessed. There simply are no "considerations, which would settle the issue [...]. If that is thought to be a relativist conclusion, then I do indeed think there is that much truth in relativism".[46]

Of course, this *is* a relativist conclusion. On Winch's account, the proper understanding of the fundamental features of life is relative to one's language game. Winch balks at saying that the decisions between alternative understandings are merely preferential, but it is clear that they are rationally arbitrary. Consequently, Winch's position ought to be understood as one that recognizes cultural universals but is nevertheless relativistic.

How might Winch avoid this conclusion? One possibility for avoiding relativism, a possibility that Winch rejects, would be to identify some standard by which claims about life as such can be assessed, not only in their form but also in their substance. If one could identify a culturally invariant claim that identifies some *content* of life as such, then different language games could then be assessed by the adequacy with which they understood that content. Such a claim would be a substantive rather than merely a formal universal. It is because Winch denies the possibility of *this* kind of universal that his position is relativistic. However, one should note that it is precisely this substantive sort of claim which both Orwell and Gandhi see themselves as making. That is, both believed that their understandings of the proper role of friendship in life follow from *substantive* claims about human nature and the ultimate context of human action. If this is so, Winch's position does not really provide a neutral framework within which their rival claims can be understood. Rather, it provides a framework that rejects the cognitive status of the claims that cultures make.

It seems that there are two general routes one might take to find such a substantive universal: one concerns contingent claims about the world and the other necessary ones. The first route would be to argue that in order to understand another at all, one must assume that one shares with that person a relation to a common world. This is the approach of Hollis and Lukes, who argue that to translate statements like "Yes, this is a brown cow" requires that one assume that others perceive brown cows as one does. A substantive universal is therefore found in shared, logically contingent perceptions.[47] Winch rejects this suggestion for the simple reason that not all uses of language concern material objects and their attributes. Statements like "Yes, this is a sacred cow", for example, do not presuppose shared percepts.

The second route to a substantive, culturally invariant claim would be to argue that there are characteristics which are common to the various things which make up the world, simply by virtue of being anything at all, characteristics of being, simply qua being. This would be some version of a metaphysical approach. One way to argue for a metaphysical claim about being qua being, though not the only way, is to argue transcendentally that some claims about the world cannot be conceivably falsified.[48] On this understanding, metaphysical claims are logically necessary. They describe the generic features of what there is and therefore ingredient in the description of anything whatsoever. Consequently, such claims are both substantive and universal.

Unfortunately, Winch rejects the possibility of metaphysics because he sees it (as many today do) as part of a certain discredited picture of how language works, namely, the picture in which language serves to describe or represent an objective reality, "there and given quite independently of our methods of conceiving and discovering it".[49] Since there is no access to the world as it is 'in itself,' there can be no descriptions of being qua being. Instead, "[o]ur idea of what belongs to the realm of reality shows itself *in* the language we use".[50] No language game houses an absolute or unmediated perspective on the world.

Though this reasoning is valid, it does not seem to be decisive, for there may be forms of metaphysics that do not claim or require an absolute or unmediated perspective.[51] Winch grants that there are claims like the existential universals that are fundamental to the very sense of what a member of a certain culture says. And he grants that as such, these claims are not falsifiable. But he insists that it is inappropriate to ask whether these claims correspond to the world. They are not true (or false). "To say they were open to the question: True or False? would be to call in question the truth of an entire *Weltbild* and give truth a metaphysical emphasis of which it is not susceptible."[52]

Why is there no metaphysical truth? Why are claims about the general character of human life, like those made by Gandhi and Orwell, irresolvable? Although Winch almost never argues against metaphysics (presumably, because he believes that its discreditation was accomplished by Wittgenstein), one can find in his writings two arguments against its possibility. First, Winch believes that a pluralistic understanding of rationality excludes the possibility of metaphysics. If all knowledge of reality is from a particular perspective, then no language game can house the one true viewpoint. One ought therefore "to be alert to the pretensions of any form of enquiry to enshrine the essence of intelligibility as such, to possess the key to reality. For connected with the realization that intelligibility takes many and varied forms is the realization that reality has no key".[53]

Now, these reasoning rules out only the possibility of a language game that claims to possess the only true perspective on the world but it does not rule out the possibility of post-Wittgensteinian metaphysics as given above. To be sure, there have been metaphysical proposals which claimed to provide the perspective which replaces all others or to which all others can be reduced or which claimed to be in some other way final or privileged. These are rightly rejected. But metaphysics need not deny that the world may be real in many ways. To return to Winch's example of the mountain, it may be 4,406 feet tall, and it may also be holy, rather far from where I am now, primarily granite, and your third favourite. These claims will be made from different forms of inquiry, carried out with different cognitive tools for different purposes, and none contains the one true reality. Metaphysics can agree with this. Metaphysics need only claim that it provides one particular perspective on the world, namely, the perspective that seeks to identify what features, if any, the mountain shares with all other things. A nonreductive or nonexclusive metaphysics is completely compatible with a pluralistic understanding of rationality.

Winch's second argument is that the possibility of metaphysics is ruled out by the fact that all knowledge is linguistically mediated. "Our idea of what belongs to the realm of reality is given for us in the language we use."[54] This does not rule out the possibility that the world exists independently of language, but it does rule out the possibility that one might describe it independently of language. There is no access to reality "in itself".

Again, this reasoning rule out the possibility of a language game that claims some extra-linguistic access to the world, but it does not rule out the possibility of the kind of metaphysics I have suggested in this paper. To be sure, there have been metaphysical proposals that claimed to be based on immediate knowledge or some other form of foundationalism. These are rightly rejected. Metaphysics need not deny that all knowledge is linguistically (and therefore socially and historically) mediated. Metaphysics need only claim that there may be some linguistic, historical and social contexts in which it is legitimate to ask about what all contexts have in common.[55]

Whether some metaphysics might provide cultural universals within the strictures of Winch's philosophy I therefore leave as an open question. I do not suppose that these brief comments would persuade Winch to find a place for metaphysics in his approach to cross-cultural comparisons. He may be convinced that the most accurate understanding of the differences between language games and those between cultures is one that ends in relativism. But I hope it is clear that Winch's position ends in relativism not because it fails to recognize universal features of rationality and morality, but rather despite this recognition. In order to avoid relativism, however, a position requires substantive universals.[56]

NOTES

1. Peter Winch, *The Idea of a Social Science and Its Relation to Philosophy*, Second edition (Atlantic Highlands, NJ: Humanities Press International, 1989). The claim that this work gave rise to this debate is made by Richard J. Bernstein, *The Restructuring of Social and Political Theory* (Philadelphia: University of Pennsylvania Press, 1976), 241, fn. 10. In my judgment, the most careful readings of Winch can be found in A.A. Derksen, "On an Unnoticed Key to Reality", *Philosophy of the Social Sciences* 8: 3 (September 1978): 209–25, in Richard J. Bernstein, *Beyond Objectivism and Relativism: Science, Hermeneutics, and Praxis* (Philadelphia: University of Pennsylvania Press, 1983), 25–30, 93–108; and in D.Z. Phillips, *Religion and the Hermeneutics of Contemplation* (Cambridge: Cambridge University Press, 2001), ch. 12. Two book-length treatments, both good, are: Colin Lyas, *Peter Winch* (Teddington: Acumen, 1999), and Berel Dov Lerner, *Rules, Magic, and Instrumental Reason* (London: Routledge, 2002).
2. Winch, "Understanding a Primitive Society", in *Rationality*, edited by Bryan R. Wilson (Oxford: Basil Blackwell, 1970), 78–111.
3. Winch criticizes Apel on this point, in "Apel's Transcendental Pragmatics", in *Philosophical Disputes in the Social Sciences*, edited by Stuart C. Brown (Sussex: Harvester Press, 1979), 51–73, especially 57–58. Apel responds to Winch in the same work, 74–86, and again in "Universal Principles and Particular Decisions and Forms of Life", in *Value and Understanding: Essays for Peter Winch*, edited by Raimond Gaita (London: Routledge, 1990), 72–101. For Habermas' critical reading of Winch, see Habermas, *The Theory of Communicative Action, Vol. 1: Reason and the Rationalization of Society*, translated by Thomas McCarthy (Boston: Beacon Press, 1980), 53–67. One should keep in mind that for Winch "language game" refers not only to a kind of discourse but also to the social practice (a "form of life") of which the

discourse is a part. See Winch, "Darwin, *Genesis*, and Contradiction", *Trying to Make Sense* (Oxford: Basil Blackwell, 1987), 132–133.

4. For the relation of language games to cultures, see Winch, "Language, Belief, and Relativism", *Trying to Make Sense*, esp. 198.
5. Winch, *The Idea of a Social Science*, 15.
6. Winch, *The Idea of a Social Science*, 101–1.
7. One or more of these criticisms can be found in each of the following: Steven Lukes, "Some Problems about Rationality", in *Rationality*, edited by Wilson, 194–213; Alasdair MacIntyre, "The Idea of a Social Science", in *Rationality,* edited by Wilson, 112–30; I.C. Jarvie, "Understanding and Explanation in Sociology and Social Anthropology", in *Explanation in the Behavioral Sciences*, edited by Robert Borger and Frank Cioffi (Cambridge: Cambridge University Press, 1970), 231–248; Martin Hollis, "Witchcraft and Winchcraft", *Philosophy of the Social Sciences* 2: 3 (June 1972): 89–103; Roger Trigg, *Reason and Commitment* (Cambridge: Cambridge University Press, 1973), 14–22; John Kekes, "Towards a Theory of Rationality", *Philosophy of the Social Sciences* 3: 4 (December 1973): 275–88; Robin Horton, "Professor Winch on Safari", *Archives Europées de Sociologie* 17: 1 (1976): 157–80; Keith Dixon, "Is Cultural Relativism Self-Refuting?" *British Journal of Sociology* 28: 1 (March 1977): 75–88; Lars Hertzberg, "Winch on Social Interpretation", *Philosophy of the Social Sciences* 10: 2 (1980): 151–171; J.H.M. Beattie, "Objectivity and Social Anthropology", in *Objectivity and Cultural Divergence*, edited by S.C. Brown (Cambridge: Cambridge University Press, 1984), 12ff; Harold I. Brown, *Rationality* (London: Routledge, 1988), 122–133; James F. Harris, *Against Relativism: A Philosophical Defense of Method* (LaSalle, IL: Open Court, 1992), 95–102. Some of these authors make further criticisms of Winch that I do not consider here.
8. Winch, "Understanding a Primitive Society", 82; *The Idea of a Social Science*, 15.
9. Winch, "Understanding a Primitive Society", 93.
10. Winch, "Understanding a Primitive Society", 82.
11. Winch, *The Idea of a Social Science*, 13.
12. See, for example, Winch, "Understanding a Primitive Society", 81–82, 100; "Language, Belief, and Relativism", 194; and Winch's "Comment", in *Explanation in the Behavioral Sciences*, edited by Borger and Cioffi, 255.
13. Winch, "Comment", 254–255. Winch explicitly distinguishes his arguments in "Understanding a Primitive Society" from "the sort of

relativism concerning *truth*" in "Language, Belief, and Relativism", 195 (emphasis added).

14. Similarly, the *discovery* of facts depends on the goals of an inquiry and the conceptual tools involved, but the *existence* of the facts does not. See Winch, "Darwin, *Genesis*, and Contradiction", 136.
15. Winch, "Understanding a Primitive Society", 81–82.
16. Roy Bhaskar, *A Realist Theory of Science* (London: Harvester, 1975), 250.
17. Letter to the author, July 7, 1993. The letter continues: "I am always relieved when someone realizes that my position is *not* a relativist one. It happens all too seldom. [...] On the other hand, I should be reluctant to accept the label 'realist'. The root of the whole trouble is that these labels convey the false impression that they designate two genuinely distinct theories, whereas *that* is where the fundamental confusion lies. In *Tractatus* §5.641 Wittgenstein wrote: 'solipsism strictly carried out coincides with pure realism'. Substitute 'relativism' for 'solipsism' and I think this remains true."
18. Winch's strongest statement of this position is the following. "Within [social practices such as] science and religion, actions can be logical or illogical. [...] But we cannot sensibly say that the practice of science itself or that of religion is either logical or illogical; both are non-logical" (Winch, *The Idea of a Social Science*, 100–101). Although Winch has distanced himself from the claim that social practices are *autonomous* wholes, he continues to argue that "the logico-conceptual difficulties which arise when ways of thinking which have their roots in different reaches of human life are brought to bear on each other cannot be resolved by any appeal to a formal system" (Winch, "Preface to the Second Edition", *The Idea of a Social Science*, xvi).
19. Winch, *The Idea of a Social Science*, 57, 134. In my opinion, this is the best way to understand Winch's notorious comments that logical principles "arise out of" or "depend on" social relations (Winch, *The Idea of a Social Science*, 100, 126).
20. Winch, *The Idea of a Social Science*, 126.
21. Winch, *The Idea of a Social Science*, 27.
22. E.E. Evans-Pritchard, *Witchcraft, Oracles, and Magic among the Azande* (Oxford: Clarendon Press, 1965), 24. Quoted in Winch, "Understanding a Primitive Society", 91.
23. Winch, "Understanding a Primitive Society", 91–92. Phillips gives on overview of Winch's response to three alleged contradictions in Zande practice (2001: 300–4).

24. Winch, "Understanding a Primitive Society", 93.
25 It is important to note that Winch does not argue, as some of his supporters and critics have claimed that there are social practices in which contradiction is not significant. For an example of supporters who say that contradiction is just the philosopher's hobgoblin, see W.W. Sharrock and R.J. Anderson, "Magic, Witchcraft, and the Materialist Mentality", *Human Studies* 8: 4 (1985): 369; for a critic, see Charles Taylor, "Rationality", in *Rationality and Relativism*, edited by Hollis and Lukes, 91.
26. Winch, "Understanding a Primitive Society", 105.
27. Winch, "Comment", 254.
28. Winch, "Comment", 250.
29. Winch, *The Idea of a Social Science*, 89. See also 45–51 and "Understanding a Primitive Society", 96, 107–8.
30. For example, *The Idea of a Social Science*, 72, 78, 117.
31. For example, *The Idea of a Social Science*, 89–90; see also 58.
32. Winch, "Comment", 258, emphasis in the original (see also "Language, Belief, and Relativism", 207) and Winch, *Ethics and Action* (London: Routledge and Kegan Paul, 1972), 3.
33. Winch, "Understanding a Primitive Society", 100.
34. Winch, "Understanding a Primitive Society", 99, 100.
35. Winch, "Understanding a Primitive Society", 87.
36. Winch, "Understanding a Primitive Society", 99.
37. Winch, "Understanding a Primitive Society", 100–1. This criticism is specifically aimed at Alasdair MacIntyre.
38. Winch, "Understanding a Primitive Society", 100.
39. See the essays by Hollis and Lukes in footnote 7.
40. For example, Winch writes that "the forms in which rationality expresses itself in the culture of a human society cannot be elucidated *simply* in terms of [...] logical coherence" ("Understanding a Primitive Society", 93; emphasis in the original). Believing that he is reproaching Winch, Hollis says, "Rationality may refer to two different things. On the one hand a man's beliefs and practices must be coherent. [...] On the other hand to show why a man's actions are rational we must give *his* reasons for performing them. This involves an appeal to his culture" ("Witchcraft and Winchcraft", 100; emphasis in the original).

41. I do not have the space here to assess the relative merits of these two positions, but it is worth noting that Hollis but not Winch is saddled with the task of tracing all cognitive claims to their "literal" or empirical meaning. Hollis tries to do this with religious claims in "Reason and Ritual", in *Rationality*, edited by Wilson, 221–39.
42. Winch, "Understanding a Primitive Society", 83. Also "Comment", 240.
43. Winch, "Understanding a Primitive Society", 107.
44. Winch, "Understanding a Primitive Society", 107.
45. Winch, "Apel's Transcendental Pragmatics", 61.
46. Winch, "Ethical Relativism", *Trying to Make Sense*, 189.
47. On Martin Hollis's construal, *that* there are shared percepts is logically necessary, but what they are is always logically contingent. See Hollis, "The Limits of Irrationality", in *Rationality*, edited by Wilson, 214–20, and "The Epistemological Unity of Mankind", in *Philosophical Disputes in the Social Sciences*, edited by Brown, 225–32. In the language of this paper, "that there are shared percepts" is a formal and not a substantive claim.
48. Charles Hartshorne develops this understanding of metaphysics. See especially his "What Metaphysics Is" and "Non-restrictive Existential Statements", in *Creative Synthesis and Philosophic Method* (LaSalle, IL: Open Court Press, 1970), 19–42, 159–72.
49. Winch, "Comment", 253.
50. Winch, *The Idea of a Social Science*, 15.
51. Hartshorne's approach is an example of this, as is the revisionary or post-foundationalist metaphysics of John Post. See John F. Post, *Faces of Existence: An Essay in Nonreductive Metaphysics* (Ithaca: Cornell University Press, 1987), and *Metaphysics: A Contemporary Introduction* (New York: Paragon House, 1991), especially 5–10, 33–36.
52. Winch, "True or False?" *Inquiry* 31: 3 (September 1988): 265.
53. Winch, *The Idea of a Social Science*, 102.
54. Winch, *The Idea of a Social Science*, 15.
55. For some suggestive thoughts on metaphysics as grammar, see Charles Hartshorne, "Wittgenstein and Tillich: Reflections on Metaphysics and Language", *Creative Synthesis and Philosophic Method* (Lanham, MD: University Press of America, 1970), 131–48. For more common ground between neoclassical metaphysics and Wittgenstein, see Hartshorne, "Reflections on Wittgenstein", *Insights and Oversights of Great*

Thinkers: An Evaluation of Western Philosophy (Albany: State University of New York Press, 1983), 293–305.

56. This paper previously appeared in *Sophia: International Journal for Philosophy of Religion, Metaphysical Theology and Ethics* and I kindly thank its editor, Purushottama Bilimoria, for the chance to republish it here.

REFERENCES

Apel, Karl Otto. "Universal Principles and Particular Decisions and Forms of Life", in *Value and Understanding: Essays for Peter Winch,* edited by Raimond Gaita. London: Routledge, 1990.

Beattie, J.H.M. "Objectivity and Social Anthropology", in *Objectivity and Cultural Divergence*, edited by Stuart C. Brown. Cambridge: Cambridge University Press, 1984.

Bernstein, Richard J. *The Restructuring of Social and Political Theory*. Philadelphia: University of Pennsylvania Press, 1976.

——. *Beyond Objectivism and Relativism: Science, Hermeneutics, and Praxis*. Philadelphia: University of Pennsylvania Press, 1983.

Bhaskar, Roy. *A Realist Theory of Science*. London: Harvester, 1975.

Brown, Harold I. *Rationality*. London: Routledge, 1988.

Derksen, A.A. "On an Unnoticed Key to Reality". *Philosophy of the Social Sciences* 8: 3 (September), (1978): 209–225.

Evans-Pritchard, E.E. *Witchcraft, Oracles, and Magic among the Azande*. Oxford: Clarendon Press, 1965.

Dixon, Keith. "Is Cultural Relativism Self-Refuting?" *British Journal of Sociology* 28: 1 (March), (1977): 75–88.

Habermas, Jurgen. *The Theory of Communicative Action, Vol. 1: Reason and the Rationalization of Society*, translated by Thomas McCarthy. Boston: Beacon Press, 1980.

Harris, James F. *Against Relativism: A Philosophical Defense of Method*. LaSalle, IL: Open Court, 1992.

Hartshorne, Charles. *Creative Synthesis and Philosophic Method*. Lanham, MD: University Press of America, 1970.

——. *Insights and Oversights of Great Thinkers: An Evaluation of Western Philosophy*. Albany: State University of New York Press, 1983.

Hertzberg, Lars. "Winch on Social Interpretation". *Philosophy of the Social Sciences,* 10: 2 (1980): 151–171.

Hollis, Martin. "The Limits of Irrationality", in *Rationality*, edited by Bryan R. Wilson. Oxford: Basil Blackwell, 1970.

——. "Witchcraft and Winchcraft". *Philosophy of the Social Sciences* 2: 3 (June), (1972): 89–103.

——. "The Epistemological Unity of Mankind", in *Philosophical Disputes in the Social Sciences.* Edited by Stuart Brown. Brighton, Sussex: Harvester Press, 1979.

Horton, Robin "Professor Winch on Safari". *Archives Européenes de Sociologie* 17: 1 (1976): 157–80.

Jarvie, I.C. "Understanding and Explanation in Sociology and Social Anthropology", in *Explanation in the Behavioral Sciences*. Edited by Robert Borger and Frank Cioffi. Cambridge: Cambridge University Press, 1970.

Kekes, John. "Towards a Theory of Rationality". *Philosophy of the Social Sciences* 3: 4 (December), (1983): 275–88.

Lerner, Berel Dov. *Rules, Magic, and Instrumental Reason.* London: Routledge, 2002.

Lukes, Steven. "Some Problems about Rationality", in *Rationality*. Edited by Bryan Wilson. Oxford: Basil Blackwell, 1970.

Lyas, Colin. *Peter Winch*. Teddington: Acumen, 1999.

MacIntyre, Alasdair. "The Idea of a Social Science", in *Rationality*. Edited by Bryan Wilson. Oxford: Basil Blackwell, 1970.

Phillips, D.Z. *Religion and the Hermeneutics of Contemplation.* Cambridge: Cambridge University Press, 2001.

Post, John F. *Faces of Existence: An Essay in Nonreductive Metaphysics*. Ithaca: Cornell University Press, 1987.

——. *Metaphysics: A Contemporary Introduction*. New York: Paragon House, 1991.

Sharrock, W.W. and R.J. Anderson. "Magic, Witchcraft, and the Materialist Mentality", *Human Studies* 8: 4, 1985.

Taylor, Charles. "Rationality", in *Rationality and Relativism*. Edited by Martin Hollis and Steven Lukes. Oxford: Blackwell, 1982.

Trigg, Roger. *Reason and Commitment*. Cambridge: Cambridge University Press, 1973.

Winch, Peter. "Understanding a Primitive Society", in *Rationality*. Edited by Bryan R. Wilson. Oxford: Basil Blackwell, 1970a.

——. "Comment", in *Explanation in the Behavioral Sciences.* Edited by Robert Borger and Frank Cioffi. Cambridge: Cambridge University Press, 1970b.

——. *Ethics and Action*. London: Routledge and Kegan Paul, 1972.

——. "Apel's Transcendental Pragmatics", in *Philosophical Disputes in the Social Sciences,* edited by Stuart C. Brown. Sussex: Harvester Press, 1979.

——. *Trying to Make Sense*. Oxford: Basil Blackwell, 1987.

——. "True or False?" *Inquiry* 31: 3, September 1988.

——. *The Idea of a Social Science and Its Relation to Philosophy*, Second edition. Atlantic Highlands, NJ: Humanities Press International, 1989.

CHAPTER 7

Buddhist Images of the Body

A study of different patterns of human embodiment and performance

CARL OLSON

Within the context of ancient Indian culture, the body was a powerful metaphor for the cosmos and human beings. In the Rig Vedic hymn (10.90), a creation narrative centres on a primordial body from which the cosmos is created and society structured by reinforcing the social structure, or what the learned Brahmin priestly caste considered the correct social order, with the priestly caste at the top and the lowest caste at the feet of the primordial being. This image emphatically suggests that the body is hierarchically ordered with the head being the most exalted part of the body and the feet the lowest part of the body.

Within this cosmological structure, ancient Indians were deeply concerned about issues of pollution and purity because they played an important role in sacrificial activity, and a patron or priest could not perform a given ritual unless they were in a purified condition because of the fear of polluting the gods and goddesses and motivating them to retaliate against the impure party. Around the same time, there was a developing tradition of wandering holy persons, who were mostly males and lived on the fringe of orthodox culture. These wandering figures and renouncers of the world practised various forms of asceticism that included mortification of their bodies in order to bring their bodies under control for a higher spiritual purpose or for the acquisition of certain powers. Into this religious milieu, Buddhism was born, nurtured, and adopted the discourse about the hierarchical nature of the body, a conviction that the body was a trap, the body was foul and impermanent, served as a hindrance to the attainment of spiritual goals, and needed to be controlled.

If we examine Pali scriptures that are the bases of the Theraväda tradition, we find that they reflect an ambiguous attitude and that a particular characterization of the body needs to be contextualized. The most common term for body is *käya* – a term that can refer to the physical body, a collection of aggregates, or something like the body of a text that implies its essence or main part.[1] Pali texts also indicate that the body does not represent an independent entity because it represents a merging of other aggregates or material elements to constitute a self, which possesses no enduring existence, according to the necessary and independent operation of the law of karma and previous karmic volitions. Another term used to designate the body is *śarīra*, which applies to both the human body and a bodily relic.

From within the context of a western culture that stresses beautifying the body and spending unimaginable amounts of money attempting to created the desired bodily appearance with various products and medical procedures, the Pali Buddhist's negative references to the human body are striking in their negativity. Pali Nikäya texts refer to the human body as a wound, a boil with nine open wounds, a bag of excrement, heap of corruption, impure, foul-smelling, and prone to discharging elements. Buddhist monks, who are the authors of these texts, also used similes to capture their grasp of the body, such as village sewage, a dunghill, or a charnel ground.

Along with feelings, perceptions, mental constituents, and consciousness, the body contributes to the five aggregates that create a false sense of the self. Similar to the other aggregates that constitute the self, the body is impermanent, and it is eventually vulnerable to sickness, old age, and death. The impermanent nature of the body is most evident when considered within the chain of causation, or dependent origination (*paṭiccasamppāda*), representing the fourth link of the chain along with the mind. Within the karmic formation of the law of cause and effect, the body and mind are products of causation as a direct result of ignorance.

From a metaphorical perspective, the Buddhist depiction of the body focuses on its impurity. The Milindapañha – a postcanonical work that can be translated as the Questions for King Milinda – refers to thirty-two loathsome constituent parts of the human body: head hair, body hair, nails, teeth, skin, flesh, sinews, bones, marrow, kidneys, heart, liver, pleura, spleen, lungs, colour, intestines, stomach, feces, bile, phlegm, pus, blood, sweat, fat, tears, lymph, saliva, snot, synovia, urine, and brain.[2] Many of these parts, such as hair, nails, teeth, and skin are considered dead matter that in the prevailing Brahmanical culture are considered polluting, while other material that oozes from the body is equally dirty and polluting.

The popular *Dhammapada* – another postcanonical text – stresses the fragile and impermanent nature of the body. The human body is compared to foam and a mirage (4. 46), a useless chip of wood (3.41), a discarded pot (11.149), and a dilapidated chariot (11.151). The body may appear to be beautiful eternally, but it is full of sores, illness, and impermanent (11.147).

The body is our vehicle that transports humans to death:

> Quite wasted away in this form,
> A nest for disease, perishable.
> This putrid accumulation breaks up,
> For life has its end in death. (11.148)[3]

Therefore, the human body is directly connected with suffering of various kinds with human embodiness making pain possible for the individual and enabling one body to harm another thereby increasing suffering.

The apparent Buddhist negative attitude towards the human body is also historically carried forward by Buddhaghosa (fifth century CE), who is the greatest commentator of the Pali canon and author of the *Visuddhimagga* (*The Path of Purification*). In this important text, Buddhaghosa, whose name means "voice of the Buddha" conveying his importance in the tradition, refers to the "filthy body", and instructs monks to be mindful of the thirty-two repulsive aspects of the body beginning with the feet and up to the head, which is for the most part identical with the items already mentioned in the *Milindapañha*.[4] In a second example, Buddhaghosa calls attention to the location of the origin of the human body within a womb surrounded by undigested food, behind the lining of the stomach, in front of the spinal cord, surrounded by the bowels and entrails, cramped, being itself stinking, disgusting, and repulsive.[5] In other words, the body is conceived, nurtured, and born within filth, a process of an impure body nurturing a foetus within an impure condition, and finally producing another impure body. Therefore, it is impure even before it appears in the world and continues to spread pollution even when finally dead.

If the human body in general is conceived by the Pali literature as a leaky container that is continually emitting defiling substances that flow from the various orifices of the body, the body of a woman is even more impure and dangerous. In the Buddhist monastic literature, women are selected for special attention because they present a danger to the purity of monks and a trap that could divert them from the path to liberation. Pali literature uses horrific imagery, such as equating a woman's sexual organ to a poisonous snake or a cave inhabited by snakes, to scare monks from deviating from the practice of celibacy. The impurity of the human body is taken to extremes with descriptions of the bodies of women. Attractive women are especially the focus of the monastic scrutiny in the post-Aśokan era when their bodies are mutilated and disfigured to destroy any sense of attachment or erotic feelings towards these beautiful women. A commentary on the *Dhammapada* tells the story of the comely Sirimā and a lovesick monk who is obsessed with her. As the narrative unfolds, the monk finally encounters her dead body, which becomes an ideal object for meditation on the impermanence of the body.[6] While practising cremation ground meditation on an undecayed female body in another episode, several monks confess later to engaging in necrophilia with the body.[7] Because of the possibility of this type of abuse, Buddhaghosa prohibits monks from meditating on the deceased bodies of females and vice versa. There is also the famous narrative about a courtesan named Vāsavadattā of the city of Mathura and the monk Upagupta, who becomes an object of obsession by the courtesan because he so handsome, but he is not seduced by her. After getting involved in a love triangle that involves the murder of a lover, the courtesan is convicted of the crime, and she is punished by having her hands, feet, nose, and ears cut off by authorities. Confined to a cremation ground, she is astonished when Upagupta comes to visit her because she thinks that he is finally coming for sex. To the courtesan's embarrassment and surprise, the monk proceeds to launch into a diatribe about the impermanence and repulsive nature of the body. This diatribe possesses a double effect because she realizes the truth of the Buddha's teachings that all life is suffering, and she becomes a stream enterer.[8] From the Buddhist perspective, if attractive women are grotesquely transformed, their horrific appearance operates to promote detachment from the female body by monks trying to adhere to a celibate injunction and to teach women the truth of Buddhism.

An inquiring reader might ponder the motivation for such a negative attitude towards the human body and especially the female body. Western Buddhist scholars have offered a variety of opinions about the reasons for the negative depiction of the body in the Pali tradition. Hamilton argues that the negative statement about the body in the Pali canon can be attributed to Brahmanical or culturally non-doctrinal influences on Buddhism. She also claims that the Buddhist position is not negative or positive with respect to the body, but it is rather analytical. And, she asserts that Buddhaghosa diverges from the original material.[9] Although there is some truth in Hamilton's position about the analytical nature of the Buddhist position, the negative references to the human body are pervasive in Pali literature, and Hamilton seems to be engaging in revisionist interpretation. In fact, negative depictions about the body make logically consistent sense when viewed within the purview of the three marks of existence: suffering (*dukkha*), impermanence (*anicca*), and non-self (*anatta*).

With respect to the female body, some women scholars have indicated that the Buddhist attitude toward the female body exhibits a blatant misogyny by monkish writers.[10] Wilson finds something ever more sinister: "By constituting the female body as deceitful and dangerous, the redactors of these texts seek to reconstitute the male gaze and reconfigure the male body".[11] In fact, the biography of the Buddha provides a paradigm for the "gynophobic horror" with its repulsive description of the female body.[12] Wilson and some other female scholars reach their positions on the basis of textual material that they look through feminist and liberal political perspectives. In other words, their prejudgments, presuppositions, biases, and pre-understandings shape what they encounter in the texts and their interpretation. This is not to say that misogynist or gynophobic attitudes among Buddhist monks cannot be discovered in the Pali literature, it is just that such critics are superimposing western attitudes on the textual material.

Several other Buddhist scholars have criticized positions of some female scholars about the worthless nature of the female body. Rita Gross defends the Buddhist affirming that "except when resisting temptation to a specific woman, contemplations on the body usually do not distinguish between a male and female body".[13] From another perspective, Steven Collins finds Lang's position that nuns did not reflect on the attractiveness of men as overstated and the difference between men and women is not confined to Buddhist texts.[14]

In another essay, Kevin Trainor examines the story of the nun Subhā in the *Therīgāthā* (71), who confronts a male rogue in an isolated location. The male attempts to seduce her, but she maintains her monastic status and detachment from promises of worldly leisure, pleasure, and wealth. When her antagonist flattery turns to the beauty of her eyes, she gouges out her eyeball and offers it to the rogue. After Subhā sees a vision of the Buddha's peerless body, her eye is restored. Trainor draws the conclusion as under:

> Finally, recognizing that the experience of Theravāda monks and nuns has been shaped in significant ways by gender differences, we must work through the interpretive implications of the tradition's unambiguous affirmation that the state of one who has reached the goal of arahantship by definition transcends the category of gender.[15]

Working with Theravāda Buddhist hagiographical texts, Jonathan S. Walters argues that it is essential not to conflate early Buddhism with all Theravādin thought. Otherwise, women's voices are silenced, and their striving to realize the equalitarian ideal of early Buddhism is lost. He concludes that "even in the Theravādin tradition some women successfully launched a powerful challenge to early Buddhist androcentrism".[16]

In contrast to these scholars, Reiko Ohnuma thinks that the negative attitudes to the body in Buddhism coalesce around notions of impurity, impermanence, fragility of the body, and its role in promoting delusions and passions that lead to attachment to the body, which monks are encouraged to conquer by the practice of mindfulness (*sati*) in order to bring the body under control for the purpose of facilitating meditative progress. This control of the body is not attained by mortification of the body as evident in the biography of the Buddha and his fruitless quest for liberation by practicing extreme forms of asceticism. Ohmuna makes a distinction between the worth and the worthlessness of the body that forms the context of two kinds of thinking that she finds is complementary rather than contradictory. When a monk is motivated to overcome his attachment to his delusional self, he emphasizes the worthless nature of the body, whereas when he is motivated to attain higher spiritual goals there is stress place on care of the body and its worth.[17] It is possible to use the worthless body for a positive purpose by sacrificing it, for instance, and to transform it from a vehicle of bondage without worth to one of freedom, which enables one to achieve an ideal body. The apparent negative act of abandoning the body thus becomes something positive and rewarding. Hence, by reviewing Buddhist literature about making a gift of the body, Ohmuna is able to demonstrate that the negative and positive views of the body are mutually related, if one examines their context.

Pali Buddhist meditation practice teaches the importance of practising mindfulness (*sati*), which initially calls for being mindful of the body because without bringing the body under control a monk cannot make any progress. Besides proper bodily meditative postures, such as the lotus position, more advance progress is impossible. The *Mahāsatipatthāna Sutta* (D.2.294) relates that the Buddha instructed his monks to assume the role of a butcher by mentally cutting their bodies into pieces and analyzing the parts.[18] According to Buddhaghosa, by practising mindfulness of the body, this practice will lead to a "supreme sense of urgency, to supreme benefit, to supreme surcease of bondage, to supreme mindfulness and full-awareness, to acquisition of knowledge and vision, to a happy life, here and now, to realization of the fruit of clear vision and deliverance" on the part of the meditator.[19]

With a similar purpose of a butcher, a monk can practise mindfulness using the human body as an object upon which to concentrate. A meditator is instructed to mediate on a dead body at various stages of decomposition and the remains thereafter. There are nine of these so-called "cemetery contemplations": a discarded, swollen body, a body eaten by crows, a heap of bones smeared with blood, a heap of bones without flesh or blood, scattered bones, bones a year old, bones stacked in a heap, and finally bones decayed and turned to powder.[20] These cemetery contemplations are intended to make a monk aware of the impermanent nature of the body, its vile nature, and its lack of self or ego with the ultimate purpose of becoming detached from it, which allows one to recognize that Buddhist could use the body as a pedagogical device.

The ambiguous nature of the Buddhist attitude towards the body is evident when one considers the ideal body of the Buddha, who is called the Mahapurisa (literally, Great Man or Superman). This person is characterized by thirty-two physical characteristics that include projecting heels, hands and feet like a web, legs like those of an antelope, his male organs concealed in a sheath, a halo, body hairs pointing upward, smooth and golden skin, forty even, gapless, and white teeth, jaws like those of a lion, a voice like that of the god Brahmā, blue eyes, eyelashes like a cow's, a white, soft hair growing between his eyebrows, a long tongue, symmetrical bodily proportions and so forth.[21] The Buddha's body was also considered to be pure, which negated the necessity to wash his corpse after death.[22] In his book on images of Indian Buddhist masculinity, John Powers insightfully indicates what was at stake: "The ideal body of

Indian Buddhism was a public terrain on which social truths were inscribed and also a place on which [...] social contradictions were played out."[23] Within the overall context of Mahāyāna literature, this Pali tradition about the Buddha's body is continued when the Buddha is described as possessing no polluting elements.[24] The bodily perfection of the Buddha suggests a connection between his physical appearance and other kinds of perfection that are connected to his action, cognition, attitude, and control, and they also indicate that his physical characteristics are auspicious and pleasing to others.

The positive attitude towards and veneration of the Buddha's body is carried over to his relics that served to embody and objectify his charisma. Because the Buddha's relics embody the same qualities as the historical Buddha, they are considered alive, own property, and perform miracles. Moreover, although the relics are not precisely the historical figure, they render him present, and even continue to spread his presence to other countries housed in memorial structures (*stūpas*). Not only did the Buddha have a biography, but his relics also possessed biographies, although the relics operated as episodic biographies by recalling specific events in his life.[25]

Tantric perspectives on the body

It is impossible to determine precisely the origin of Śaiva and Buddhist Tantra. There is evidence in China of Tantric notions several centuries before the earliest Indian evidence, and we, moreover, know that there had been several centuries of active interchange between Chinese and Indian trade routes. It is possible that Chinese notions were conceptualized within a specific Indic vocabulary. In retrospect, there was a gradual development toward a yoga tantra (c. 700–c. 750).[26] For the subsequent discussion of this essay, I have utilized three Tantric texts from the Yoginī Tantra classification: *Hevajra Tantra* (late eight or early ninth century), *Cakrasamvara Tantra* (late eight or early ninth century), and the *Kālacakratantra* (mid-eleventh century). In addition, I have also used the *Caṇḍamahṛroṣaṇa Tantra* (late thirteenth century).

An aspirant gains admission into the tantric path by initiation provided by a master practitioner. During the initiation ceremony (*guhyābhiṣeka*), the initiate consumes a drop of the combined sexual fluids – semen and blood – of the tantric master and his consort. This part of the initiation is historically indicative of the importance that sexual fluids played in Tantra from a very early period. In fact, David Gordon White thinks that the consumption of sexual fluids represents the origin of Tantric practice.[27] The original rationale for the ingestion of sexual fluids is related to their extremely polluting and powerful effectiveness. Thus, it is a misconception to concentrate on the spiritual fulfilment of sexual activity as the motivation for the consuming of fluids, but their polluting nature made them transgressive and thus powerful.[28]

Tantric Buddhist texts take a very different view of the human body, which is conceived as a microcosm of the macrocosmic universe, implying that what can be discovered in the universe can also be found within the human body, such as mountains, rivers, the sun, and the moon. *The Kalacakratantra* states, "As it is in the external world so it is in the body" (4.66). There are two kinds of body distinguished by Tantric texts: the gross material body and the innate subtle body. The physical body can be seen and touched by oneself and others, and it consists of the four elements: earth, water, fire, and wind along with their derivatives. Within the physical body is the subtle or innate body that cannot be seen because it consists of 72,000 channels (*nāḍīs*) that is supported and sustained by the gross body. The subtle body is akin to a psycho-physical complex that consists of fine breath power (sometimes called winds or rivers) and functions as a vehicle of mental energy. These winds, or various kinds of breaths, are located within the centre of the *nāḍīs* according to their functions, and they pervade the 72,000 *nāḍīs*.[29]

At the centre of the subtle body, there is the spinal cord that is analogous to Mount Meru, a symbolic centre of the Buddhist universe, which is called the Merudanda. Surrounding the central column of the subtle body, there are the four wheels (*cakras*), representing centres of energy. Beginning with the navel region of the subtle body, there is located the *nirmana-kāya*, in the heart is located the *dharma-kāya*, at the juncture of the spinal cord and medulla oblongata is the *sambhoga-kāya*, and at the top of the head is the *mahāsukha-kāya* (body of great bliss).[30] By carrying substances, such as phlegm, bile, wind, and the three humors, the *nāḍīs* (breath channels) lock the *cakras* (centres) and cause an imbalance in the subtle body.[31]

The subtle body is united by a complex web of interlocking nerves that manifest three major nerves: *lalanā* (located on the left side of the body and symbolically identified with wisdom); *rasanā* (located on the right side of the body and is identified with skilful means); and the *avadhūti* (located in the centre that passes through the heart along with mental energy). The *lalanā*, which represents wisdom (*prajñā*), carries the female egg or energy, whereas the *rasanā*, which is identified with *upāya* (skilful means) transports male sperm or energy. These two complementary energies are united in the central nerve that ascends to the head to unite with the body of bliss, which represents a union of wisdom (female principle *prajñā*) and skilful means (male principle *upāya*). In the final analysis, the mind (*bodhicitta*) is a combination of egg and sperm at the instant of enlightenment.

The distinction between the physical and subtle bodies is also related to two kinds of mind: mental body and innate body (referring to transcendent consciousness). Because of experiences of pleasure and pain, the mental body contributes to the creation of rebirth (*saṃsāra*), is considered contaminated, and in a state of bondage to the law of karma, whereas the innate mind creates what is beyond rebirth, is free from any kind of defilement, and is free to perform good deeds that contribute to positive personal and social outcomes. The innate mind represents a union of emptiness (*śūnyatā*) and compassion (*karunā*). Emptiness is associated with wisdom (*prajñā*), which is defined as passive, feminine, and universal principle underlying the diversity of the universe, because it represents perfect knowledge, whereas compassion is connected to skilful means (*upāya*) that is able to bring the mind into contact with the world of particulars, representing the male principle called the thunderbolt (*vajra*).

From the Tantric perspective, if the human body is a microcosm of the universe, the body represents the abode of all truth, which is a fundamental Tantric presupposition. Another presupposition of Tantric thought is that it is possible to use worldly (*samsāric*) means to reach the goal of liberation. From the Tantric perspective, the human body is an absolute necessity for spiritual attainment. According to The *Kalacakratantra* (6.107), "In the absence of the body, neither a *siddhi* (power) nor supreme bliss is attained in this life". Although this is a secretive and dangerous path, it is also considered a more rapid path. Such a path makes use of forbidden acts and ingestion of polluting substances and fluids in conjunction with use of instinctual passions, and the practice transforms them into instruments for achieving freedom. This attitude is summarized by the *Hevajra Tantra* (2.3.51): "By passion the world is bound, by passion too it is released, but by the heretic Buddhists this practice of reversals is not known." This position is difficult for the uninitiated to understand.

It is also difficult for the uninitiated to grasp that by indulging the physical body in forbidden substances, fluids, and actions that this assists the subtle body untie knots, which are due to emotional and cognitive problems that form around the various energy channels and prohibits spiritual progress. When the nerve channels are unblocked energy is able to flow into the central channel. Not only do forbidden, impure liquids and substances eliminate disease, but also, according to the *Kalacakratantra* (6.125), "Feces, urine, semen, and blood ingested together with human flesh give life". To cite another example of impure, disgusting material used in a ritualistic context, the *Cakrasamvara* Tantra instructs one to overpower the body with vomit of food eaten. After seven nights the vomit should be added to one's food, drink, and used to anoint one's face.[32] Ideally, the forbidden liquid includes menstrual blood and semen, whereas the substance is the feces of the female partner eaten by the male, which is accompanied by sexual congress in secret. This entire procedure is for advanced practitioners, and it occurs within a highly ritualistic context with the male aspirant using the energy of the female to unlock the channels of his subtle body – a practice believed to be superior to ordinary solitary meditation because it adds the energy of the partner to achieving one's goal.

From a metaphorical perspective, sexual congress is similar to the union of the lotus (female organ) and diamond scepter (male organ), which from a philosophical perspective represents the union of wisdom and compassion. The metaphor entails the diamond scepter churning the lotus of the female partner, functioning thereby as the efficient cause of the nectar of Buddhahood. What this churning process creates is bliss, which leads to enlightenment and concomitant realization that everything is emptiness, including sexual congress.

According to the *Caṇḍamahāroṣana Tantra* (6.20–180), assuming the secret nature of the practice, the female partner sits before the male with each gazing at each other. Falling at the female partner's feet with palms pressed together, the partners should identify each other imaginatively with family members, such as mothers, fathers, sisters, and brothers, which increases the forbidden nature of the rite by transforming the relationship into an incestuous one. Kissing her partner, placing three syllables on his head, and saliva into his mouth, the male figure responds by sucking the lotus (vagina) of his partner, which is followed by her pinching him on the chest and inviting him to consume her *Vairocana* (feces) and drink her water of *Akṣobhya* (urine). If a male aspirant thinks that these bodily waste products are repulsive that person is still stuck in ignorance and bondage.[33] After informing her partner that she is his slave, wife, mother, and refuge, she requests the pleasure of his *vajra* (penis).

With his mind fixed on the pleasure, the male is commanded to examine his partner's sexual organ and to enter it with thousands of strokes. Besides trying various sexual positions, the male is instructed to suck her tongue, drink her saliva, consume any waste in her teeth, clean her nostrils and corners of her eyes with his tongue, and finally he cleans her vagina with his tongue and drinks the white drops (semen) and red drops (blood) of the lotus. In order to increase desire, the male aspirant eats meat, fish, and drinks wine, which are normally forbidden substances and liquids for a Buddhist. The consumption of meat, for instance, is believed to stimulate the production and flow of sexual fluids needed by the yogin.

The stimulation of the clitoris and sexual orgasm need further clarification. By stimulating the female partner's clitoris, this energizes the flow of female sexual fluid. Some commentators call for a menstruating woman in order to ensure that the feminine fluid contains blood. With respect to sexual orgasm, the *Hevajra Tantra* advocates a controlled ejaculation by the male partner in conjunction with yogic postures, and placement of seed syllables. This is followed by the reabsorption of the mixed fluids by the yogin using a technique of reverse uretheral suction (*vajralimudrā*).[34] From a historical perspective, White argues that the ejaculation requirement is an older Hindu practice, whereas Buddhists rejected ejaculation at a later time.[35]

The ethically transgressive and radical nature of the secret rite continues in the text when the male practitioner is instructed to visualize entering the top of the head of the Buddha Akṣobhya and the womb of the goddess Māmakī in the form of a sperm. This is followed by a radical visualization when the male figure visualizes killing his father Akṣobhya and eating his flesh, while also visualizing having sexual congress with his mother.[36] Therefore, this radical scenario combines cannibalism, murder, and incest – a triple transgression intended to not simply violate ethical standards but to transcend distinctions such as good and evil.

Although women and their bodies played a significant role in Tantric Buddhism, the textual evidence exhibits an androcentric perspective. As with the Theravāda tradition, women are portrayed from a male viewpoint because men wrote and preserved the texts according to patriarchal norms.[37] A woman did not assume a role as a genuine and equal partner to her male counterpart, even though she did play an instrumental role.[38] It is this type of role the Shaw uses to indicate the central role of women in Tantric Buddhism as teachers and organizers of Tantric lineages.[39] Samuel and Davidson disagree because of a lack of widespread evidence and the dominance of males.[40] These scholars agree that the role of women was diminishing in everyday life as evident by the lack of the names of female donors in significant numbers inscribed at Buddhist holy sites.

Dōgen's Zen perspective on the body

Dōgen Kigen Zenji (1200–1253) is arguably the most gifted thinker within the Japanese Zen Buddhist tradition, who is credited with founding the Sōtō Zen School after his return from China where he attained enlightenment under the tutelage of Ju-ching (1163–1268), a master of the Ts'ao-tung school. In the remote mountainous region location of Fukui Prefecture, he established the Eihei-ji ("Temple of Eternal Peace"), a place from which he trained monks and where he composed the *Shōbōgenzō* (The Treasury of the True Dharma Eye) towards the end of his life, representing his mature thought. In this monumental philosophical work written from the perspective of an enlightened Zen master, he expounded his non-dualistic philosophy that argued that the Buddha-nature was equivalent to all existence including plants, animals, and the inanimate world. Although he occasionally did refer to kōans (enigmatic statements made by previous masters), he stressed seated meditation (*zazen*) as his primary practice for achieving enlightenment. Dōgen indicated that a monk practices seated meditation with his body, and thus quests for liberation in an embodied condition. Thus, one is hard pressed to find negative statements about the human body in Dōgen's works as compared to the Theravāda tradition because the human body is not a hindrance to realization, but it rather serves as a vehicle through which enlightenment is realized by the aspirant devoid of the forbidden practices of Tantric Buddhism. Therefore, a person's body plays a pivotal role in the quest, practice of meditation, understanding, and attaining enlightenment. In short, the human body assumes a metaphysico-religious status for Dōgen.[41] It is possible to witness this in the body's relationship to the world, consciousness, perception, time, and reality.

Grasping the body as subject, object, and something additional, Dōgen explains that the body is not merely a subject and an object, but it is, along with the mind, also equivalent with grass, trees, wall rubble, wind, rain, water, and fire.[42] By affirming this position from his enlightened perspective, Dōgen is stating that everything represents a single and total body. According to Dōgen, if this is not true, a monk's body and mind is not his own, and if body and mind fail to exist, grass, wood, and everything else do not exist.[43] Since body and mind represent the entire world and its contents, human beings are not separated from the world by their bodies. Moreover, it is impossible for anyone to know precisely where the body begins and ends and where the world begins and ends. From a slightly different perspective, Dōgen thinks that the human body participates in the world in the sense that the mind, body, and things of the world interpenetrate each other in such a way that it is impossible to differentiate among them.

By affirming the inseparable interconnection between the body, mind, and world, Dōgen also wants to call attention to the dynamic nature of the body for which he utilizes sailing in a boat. Dōgen metaphorically indicates that life is analogous to riding in a boat in which the voyager uses the boat's sails to power the vessel and its tiller to guide it to its intended destination. Although the sailor can perform certain tasks to assist him in his journey, it is the boat that carries him. The boat is not merely the sailor's mode of transportation, it is also he who makes it a boat, which becomes a world for the sailor. From this boat metaphor, Dōgen draws the lesson that life is what a person makes to exist, and person is what life makes me. When the sailor boards the boat his body, mind, and the total environment represents the boat's dynamic working, which implies that the entire world of earth and space are the boat's dynamic working. What Dōgen intends to indicate with his boat metaphor is that the body, mind, and world are nondual and dynamic. Dōgen's philosophical position implies, although he does not say this explicitly, that a writer can only use a metaphor in an embodied condition.

Because the human body participates in the inner world of the individual for Dōgen, it is interrelated with consciousness. Thus consciousness is incarnate, although Dōgen is not simply interested in intentional or worldly consciousness. Dōgen is more concerned with non-thinking (*hishiryō*), a simple acceptance of ideas without affirming or denying them, that unites thinking, an intentional weighting of ideas, and unthinking, a negation of mental acts. Non-thinking possesses no form, purpose, object, or subject. As a pure presence of things as they are, non-thinking is realized in *zazen* (seated meditation) that represents in a non-representational way the thinking of the unthinkable or emptiness. Within the state of non-thinking, there is no bifurcation or differentiation between the human body and mind.

For Dōgen, the human body forms the foundation from which consciousness arises. Similar to the totality of the world, the body and consciousness are non-dual because they penetrate each other and are inextricably interconnected: "The principle that body and mind are one reality is being constantly spoken by the Buddha-Dharma."[44] Even though the mind ultimately transcends the body, substance, and form, it remains subject and object, consciousness and nonconsciousness.

Just as consciousness is embodied for Dōgen, the same holds true of perception and other senses. In the *Shōbōgenzō*, Dōgen refers to seeing forms and hearing sounds with the body and mind.[45] In a lucid way of illustrating this way of using one's senses, Dōgen quotes a Ch'an master statement: "A painting of a rice cake cannot satisfy hunger." Offering his own interpretation of this authoritative statement, Dōgen claims non-dualistically that the rice cake is equivalent to everything else, and he denies the common sense view that the painting is unreal, whereas the rice cake is real. If the painting of a rice cake is not different from other forms of existence, an actual rice cake is not different from a painting of a rice cake. Dōgen warns that if you do not know what the painting signifies it is fruitless to discover a real rice cake outside of the painting.[46] Although it is possible that the painting may or may not appear in its true form, any genuine meaning of a rice cake transcends the distinction between past and present, or birth and destruction.[47] What relieves a person's hunger is not necessarily a real rice cake or a painting of a rice cake, but it is rather becoming detached from the opposites of enlightenment and illusion. Dōgen's position is that an eatable rice cake and a pictorial representation of a consumable rice cake are empty, which suggests that either one can satisfy a person's hunger. The satisfied hunger to which Dōgen is referring pertains to the fact that viewing the painting possesses the potential to lead a viewer to an awakening, which functions to actualize the painting. It is in this sense that a painting of a rice cake can satisfy a person's hunger. Therefore, the perception to which Dōgen alludes in his essay is not the subject/object type of perception that leads to representational modes of thinking.[48]

Overcoming perceptive experience that leads to a representational mode of thinking is achieved by *zazen* (seated meditation), which enables the body to actualize itself and achieve a pre-established harmony. Nonetheless, *zazen* is not entering into realization because it is already realization even when one begins to sit for the first time. This is possible because *zazen* is the non-thinking mode of consciousness where body and mind are cast off, and one makes a leap to enlightenment. The casting off of body and mind are analogous to climbing to the top of a hundred foot pole using one's body and mind. What does a person do when reaching the top of the pole? The successful climber leaps from the top of the pole and thereby casts off body and mind. To make such a radical leap is to think the unthinkable, which suggests non-thinking. This non-thinking is not a transcendental type of thinking because there is nothing to transcend in Dōgen's philosophy. It is best grasped as a realizational seeing, which opens the universal horizon of Buddha-nature that is being and being itself, emptiness, impermanence, existence, and time.[49]

According to Dōgen, the body and mind do not dwell in space and time, but they are time just as all things are manifestations of being-time (*uji*): "Because [real existence] is only this exact moment, all moments of existence-time are the whole of time, and all existent things and all existent phenomena are time. The whole of existence, the whole universe, exist in individual moments of time."[50] It is possible to state that time is within my body, my body is in time, or that, more accurately, my body is time. This implies that the mind, being, world, and time form a unity. This position involves important consequences for one's natural environment because,

> the mountains are time, and the seas are time. Without time, the mountains and the seas could not exist: we should not deny that time exists in the mountains and the seas here and now. If time decays, the mountains and the seas decay. If time is not subject to decay, the mountains and the seas are not subject to decay.[51]

Dwelling with space and time, the human body necessarily encounters other bodies within a common and shared world. If there is no separation between body and mind as Dōgen argues, there is no distinction between one's body and the bodies of others just as there is no distinction between one's body and time and that of other bodies. Moreover, when a monk cleans his body he is washing his mind and vice versa. In fact, to wash one's body is to cleanse other bodies and the world.[52]

The unity of time, human body, and the totality of all things is most clearly evident within the context of an understanding of the Buddha-nature, whose being is time itself. Within the Buddha-nature, both future and past signify the present, even though Dōgen emphasizes the 'now' moment because there is never a time that has not been or a time that is coming. Within the being-time of the 'now' moment, everything is immediate presencing at this 'here and now', suggesting that time is a continuous occurrence of 'now' moments. For Buddha-nature, this position means that it is not a potentiality to be actualized in the future, but it is rather a present actuality that renders every moment of illusion and enlightenment a container of all reality, making Buddha-nature an embodiment of illusion and enlightenment.

The human body, for Dōgen, is impermanent, a feature of the body that necessitates becoming detached from one's body. This impermanence is also true of the Buddha-nature, which is equated with reality. This implies that the Buddha-body is the manifesting body, while there is always a body manifesting Buddha-nature.[53] Because the Buddha-nature is always eluding the grasp of knowledge, this revealing is also simultaneously a concealing. The Buddha-nature possesses the power to subsume and transcend being and non-being, which suggests that the manifesting of Buddha-nature by the human body both negates and transcends it.

Consequently, to grasp the essence of the body truly is intuitively to grasp emptiness, the creative and dynamic aspect of Buddha-nature.

Dōgen denies that Buddha-nature is something to be achieved because it already is. It is neither a process nor an entity, and it is not a potentiality possessed by sentient beings because it is all-inclusive, encompassing both sentient and insentient beings. Thus, the Buddha-nature is absolutely inclusive, yet it is beyond existence and non-existence. Dōgen elucidates his point as it pertains to the body:

> In short, "total existence" is "the Buddha-nature", and the perfect totality of "total existence" is called "living beings". At just this moment, the inside and outside of living beings are the "total existence" of "the Buddha-nature". The state is more than only the skin, flesh, bones, and marrow that are transmitted one-to-one, because "you have got" skin, flesh, bones and marrow.[54]

Since Dōgen equates all existence and insentient beings, the Buddha thus includes plant life, animal life, and the inanimate world. None of these entities possess the Buddha-nature because it is both beings and being itself, making the Buddha-nature immanent in all existence, instead of all existences being immanent in it.

The distinction between purity and pollution, evident in the Theravāda and Tantric positions with the former stressing the need for purity and the latter embracing the transgressive nature of pollution, is missing in the thought of Dōgen, even though he sees a need for cleanliness. In his essay *Senjō* (Washing) in the *Shōbōgenzō*, he describes the way for a monk to care for his hair, nails, urine, and feces, but he does not emphasize their impure nature as the Theravāda tradition did.[55] Dōgen does stress, however, that a monk should exercise proper decorum when attending to these waste products because this is in accord with the Buddha dharma (teaching) and is thus what is traditionally expected.

Concluding remarks

Although Dōgen negatively mentions the human body on occasion and certainly recognizes its impure aspects centred on hair, nails, and other waste products, he never approaches the many negative assaults on the body that one can find in the Theravāda tradition. And, Dōgen does not advocate any kind of method approaching the transgressive approach of Tantric Buddhism. All three types of Buddhism, however, share a common feature, even though it is defined differently, that culminates with a non-dualistic position. This non-dualistic position is arrived at in spite of the Theravāda rejection of the body, an embrace of the body in Tantric Buddhism, and an acceptance of the body by Dōgen.

The Theravādin negative attitudes towards the body seem intended to service the monk's vow of celibacy, an attempt to exercise discipline and control upon the body, and the monastic sense of purity that accompanies the vow that involves becoming detached from the body. Tantra is intentionally transgressive and embraces impure bodily substances by turning them into sacred substances and liquids consumed to attain liberation, whereas Dōgen recognizes bodily waste, but he just let it be in the sense of not advocating for or against it.

The three examples of Buddhist thought examined in this essay indicate that they were aware that our understanding of the world, ourselves, and others is conceptualized from within an embodied condition. These three forms of Buddhist thought agree that in a sense the body is in the mind in different degrees and that the body undergoes changes throughout its life unto and including death. Each example represents an attempt to socially construct a new body by means of celibacy for Theravādins and Dōgen, whereas Tantra alters, or more precisely reconstructs, the body to conform to divine, copulating consorts.

As we have noted previously, Buddhist attitudes to the body are grounded in the distinction between purity and pollution inherited from the Indian cultural milieu. Purity is related to holiness, which is characterized by wholeness, order, unity, and perfection. The Tantric exception turns the notion of purity upside down, but it results in a new understanding of purity and completeness in spite of its dangerous practices that run counter to social and monastic norms.

As reviewed in this essay, the three forms of Buddhism agree, although in different ways, that the human body can be used in performative ways in the sense that the human body can be used to make something happen. In the Theravāda tradition, the performance of cemetery contemplation of decomposing bodies are used as objects upon which to concentrate during the process of meditation, which helps a meditator achieve detachment from his body. The bodily relics of the Buddha and saints of the tradition involve the performance of pilgrimage, veneration, prostrations, and circumambulation of stūpas housing the relics by the faithful. Tantric Buddhism calls for consuming normally impure liquids and substances and performing sexual congress within a ritualistic context. Instead of fleeing from the body or becoming detached from it as in Theravāda Buddhism, or using it to perform transgressive acts as in Tantra, the Zen of Dōgen acknowledges that the body is an instrument in one's quest for liberation. For Dōgen, a person performs meditation with one's body that is identical to the Buddha-nature, although all three traditions agree that a person gains liberation in an embodied condition.

NOTES

1. Paul Williams, "Some Mahāyāna Buddhist Perspectives on the Body", in *Religion and the Body*, edited by Sarah Coakley (Cambridge: Cambridge University Press, 1997), 207.
2. *Milinda's Questions*, trans. I.B. Horner, *Sacred Books of the Buddhists*, Vols. 22–23 (London: Luzac and Company, Ltd., 1963, 1964), Series 26, pp. 1–42.
3. John Strong and Mahinda Patihawadana, trans. *The Dhammapada* (New York, Oxford: Oxford University Press, 1987).
4. Buddhaghosa, *The Path of Purification*, trans. by Bkikhu Ñyāṇamoli (Colombo: M.D. Gunasena & Company, Ltd., 1964), 8.45.
5. Buddhaghosa, *The Path of Purification*, trans. by Bkikhu Ñyāṇamoli (Colombo: M.D. Gunasena & Company, Ltd., 1964), 19.4.
6. *Dhammapada Commentary in Buddhist Legends*, 3 vols. trans. by Eugene Watson Burlingame, Harvard: Oriental Series, Vol. 28–30 (London: Luzac and Company, Ltd., 1969), 17.3b, Vol. 3, 103–107.

7. C.A.F. Rhys Davids, trans. *Psalms of the Early Buddhists: I Psalms of the Sisters* (London: Pali Text Society, 1909), 189–190.
8. John Strong, *The Legend and Cult of Upagupta: Sanskrit Buddhism in North India and Southeast Asia* (Princeton: Princeton University Press, 1992), 76–78.
9. Sue Hamilton, "From the Buddha to Buddhaghosa: Changing Attitudes toward the Human Body in Theravāda Buddhism", in *Religious Reflections on the Human Body*, edited by Jane Marie Law (Bloomington: Indiana University Press, 1995), 61.
10. Karen Christina Lang, "Lord Death's Snare: Gender-Related Imagery in the Therigāthā and the Therigāthā", *Journal of Feminist Studies in Religion* 11.2 (1986): 63–79. Kathryn R. Blackstone, *Women in the Footsteps of the Buddha: Struggle for Liberation in the Therigāthā* (Surrey, UK: Curzon Press, 1998), 59–81.
11. Elizabeth Wilson, "The Female Body as a Source of Horror and Insight in Post-Ashokan Indian Buddhism", in *Religious Reflections on the Human Body,* edited by Jane Marie Law (Bloomington: Indiana University Press, 1995), 93. Wilson makes similar claims in her *Charming Cadavers: Horrific Figurations of the Feminine in Indian Buddhist Hagiographic Literature* (Chicago: The University of Chicago Press, 1996).
12. Elizabeth Wilson, "The Female Body as a Source of Horror and Insight in Post-Ashokan Indian Buddhism", 77.
13. Gita Gross, *Buddhism after Patriarchy: A Feminist History, Analysis, and Reconstruction of Buddhism* (Albany: State University of New York Press, 1993), 47.
14. Steven Collins, "The Body in Theravāda Buddhist Monasticism", in *Religion and the Body,* edited by Sarah Coakley (Cambridge: Cambridge University Press, 1997), 191.
15. Kevin Trainor, "In the Eye of the Beholder: Nonattachment and the Body in Subhā'a Verse (Therīgāthā 71), *Journal of the American Academy of Religion* 61.1 (1993): 69.
16. Jonathan S. Walters, "A Voice from the Silence: The Buddha's Mother's Story, *History of Religions*, 33. 4 (1994): 377.
17. Reiko Ohnuma, *Head, Eyes, Flesh, and Blood: Giving Away the Body in Indian Buddhist Literature* (New York: Columbia University Press, 2007), 205–208.

18. *The Dīgha Nikāya*, T.W. Rhys Davids and J. Estlin Carpenter (eds.), 2 vols. (London: Luzac and Company, Ltd., 1890, 1903; reprint 1967, 1966), 2, 294.
19. Buddhaghosa, 8.42.
20. *Dīgha Nikya*, 252. 7–13.
21. *Dīgha Nikya*, 2. 16–17; 3.2, 143–144.
22. Jean Pryzyluski, *Le parinirvāna et les funérailles du Buddha* (Paris: Imprimerie Natrionale, 1920), 179–180; Etienne Lamotte, *La traité de la grande vertu de sagesse*, 5 vols. (Louvain: Institut Orientaliste, 1949–1980), 271–282.
23. John Powers, *A Bull of a Man: Images of Masculinity, Sex, and the Body in Indian Buddhism* (Cambridge: Harvard University Press, 2009), 19.
24. Williams, "Some Mahāyāna Buddhist Perspectives on the Body", 219.
25. For more complete discussions of the Buddha's relics, see Gregory Schopen, *Bones, Stones, and Buddhist Monks: Collected Papers on the Archaeology Epigraphy and Texts of Monastic Buddhism in India* (Honolulu: University of Hawaii Press, 1997) and John S. Strong, *Relics of the Buddha* (Princeton: Princeton University Press, 2004).
26. Geoffrey Samuel, *The Origins of Yoga and Tantra: Indic Religions to the Thirteenth Century* (Cambridge: Cambridge University Press, 2008), 285–286.
27. David Gordon White, *The Alchemical Body: Siddha Traditions in Medieval India* (Chicago: The University of Chicago Press, 1996).
28. Samuel, *The Origins of Yoga and Tantra*, 269.
29. *The Kālacakratantra*, trans. Vesna A. Wallace (New York: American Institute of Buddhist Studies, 2004), 2.42.
30. *The Kālacakratantra*, 2.27.
31. *The Kālacakratantra*, 3.59.
32. *Cakrasamvara Tantra (The Discourse of Śrī Heruka)*, trans. David B. Gray (New York: The American Institute of Buddhist Studies, 2007), 320–321.
33. D.L. Snellgrove, trans. *The Hevajra Tantra: A Critical Study*, London: Oriental Series 6 (London: Oxford University Press [1959], 1971), 2.3.48.
34. D.L. Snellgrove, trans. *The Hevajra Tantra*, 262–266; this is discussed by White in *The Alchemical Body*, 199–202.
35. David Gordon White, *The Kiss of the Yogini: 'Tantric Sex' in its South Asian Context* (Chicago: The University of Chicago Press, 2003), 109.

36. *The Caṇḍamahāroṣaṇa Tantra*, trans. Christopher S. George (New Haven, CT: American Oriental Society, 1974), 4.33–34, 36, 38.

37. José Ignacio Cabezón, "Mother Wisdom, Father Love: Gender-based Imagery in Mahāyāna Buddhist Thought", in *Buddhism, Sexuality, and Gender*, edited by José Ignacio Cabezón (Albany: State University of New York Press, 1982), 189.

38. Gross, *Buddhism after Patriarchy*, 105.

39. Miranda Shaw, *Passionate Enlightenment: Women in Tantric Buddhism* (Princeton: Princeton University Press, 1994).

40. Samuel, *The Origins of Yoga and Tantra*, 302–303; Ronald M. Davidson, *Indian Esoteric Buddhism: A Social History of the Tantric Movement* (New York: Columbia University Press, 2002), 91–98.

41. Hee-jin Kim, *Dōgen Kigen: Mystical Realist* (Tucson, AZ: The University of Arizona Press, 1975), 128.

42. Dōgen, *Shōbōgenzō: The True Dharma-Eye Treasury,* 4 vols., trans. Gudo Wafu Nishijima and Chodo Cross (Berkeley: Numata Center for Buddhist Translation and Research, 2007), III. 336.

43. Dōgen, *Shōbōgenzō: The True Dharma-Eye Treasury*, III, 336.

44. Dōgen, *Shōbōgenzō: The True Dharma-Eye Treasury*, I. 15.

45. Dōgen, *Shōbōgenzō: The True Dharma-Eye Treasury*, I. 42.

46. Dōgen, *Shōbōgenzō: The True Dharma-Eye Treasury*, II. 344.

47. Dōgen, *Shōbōgenzō: The True Dharma-Eye Treasury*, II. 345

48. For a book length discussion of this problem, see Carl Olson, *Zen and the Art of Postmodern Philosophy: Two Paths of Liberation from the Representational Mode of Thinking* (Albany: State University of New York Press, 2000).

49. Kim, *Dōgen Kigen: Mystical Realist*, 77.

50. Dōgen, *Shōbōgenzō: The True Dharma-Eye Treasury*, I. 144.

51. Dōgen, *Shōbōgenzō: The True Dharma-Eye Treasury*, I. 148.

52. Dōgen, *Shōbōgenzō: The True Dharma-Eye Treasury*, I. 75.

53. Dōgen, *Shōbōgenzō: The True Dharma-Eye Treasury*, II. 18.

54. Dōgen, *Shōbōgenzō: The True Dharma-Eye Treasury*, II. 4.

55. Dōgen, *Shōbōgenzō: The True Dharma-Eye Treasury*, I. 75–84.

REFERENCES

Blackstone, Kathryn R. *Women in the Footsteps of the Buddha: Struggle for Liberation in the Therigāthā*. Surrey, UK: Curzon Press, 1998.

Buddhaghosa, *The Path of Purification*. Trans. Bhikhu Ñyāṇamoli. Colombo: M.D. Gunasena & Company, Ltd., 1964.

Burlingame, Eugene Warren. Trans. *Buddhist Legends*. 3 vols. Harvard Oriental Series, Vols. 28–30, London: Luzac and Company, Ltd., 1967.

Cabezón, José Ignacio "Mother Wisdom, Father Love: Gender-based Imagery in Mahāyāna Buddhist Thought", in *Buddhism, Sexuality, and Gender*. Edited by José Ignacio Cabezón. Albany: State University of New York Press, 1992, pp. 181–199.

Collins, Steven "The Body in Theravāda Buddhism", in *Religion and the Body*. Edited by Sarah Coakley. Cambridge: Cambridge University Press, 1997.

Davidson, Ronald M. *Indian Esoteric Buddhism: A Social History of the Tantric Movement*. New York: Columbia University Press, 2002.

Dōgen. *Shōbōgenzō: The True Dharma Eye Treasury*. 4 vols. Trans. Gudo Wafu Nishijima and Chodo Cross. Berkeley: Numata Center for Buddhist Translation and Research, 2007.

George, Christopher S. Trans. *The Caṇḍamahāroṣaṇa Tantra*. New Haven, CT: American Oriental Society, 1974.

Gray, David B. Trans. *Cakrasamvara Tantra (The Discourse of Śrī Heruka)*. New York: The American Institute of Buddhist Studies, 2007.

Gross, Rita. *Buddhism after Patriarchy: A Feminist History, Analysis and Reconstruction of Buddhism*. Albany: State University of New York Press, 1993.

Hamilton, Sue. "From the Buddha to Buddhaghosa: Changing Attitudes toward the Human Body in Theravāda Buddhism", in *Religious Reflections on the Human Body*. Edited by Jane Marie Law. Bloomington: Indiana University Press, 1995.

Horner, I.B. Trans. *Milinda's Questions*. 2 vols. *Sacred Books of the Buddhists*, Vols. 22–23, London: Luzac and Company Ltd., 1963, 1964; reprint 1969.

Kim, Hee-jin. *Dōgen Kigen: Mystical Realist*. Tucson, AZ: The University of Arizona Press, 1975.

Lamotte, Etienne. *La traité de la grande vertu de sagesse*. 5 vols. Louvain: Institut Orientaliste, 1949–1980.

Lang, Karen Christina. "Lord Death's Snare: Gender Related Imagery in the Therigāthā and the Therigāthā". *Journal of Feminist Studies in Religion* 11.2 (1986).

Ohnuma, Reiko. *Head, Eyes, Flesh, and Blood: Giving Away the Body in Indian Buddhist Literature*. New York: Columbia University Press, 2007.

Olson, Carl. *Zen and the Art of Postmodern Philosophy: Two Paths of Liberation from the Representational Mode of Thinking*. Albany: State University of New York Press, 2000.

Powers, John. *A Bull of a Man: Images of Masculinity, Sex, and the Body in Indian Buddhism*. Cambridge: Harvard University Press, 2009.

Pryzyluski, Jean. *Le parinirvāna et les funérailles du Buddha*. Paris: Imprimeire Nationale, 1949–1980.

Rhys Davids, C.A.F. Trans. *Psalms of the Early Buddhists: I Psalms of the Sisters*. London: Pali Text Society, 1909.

Rhys Davids, T.W. and J. Estlin Carpenter (eds.). *The Dīgha Nikāya*. 2 vols. London: Luzac and Company, Ltd., 1966, 1967.

Samuel, Geoffrey. *The Origins of Yoga and Tantra: Indic Religions to the Thirteenth Century*. Cambridge: Cambridge University Press, 2008.

Schopen, Gregory. *Bones, Stones, and Buddhist Monks: Collected Papers on the Archaeology, Epigraphy, and Texts of Monastic Buddhism in India*. Honolulu: University of Hawaii Press, 1997.

Shaw, Miranda. *Passionate Enlightenment: Women in Tantric Buddhism*. Princeton: Princeton University Press, 1994.

Snellgrove, D.I. Trans. *The Hevajra Tantra: A Critical Study*. London: Oriental Series 6. London: Oxford University Press, 1959.

Strong, John. *The Legend and Cult of Upagupta: Sanskrit Buddhism in North India and Southeast Asia*. Princeton: Princeton University Press, 1992.

——. *Relics of the Buddha*. Princeton: Princeton University Press, 2004.

Strong, John and Mahinda Panhawadana. Trans. *The Dhammapada*. New York: Oxford University Press, 1987.

Trainor, Kevin. "In the Eye of the Beholder: Nonattachment and the Body in Subhā's Verse (Therīgāthā 71)". *Journal of the American Academy of Religion* 61.1 (1993): 57–79.

Wallace, Vesna A. Trans. *The Kālacakratantra*. New York: American Institute of Buddhist Studies, 2004.

Walters, Jonathan S. "A Voice from the Silence: The Buddha's Mother's Story". *History of Religions* 33.3, pp. 358–379.

White, David Gordon. *The Alchemical Body: Siddha Traditions in Medieval India*. Chicago: The University of Chicago Press, 1996.

——. *The Kiss of the Yogini: 'Tantric Sex' in Its South Asian Context*. Chicago: The University of Chicago Press, 2003.

Williams, Paul. "Some Mahāyāna Buddhist Perspectives on the Body", in *Religion and the Body*. Edited by Sarah Coakley. Cambridge: Cambridge University Press, 1997, pp. 205–230.

Wilson, Elizabeth. *Charming Cadavers: Horrific Figurations of the Feminine in Indian Buddhist Hagiographic Literature*. Chicago: The University of Chicago Press, 1996.

——. "The Female Body as a Source of Horror and Insight in Post-Ashokan Indian Buddhism", in *Religious Reflections on the Human Body*. Edited by Jane Marie Law. Bloomington: Indiana University Press, 1995, pp. 76–99.

CHAPTER 8

Bringing Peace in the World

The Buddhist way

MADHUMITA CHATTOPADHYAY

It is really very ironical that the life of a man today is not safe as it was five hundred years ago. The simple word "peace" has turned out to be a fantasy to the individual. The headlines of the morning newspaper supply us with reports of something terrible happening somewhere in the universe. No former generation had to experience so much bad news as we face today. This constant awareness and tension make any sensitive and compassionate person question the progress of modern world seriously. In the background of all this, the question that comes to the forefront is – has religion any role to play in bringing global peace? If so, how? A possible answer to this question may be explored from the standpoint of Buddhism.

Śānti (*santi* in Pāli) is described as the ideal state of man in Buddhist literature. In the *Dhammapada* Lord Buddha himself has said that there can be no happiness other than peace (*natthi santiparam sukham*/verse 202). Accordingly, it can be said that Buddhism throughout its long history has aimed at the attainment of peace. More than any other religion or philosophy, Buddhism presents a clear vision of peace. Individuals are advised to work hard for the elevation and happiness of mankind and to bring peace in the world. In order to point out the way for bringing lasting peace to the world, the Buddhists have attempted to find out the causes for social conflicts.

Causes of conflict

Generally, it is thought that conflicts arise out of some extraneous factors like a piece of land or some property. But Lord Buddha finds the root to lie deep in human nature. Greed (*lobha*), hatred (*dosa*) and delusion (*moha*) are held to be at the root of all conflicts. Greed or *lobha* is the desire to have things of one's likings. It attaches the mind to the objects of desire and allures the beings in the garb of happiness. Hatred or *dosa* is that mental state which not only hurts others but also oneself. Delusion means lack of understanding, which sometimes creates false impression about the object and conceals its true nature. *Moha* has been compared in Buddhist literature with darkness. Just as darkness draws a black curtain on the eye and allows nothing to be seen, *moha* covers the inner eye of the individual and makes him incapable of seeing the nature of objects and leads one to perform all sorts of misdeeds.

Conflict often is caused by attachment to material entities like property, territory, wealth, economic dominance or political superiority. Desires for any of them lead to further desires, which ultimately results in conflicts among groups of people including kings, emperors or rulers. In the text *Śiksāsamuccaya,* Śāntideva observes that "wherever conflict arises among living creatures, the sense of possession is the cause" (Ss 20). The sense of possession occurs in the mind of the individual when he is ignorant about the true nature of the self. We forget that nothing in the world is permanent, nor is the individual himself. Hence, there is no question of pride or vanity regarding one's own self or one's possession. Accordingly, Lord Buddha through his different dialogues and teachings tried to make people conscious of the ephemeral nature of all objects of the world.

Ignorance regarding the true nature of the self and of other objects of the universe leads the individual to get inflicted with a delusion giving rise to a false sense of "I-conceit". One believes that he has a permanent non-changing self which needs to be protected from all unwanted and awkward situations. As part of this wrong belief, he develops a sense of identity which he expresses as "my family", "my community", "my country", "my religion" etc., and when any of them is threatened or is offended, he feels threatened or hurt. Consequently, out of a false sense of ego-satisfaction, he gets involved in encounters with others – be it of a small group or another community or another country. Thus, it can be said that at the root of social conflicts lies the false belief in a fixed essence of "self" or conventional groupings of country or community which do not in reality have any permanent existence. In fact, history shows us that the political maps of the world change over time when the boundaries shift from one place to another with the rise and fall of different political rulings.

Out of such ignorance regarding the nature of self arise the feelings of hatred and aversion which like desire, greed and delusion cause unhappiness in the mind of the individual. Such ignorance leads us to believe in our permanent independent existence; we believe ourselves to be self-sufficient separate beings, who do not have any necessity for being connected with others. However, the reality is a state of interdependence and interconnectedness – we are dependent on others. Ignorance covers this truth and keeps us divided. So through proper practice we have to remove this ignorance. In the *Abhidhamma* literature, of the fourteen immoral mental states (*cetasika*), importance is given to misconception (*ditthi*), conceit (*māna*), envy (*issā*) and selfishness (*macchariya*) as these defile, debase or degenerate the mind. Because of misconception or false view man considers the wrong view to be the absolute truth and defies all other views placed before him. Under the influence of this misconception, the transitory world appears to the individual as real and permanent and the world full of sorrows and sufferings as a great repository of happiness. Consequently, his mind gets engulfed with wrong views. Conceit or *māna* is ego-consciousness, which is responsible for the notions like "I", "me", and "mine". Envy or *issā* is grudging contemplation. It cannot tolerate the happiness, fortune, fame of others. It manifests itself in blaming and finding fault with others. Selfishness, on the other hand, seeks to hide one's own possessions so that it cannot be shared with others. Thus, these four mental states totally lead a man not to remain content with his own belongings and feeling jealousy of others, try to find fault with them, and thus get involved in several forms of conflicts. Accordingly, throughout his teachings, Lord Buddha has attached much importance to removal of ignorance through purification of mind.

Some extraneous source has also been identified in Buddhist literature to be responsible for the occurrence of conflicts among people. Important among them is poverty of the members of the society. When people suffer from lack of money and do not have any other means to earn their livelihood, they take recourse to immoral acts which give rise to societal injustice. In the *Cakkavatti-Sihananda-Sutta* of the *Dīgha Nikāya* we hear of the story of a prince who was advised by his father king to rule according to *dhamma* in the sense of justice and righteousness and help the needy. The prince followed all the words of his father except that of providing financial help to the poor. As a result, poverty was in the hike in the state and people started committing immoral acts like stealing, robbery, murder etc. Such heinous acts could not be controlled either by giving property to some of them or by punishing the culprits. On the contrary, conflicts among people resulting in bloodshed of ordinary people went on increasing. The story teaches us that from the not giving of property to the needy, poverty becomes rife, from the growth of poverty, the taking of what was not given increased, from the increase of theft, the use of weapons increased, from the increased use of weapons, the taking of life increased – and from the increase in the taking of life, people's life-span decreased, their beauty decrease […].[1]

In other words, the ruler who allows his countrymen to undergo poverty cannot avoid the seeds of crime and social conflict. Systematic poverty threatens law and order and thus inhibits both social cohesion and personal morality. The same message is conveyed through another story, namely, the *Kutadanta Sutta* of the *Dīgha Nikāya*. There we find that a rich king Mahāvijita, who had an abundance of gold and silver, treasury and granary, money and riches, wanted to organize a big sacrifice in the hope of his future benefit and prolonged happiness. He then asked his minister to give shape to his thought. The minister, pointing out the situation of the country to the king, said that the country had become full of thieves, the villages and towns were being destroyed, the countryside being infected with brigands. Such a situation cannot be improved by mere executions or imprisonment or by threats and punishments. For those who would survive would later create more harm. This indicates that the Buddhists were conscious that want of money ultimately results in social conflict.

Another cause of giving rise to conflicts among people is the bad influence of some members of the community, specially the ruler, or the leader of any political party or the *guru* of a religious community. In the *Anguttara Nikāya* it has been said that if a ruler works in an immoral way, it will also encourage his ministers to follow the same immoral path and this path will subsequently spread among all the other members of the society. Thus anything bad committed by the top leaders will easily have its effect on the society at large. At the higher level the persons may be indulged in immoral activities when they do not have any strong personality and are subject to the flattering of others. Then, such flattering words close their eyes and they fail to distinguish between what is good and bad and start believing that what they are saying or doing is the only truth. Consequently, they ignore or overlook the views of others and the result is violence in some form or other.

Remedial suggestions

Recognizing that one of the causes of social unrest is financial discrimination among the members of the society, the Buddhists have recommended certain methods for removing such discrimination. For example, the ruler king should take appropriate steps for the proper distribution of wealth and property among all the members of the society. Besides it is also advised that the king should distribute grain and fodder to those engaged in cultivating crops and raising cattle, give venture capital to those engaged in trade and pay proper living wages to those in government services. This will bring contentment in the minds of the people and they will give up all unfair acts. So, proper distribution of wealth will decrease the number of social crimes and subsequent conflicts. At the same time, it will also help the government to earn more revenues and rule in a peaceful manner. In the *Rāja-parikathā-ratnamālā,* Nāgārjuna's advice to the king Udayi has been to support all the members of the society by providing them the required help and also setting the prices of commodities in a fair manner:

Provide stricken farmers
With seeds and sustenance,
Eliminate high taxes
By reducing their rate,
Eliminate thieves and robbers
In your own and other's countries.
Please set prices fairly and keep
Profits level (when things are scarce).[2]

It is the duty of a king to look after the poor and the needy in his country. In the *Mahā-Sudassana-Sutta* of the *Dīgha Nikāya* we are told of a story of the past life of Lord Buddha when he was born as a righteous king. At that time he established a beautiful lotus pond where those in need were given food, water, shelter, money etc. In the *Mahāvastu* also it has been said that one of the duties of the king is to favour the poor, but that also not at the cost of the riches. It is his utmost task to protect his people. This he has to do by giving property to the poor and punish the wicked in accordance with the law. Though one of the essential tasks of any government is to generate revenues, the Buddhists recommend that it has not to be done at the cost at the dignity of the poor. The poor people should be exempted from paying taxes only when they are badly affected by natural calamities or social unrest. If their poverty is caused by their own faults like their addiction to drinks or other illegal activities like prostitution, gambling etc., they are required to pay half of the taxes, the remaining half need to be paid by the king in the hope that the person will be able to rectify himself. The kings are requested to lend money to his countrymen so that they can engage themselves in trade. In this way, by taking recourse to the policies analogous to those of modern welfare state, the Buddhists expect to reduce the poverty level of the people and help them leading a normal life. Once the people themselves have a proper earning to maintain their family, it is hoped that the instances of adopting unfair means will decrease in the society, thereby reducing the number of social conflicts. It would also be pertinent to mention that such a method of reducing social evils with the help of providing support to the needy by the ruling class has been recommended also by Kautilya in his *Arthaśāstra* wherein he specifically identifies as the duty of the king to "provide the orphans, the aged, the infirm, the afflicted and the helpless with maintenance" along with providing "subsistence to helpless women when they are carrying and also to the [new-born] children they give birth to".[3]

Providing economic support to the needy or helping people at moments of distress may uplift the position of the people and reduce the number of social conflicts to some extent, but they cannot bring in lasting peace. In fact, the sole cause of all conflicts lies not in any external factor but in the individual himself. For bringing happiness and peace in the world, the Buddhists place more emphasis on the purification of the mind itself. Though the fundamental thesis of Buddha's teaching consists of three things, viz., the avoidance of all evil deeds, performance of morally right ones and the purification of one's own mind,[4] the last one has been considered to be the most important one since the moral quality of the action is determined by the mental factors associated with them. Any action committed with greed, aversion and delusion is said to be morally wrong and results in conflicts. Even an accidental killing can have adverse consequence on the society if it is caused through negligence or unmindfulness which is considered as delusion. Hence, to get rid of such conflicts, the Buddhists advise to control the mind and avoid the evil thoughts. "Beware of the anger of the mind, and control thy mind! Leave the sins of the mind, and practice virtue with thy mind!"[5]

In the whole Buddhist literature it has been pointed out time and again that the mind or *manas* is the most important guiding factor in a man's life. All the tasks that he performs are the result of mind and the mental states. Evil mental states lead to the performance of immoral acts which bring about unhappiness at the individual level and different forms of conflicts at the societal level. On the other hand, good mental states result in the performance of good or moral acts, which bring peace and happiness in the mind of the individual and consequently help to resolve societal conflicts.[6] Accepting the important role that mind plays in the life of the individual, it has been commented in the *Dhammapada*: "Not a mother, nor a father, nor any other relative will do so much, as a well-directed mind can do greater service".[7] Accordingly, the whole attempt of Lord Buddha and his followers has been to teach people how to control the mind. To get peace, one must restrain oneself. One must realize that there is no fire-like passion, no capturer-like hatred, no net (snare) (*jālam*)-like delusion and no current-like craving. In short, mental/psychological states like greed, passion, delusion, hatred, craving, etc., are the impurities that lead man to perform all sorts of evil acts as a result of which he undergoes suffering not only in the after-life, but even in this worldly life. But, all these impurities have their root in ignorance. Accordingly, ignorance is considered as the greatest impurity and there is no greater impurity than it (*tato malā malataram avijjā paramam malam*/verse 9 of ch. 18). In the text *Milindapañha*, the venerable Bhikkhu *Nāgasena* tells the king Milinda:

> O Maharaja, *kamma* is not said to be stored somewhere in this fleeting consciousness or in any other part of the body. But dependent on mind and matter it rests manifesting itself at opportune moment, just as mangoes are not said to be stored somewhere in the mango tree, but dependent on the mango tree they lie springing up in due season.

Ignorance is considered as the essential central fault which urgently needs to be removed. What is called ignorance is not simply the absence of knowledge of things, nor having superficial knowledge of things; it means forgetting the very reason of our existence – the truth that has to be discovered. Ignorance is considered to be the "greatest" evil because it is the root of all other evils. It is because of this ignorance that we consider something as pleasant and something as unpleasant and try to cling to what is pleasant. Hence, in the situation where there is absence of the pleasant and presence of the unpleasant, there occurs pain in us. Not only so, ignorance regarding the true nature of things brings about some other feelings like love (*piya*), affection (*pema*), enjoyment (*rati*), desire (*kāma*) and craving (*tanhā*) towards the object. All these feelings result in grief when the object remains unattained, and even when the object is attained these feelings give rise to fear in anticipation of the future loss of the object. That is, in neither of the situation can the man remain steady. In *Dhammapada* passion or craving (*tanhā*) has been regarded as the mother and pride or vanity (*asmimāna*) as the father, since these two are the main causes of all our suffering. False doctrines about the total annihilation of objects (*ucchedavāda*) or about the permanent eternal nature of objects (*śāśwatavāda*) are regarded as two valiant kings of the world of suffering and the world of sensual enjoyment as their entire kingdom. So, to get rid of the evils, one has to destroy the craving, the sense of ego, and the wrong views about the world of sensual enjoyment, along with the effects of all these things.

Apart from craving, desire, affection etc., ordinary people suffer from another important psychological disorder, namely, anger. Anger like fire not only burns the person himself but other persons associated with him also. Accordingly, anger is considered to be one of the greatest enemies of man. Along with anger another mental faculty that is detrimental to a man's happiness is his conceit which often gives rise to different types of false knowledge in man.

Buddhism highlights the belief that bad thoughts like feeling of insult (from others), feeling of humiliation, getting hurt, being robbed (by others), produce in us the feeling of hatred. On the other hand, those who do not nourish such thoughts can easily be free from the feeling of hatred, jealousy, etc., which is one of the most important causes of human misery. So long as we have the feelings of hatred, jealousy, enmity in us, we will never be able to get rid of these lower feelings. The feeling of hatred can only be countered by the feeling of love. This is the eternal truth. Such eternal truth is spoken of not only in the *Dhammapada*, but in all the sacred texts; so, the only remedy is to generate this feeling of love in all of us. In the text *Bodhicaryāvatāra* Śāntideva has also made people aware of the dangers of hatred and advised them to develop forbearance to get rid of such dangers: "One's mind finds no peace neither enjoys pleasure or delight, nor goes to sleep, nor feels secure while the dart of hatred is stuck in the heart."[8] "There is no evil equal to hatred, and no spiritual practice equal to forbearance. Therefore, one ought to develop forbearance, by various means, with great effort."[9]

In short, hatred and aversion are also the causes of unhappiness in man. Like desire, greed and delusion, the feelings of hatred and aversion arise out of ignorance regarding the nature of the self. Such ignorance leads us to believe in our permanent independent existence; we believe ourselves to be self-sufficient separate beings, who do not have any necessity for being connected with others. However, the reality is that we are all dependent on others. Ignorance covers this truth and keeps us divided. So through proper practice we have to remove this ignorance. In the *Abhidhamma* literature, of the fourteen mental states (*cetasika*), which are considered to be immoral in the sense of defiling, debasing or degeneration of the mind, misconception (*ditthi*), conceit (*māna*), envy (*issā*) and selfishness (*maccariya*) are considered to be of great importance. Because of misconception, man considers the wrong view to be the absolute truth and defies all other views placed before him. Under the influence of this misconception the transitory world appears to the individual as real and permanent and the world full of sorrows and sufferings as a great repository of happiness. Consequently, his mind gets engulfed by wrong views. *Māna* or conceit is ego-consciousness, which is responsible for the notions like "I", "me" and "mine". Envy or issā is grudging contemplation. It cannot tolerate the happiness, fortune, fame of others. It manifests itself in blaming and finding fault with others. The nature of selfishness (*macchariya*), on the other hand, is to hide one's own possessions so that it cannot be shared with others. Hence, it can be understood that selfishness, conceit, envy and false belief always lead a man not to remain contented with his own belongings and to find fault with others, which ultimately give rise to some form of conflicts. Accordingly, Lord Buddha puts much importance on the purification of the mind and that has to be done by the individual himself and not by any external agency. He emphasized time and again that the greatest friend or the foe of an individual is his own inner self. None else in the external world can be of better help or enmity to him. The Buddhists were fully aware of the value of self-reliance on the way of deliverance to obtain fundamental peace in one's mind. Hence, they recommend the practice of *panca śila.* If we look into the core moral values involved in the practice of *pañca śila*, we find that they actually contain the core moral values required for leading a good life and building a good community. These are abstention from killing and hurting living creatures, abstention from stealing, abstention from wrong indulgence in sensual pleasures, abstention from lying and abstention from taking intoxicants. Respect for life and property, truthfulness, leading a lifestyle which avoids excessive, illegitimate and harmful pleasures and awareness of the danger of social evils like alcoholism and drug addiction are the basic moral concerns of a Buddhist society. Buddha did not hesitate to condemn both the performance of animal sacrifice and the pleasure of hunting. He also pointed out the futility of warfare. Monks were prohibited from joining the army and also from digging the ground as in this process there was the possibility of hurting a being. Thus, as regards the moral values involved in the precepts, we can find pragmatism and realism in Buddha's outlook, which can help to resolve the conflicts between human needs and moral ideals.

All these precepts can be formulated in terms of rights and duties too. For example, as the right of living involves the duty to respect the life of others, similarly, the right to possess any object signifies the duty to respect the belongings of others, and the right to enjoy the pleasures of living involves the duty to recognize the same rights in respect of others. Likewise, the right to search for the highest truth implies the duty of truthfulness, and the right to maintain self-respect involves the duty of avoiding intoxicating drinks. If a man is intoxicated with drinks or with obsessions and prejudices, he will lose his self-esteem and his inhibitions will become nuisance. As human beings, we are unique in our ability to see what is good. We can choose to realize it in our speech and behaviour. So, we have to control our own behaviour as far as possible for our own sake as well as for the sake of whole society. Thus *pañca śīla*, though, primarily formulated to restrain the behaviour of the individual, it has actually a far-reaching effect on the society in general. This is because of this character of *pañca śīla* that the concept has been recognized in the political arena. They became the five principles of the international code of conduct among nations adopted in the Sino-Indian Agreement on Tibet in

1954. At the political level, the precepts have been taken to signify non-aggression, mutual respect for each other's territorial integrity and sovereignty, non-interference in other's internal affairs, equality and mutual benefit, and peaceful co-existence.

Not only the concept of *pañca śīla*, but the concept of *brahmavihāra* also is indispensable for the happiness and peace of the world. *Brahmavihāra* means the cultivation of four divine sentiments, namely, loving-kindness (*mettā* or *maitri*), compassion (*karunā*), empathetic joy (*muditā*) and equianimity (*upekkhā*). Observance of the *pañca śīla* will not only help the individual to get rid of the *micchāditthi* or wrong views, but at the same time he has to develop some good qualities in himself for his own benefit and in turn the entire society. The way the Buddhists have recommended to cultivate these virtues, shows that they were aimed to bring about peace in the universe. These virtues were first directed towards the individual himself, then towards his inner circle and ultimately to the world as a whole. These are called *brahmavihāras* or divine abiding, since when developed to a high degree in meditation, these are said to make the mind "immeasurable" like the mind of the loving *brahmā* gods. These four qualities work by rejection of adversaries, by application to all particulars and function on three foundations of beings, the *dhamma* and on no foundation at all, and by special acts on the basis of the maturity of beings. Loving-kindness is the aspiration for the true happiness of any, and ultimately all sentient beings, for all of them are like oneself in aspiring happiness and avoiding pain. It is the antidote to hatred and fear, and is to be distinguished from sentimentality. Compassion is the aspiration that beings are free from suffering, feeling for them; it is the antidote to cruelty, and is to be distinguished from sadness. Empathetic joy comes from the joy of others, happiness at their good fortune; it is the antidote to envy and discontent and is to be distinguished from giddy merriment. Equianimity is an even-minded, unruffled serenity in the face of ups and downs of life – one's own and that of others[10] – and comes from the reflection that beings suffer and are happy in accordance with their own *karmas*. It is the antidote to both aversion and approval but should be distinguished from indifference. It also ensures a feeling of impartiality towards all beings, so that loving-kindness etc., is felt towards all equally.

If we take a careful look into the nature of these four qualities as has been analyzed by the *Mahāyāna* thinkers, we will find that they expand the inner feelings of the individual to such an extent that he cannot but feel for others. For example, *karuṇā* has been described in the *Suttanipāta* as *ahita-dukkha-apanaya-kāmatā*, that is, the desire to remove bare and sorrow for one's fellow men. In the *Viśuddhimagga* it has been said, "*Paradukkhe sati sādhunām hadaya-kampanam karoti*" – when there is suffering in others, it causes good people's heart to be moved (*kampanam*) and so it is *karunā*. An alternative interpretation is that it combats others' suffering, attacks and demolishes it, thus it is compassion. So, according to *Viśuddhimagga,* compassion is characterized as promoting the aspect of allaying suffering. Its function resides in not bearing other's suffering.

Mettā or *maitri* is loving-kindness and is regarded as the complementary of *karunā*. According to *Attaśālini*, derived from the root mid (meaning "to love"), the word "*mettā*" stands for love, amity, sympathy, friendliness, active interest in others. It comes about with respect to a friend (*mitta*) or it is behaviour towards a friend, thus it is loving-kindness. As distinguished from compassion (*karunāi*), *maitrī* consists in *hita-sukha-upanaya-kāmatā* that is desire of bringing happiness and welfare to one's fellow men. It actually is a positive frame of mind promoting the aspect of welfare.

Muditā is soft-heartedness, kindliness, sympathy. Often in triad *mettā* (active love), *karunā* (preventive love), *muditā* (disinterested love), it is defined as the feeling of gladness produced by other's success. Those endowed with it are glad. Its function resides in being unenvious.

Equianimity (*upekkhā*) is characterized as promoting the aspect of neutrality towards beings. Its function is to see equality in beings. It is manifested as the quieting of resentment and approval.

In the text *Attaśālini* it has been pointed out that *mettā* signifies "one wishes well". It is so called because it goes on concerning a beloved one (*mettā*, *mitte*) or because of the state of being a loved one. *Karunā*, on the other hand, makes the heart of the good lament at the pain of others and so is pity. Or it crushes, destroys the pain of others, thus it is pity. Or it is scattered over the afflicted, stretched out over them by diffusion. It has the property of not being able to see others suffer. Sympathetic joy or *muditā* means those endowed with it rejoice.

The basic aim of these four attributes is to remove evil thoughts from the mind of the individual, for instance, love is aimed to remove ill-will, compassion cruelty, sympathetic joy from dislike/discontent and equanimity the escape from lust and aversion.[11] The way these qualities are advised to be cultivated, indicates that they always involve concern for others. In fact, the whole of Buddhist ethics is based on feeling for others. So, it is not for one's own benefit but through the feeling for others that one's inner spirit will be enlightened. It is believed that through this feeling/concern for others, the uniqueness of man is exhibited, and the goal of humanity is achieved. The cultivation of this goal in its fullest form has been exhibited in the life and teachings of Lord Buddha. In the *Mettāsutta* of the *Suttanipāta*, Buddha has advised us to extend the feeling of unlimited "care" to all beings of the universe in the same spirit as the mother extends to her child:

Mātā yathā nijam puttam āyusā ekaputtam anurakkhe/
Evampi sabbabhutesu mānasambhāvaye aparimānam//

The best form of caring in this world is expressed through the relation between the mother and the child – it is a divine relationship. Mother's caring hand protects her child from all sorts of danger; in a like manner we have to extent our caring attitude to all the beings in the world.

A person who practises any of these *brahmavihāras* will experience the happiness born of insight and will secure a happy existence. As stated earlier, the purpose of these four meditations is to eliminate ill-will, cruelty, envy and lust respectively. The practice of the four *brahmavihāras* may be divided into three stages: the duty of moral responsibility towards fellow being is the beginning: the purgation of the mind from the hindrances is the middle, and the manifestation of these qualities in thought, word and deed is the end. Unlike the other forms of meditation, this four-fold exercise in each case consists of the continual expansion of the particular sentiments involved, from the individual to the community or from a single being to the many, and then from one quarter of the world to the other, and so gradually to the whole world and all that exists in it. So, this form of meditation expands the field of its influence until the aspirant, becoming one with the whole universe, passes beyond all individual limitations. In the text *Viśuddhimagga* elaborate discussion has been made on how to cultivate these four great qualities of the mind. It has been pointed out that one has to cultivate these qualities first towards oneself. Since one's own self of is most dear to him, he who loves himself can never do any harm to another.[12]

He should next develop these feelings towards a very dearly loved friend, then towards a neutral person as a very dearly loved friend, and then towards a hostile person as neutral. And, while he does so, he should make his mind malleable and wieldy in each instance before passing on to the next. In this way, he develops his feelings towards all beings in the world. Lord Buddha has pointed out that one should not develop these feelings at the beginning towards an antipathetic person, a very dearly loved friend, a neutral person, a hostile person and specifically the opposite sex. The reason for this is that if he develops such feelings towards an antipathetic or a neutral person, there might arise fatigue in him, while towards a hostile person such feelings may bring in anger and towards a dear friend may make him depressed if anything wrong happens. And feelings towards the opposite sex may bring in lust in his mind. And so it is advised to start with one's own self first and then proceed gradually through the different stages towards all beings. Since the objective of these attributes is to make the mind free from all impurities, the attributes have to be developed in the manner stated above. Ultimately, the mind will rise to such a state that the feelings of compassion and friendliness (which we are considering as a substitute for care) may be extended not only to one particular individual man but to all beings – leg-less, two-legged, four-legged and many-legged. To quote from *Khanda Parittam:*

Apādake hi me mettam mettam dvipādake hi me/

Catuppadehi me mettam mettam vahuppadehi me//

So, the recluse is concerned not with his own welfare or the welfare of his near and dear ones, but for all beings existing in the universe. So his prayer is:

Sabbe sattā pānā sabbe bhutā ca kevalā/
Sabbe bhadrāni passantu mā kancipāpam āgamā//

Let all the beings, all the creatures, all those who are born, all those who are yet to be born be happy and let not any type of unhappiness or pain inflict upon them.

Eminent economist, Professor Amartya Sen in his *Identity and Violence* has described these qualities of "benevolence", "loving kindness" and others as "Asian values" and points out that if such qualities can be practised properly they will lead to the prosperity of the entire society. The Buddhist doctrines of *pañca śīla* and *brahmavihāra* make us aware of the idea that an individual is not a separate and isolated entity, but an aspect in the process of becoming, in which each individual action sets up a practically universal reaction. This denial of the existence of the individual ego-entity naturally leads to a broadening view of life, in which the individual is a part of a larger whole. Accordingly, peace in the individual is not to be obtained by prayer and sacrifice, but through his being in harmony with his environment. Only when the individual has attained this harmony and no longer looks upon himself as an isolated entity but truly sees himself as a force, however small, which goes to swell this greater force of life on the nation, on the universe, then alone we can expect these five principles of individual moral conduct to become effective in the international stage. Then alone individual existence will pave the way to international co-existence, and peace will come.

That the Buddhist notions of *brahmavihāra* are not mere theoretical notions but can be followed in practice has been amply demonstrated by Emperor Aśoka. A great warrior in the true sense of the term, Aśoka in his own life realized that shedding bloods in a battlefield cannot give any one satisfaction or mental peace and hence later in his life he took recourse to the doctrine of non-violence as advocated by Lord Buddha. In the rest of his life Aśoka insisted on the cultivation of virtues like compassion, liberality, truth, purity, gentleness and saintliness among all the members of his kingdom. His people were absolutely warned to abstain from speaking evil of their neighbour's faith, remembering that all forms of religion alike aim at the attainment of self-control and purity of mind, and are thus in agreement in respect of spirit, even though in respect of external rituals etc., there might be difference. For example, in the edict at Erragudi, we have the following message engraved:

> […] a man must not do reverence to his own sect or disparage that of another man without reason. Depreciation should be for specific reason only, because the sects of other people all deserve reverence for one reason or another. By thus acting, a man exalts his own sect, and at the same time does service to the sects of other people. By acting contrariwise, a man hurts his own sect, and does disservice to the sects of other people. For he who does reverence to his own sect while disparaging the sects of others wholly from attachment to his own, with intent to enhance the splendor of his own sect, in reality by such conduct inflicts the severest injury on his own sect.[13]

This inscription of Aśoka is an instance to indicate how the importance of tolerance for other religions was emphasized by the Buddhists from the third century BC both for public society and as advice for behaviour of citizens to each other. As a practitioner of this tolerance Aśoka himself used to show reverence to men of all sects whether ascetics or householder, through donations and others.[14] From the cave inscriptions we come to know that he bestowed costly gifts to the *Ājivakas*, an independent sect of self-mortifying ascetics, and thus exhibited his adoration to the principle of universal tolerance. This example indicates that if any ruler or leader shows respect or reverence to other sects by rising above his own personal belief, that attitude will inspire his followers to show respect to others. And that will definitely be a great step towards putting an end to a good number of social violence.

That the ideals of universal brotherhood, compassion, friendliness etc., as preached by Lord Buddha, are of great relevance even today has been unanimously recognized by great thinkers like Rabindranath Tagore, Sri Aurobindo, Swami Vivekananda and others to mention a few. In the present-day society, where technological advancement and economic growth go hand in hand with illiteracy, poverty, untimely death and others among the majority of population which, actually, is the cause of different sorts of cruel conflicts occurring each day, the requirement is the compassionate attitude of Buddha. Being pained by the attitude of human beings afflicted by greed, hatred and violence, the anguished soul of the poet Rabindranath Tagore cries out for the healing touch of Lord Buddha: "O Serene, O Free, in thine immeasurable mercy and goodness, wipe away all dark stains from the heart of this earth."[15] He goes on to pray to the Almighty to instil love and wisdom in the minds of the people. It is true that violence breeds violence. So, to stop violence, the only alternative is to follow the path of non-violence, to take refuge to Lord Buddha who will sow the seeds of compassion, friendliness and others in the minds of all of us so that we can show such feelings towards all. The same feeling of confidence in Buddha's doctrine of *maître* or friendliness and *karunā* has been found in the writings of Sri Aurobindo and Swami Vivekananda. In a note, Sri Aurobindo regards the "Buddhist elevation of universal compassion, *karunā* and sympathy (*vasudhaiva kutumbakam*, the whole earth is my family)" as "the highest principle of action",[16] since they bring forth "the sense of unity with all beings, the stress of a universal love and compassion, the will to spend the energies for the good of all creatures".[17] That is, Sri Aurobindo also acknowledges the Buddhist spirit that the solution for the conflicts may partially be achieved by "external means"; but for the real solution it is needed to have an "inner change, a transformation of consciousness and nature".[18] In the eyes of Swami Vivekananda love as advocated by Lord Buddha is the powerful weapon that alone has the power to change the world entirely. For love is the going out of one's narrow self. The lover, by the power of love, develops in himself a uniting/binding force by which he ties up one individual with the other, one man with another woman, one woman with another man, animals with animals, drawing the whole universe, as it were towards one centre. One who has increased this love in oneself, can rise above all selfish blemishes and expand his mentality. He can then "feel" for others. This love not only improvises the individual's own existence but also leads to the service of mankind. This service is not service in the sense of a mere external help, but it is service to man then turns out to the Ultimate Being, worship to God. Swami Vivekananda believes that the emphasis on the "heart" of man rather than on his "intellect" has been the true spirit of the teachings of Lord Buddha and that is what is required in today. That alone can elevate the human beings from the world of social conflicts and unrest to the plane of peace of harmony.

NOTES

1. *The Long Discourses of the Buddha*, 399–400.
2. See P. Harvey, *An Introduction to Buddhist Ethics*, 199.
3. Quoted by Amartya Sen in *Development as Freedom*, 237.
4. Sabba pāpasyākaranam kusalasya upasampadā/Sacittapariyopadanam etat Buddhānuśāsanam; *Dhammapada, Buddhavagga*, verse 183.
5. Manopakopam rakkheyya manasā sambuto siyā/
   Manoduccaritam hitvā manasā sucaritam care//, *Dhammapada,* verse 233.
6. Cf. Mano pubbam gamā dhammâ manosetthā manomayā/
   Manasā ce padutthena bhāsati vā karoti vā/
   Tato nam dukkham anveti cakkam'va vahato padam//
   Mano pubbam gamā dhammā manosetthā manomayā/
   Manasā ce pasannena bhāsati vā karoti vā/
   Tato nam sukham anveti cakka'va vahato padam/, *Dhammapada,* verses 1–2.
7. Na tam mātāpitā kariyā aññe vāpi ca ñātakā/
   Sammāpanihitam cittam seyyaso nam tato kare//, *Dhammapada, Cittavagga* verse 11.
8. Chapter 6, verse 3, *Bodhicaryavatara.*
9. Chapter 6, verse 2, *Bodhicaryavatara.*
10. Maitrī sattvesu sukhasamyogakārā/Karunā duhkhaviyogākārā/muditā sukhaviyogākārā. Upeksāsu vedanāsu tesām sattvānām nihkleśatopasamhārākārā. *Mahāyāsūtrālamkāra*, ch. 17, verse 18.
11. Ref *Majjhimanikāya* 62 *Mahārāhulovādasutta.*
12. *Samyukta Nikāya* i. 75.

13. Quoted by Amartya Sen in *Development as Freedom*, 236.
14. Referred to by K. Hazra in *Asoka as Depicted in his Edicts*, 96.
15. Translated by M.N. Chatterjee in *Rabindranath Tagore: Spiritual Insight in Tagore's Works,* on-line at http: //www.experiencefestival.com/a/Rabindranath_Tagore/id/221427.
16. Sri Aurobindo, *The Life Divine*, 919.
17. Sri Aurobindo, *The Life Divine*, 918–919
18. Sri Aurobindo, *The Life Divine*, 919.

REFERENCES

Asamga. *Mahāyānasūtrālamkāra*, translated by Surekha Vijay Limaye. Delhi: Sri Satguru Publications, 2000.

Barua, Beni Madhab. *Ashoka and his Inscriptions* (Parts I and II), Calcutta: New Age Publishers Pvt. Ltd., 3rd edition, 1969.

Brahmachari Silananda. *An Introduction to Abhidharma* (Buddhist Philosophy and Psychology), Calcutta: Jadab Barua Publication, 1990.

Chattopadhyay, M. "Dhammapada's Recommendation for Well-being", in *Belief and Well-being*, edited by Sadhan Chakraborty. Kolkata: Gangchil, 2009.

——. "Swami Vivekananda's System of Practical Vedanta and its Integral Values", in *Ethics and Culture,* edited by Indrani Sanyal, New Delhi: D.K. Printworld, 2009.

Harvey, P. *An Introduction to Buddhist Ethics.* Cambridge: Cambridge University Press, 2000.

Hazra, K.L. *Asoka as Depicted in his Edicts*. Delhi: Munshiram Manoharlal Publishers Pvt. Ltd., 2007.

Nanamoli, Bhikkhu. *The Path of Purification: Visuddhimagga*. Sri Lanka: Buddhist Publication Society, 1991.

Radhakrishnan, S. *The Dhammapada, with Introductory Essays, Pali Texts, English Translations and Notes*. New Delhi: Oxford University Press, 4th Impression, 1999.

Sen, Amartya. *Development as Freedom*. New Delhi: Oxford University Press, 11th Impression, 2006.

——. *Identity and Violence: The Illusion of Destiny*. Great Britain: Allen Lane, 2006.

Sri Aurobindo. *The Life Divine*. Pondicherry: Sri Aurobindo Ashram, 2nd Impression, 2004.

Walsch, M. *The Long Discourses of the Buddha: A Translation of the Digha Nikaya*. Boston: Wisdom Publications, 1995.

WEBSITES

M.N. Chatterjee. "Rabindranath Tagore: Spiritual Insight in Tagore's Works".

<http: //www.experiencefestival.com/a/Rabindranath_Tagore/id/221427> (24 October 2009)

Jan Willis. "Buddhism and Peace".

<http: //www.urbandharma.org/udharma6/peace.html> (24 October 2009)

Contributors

T.N. MADAN

T.N. Madan is Honorary Professor at the Institute of Economic Growth, New Delhi. He is an Honorary Fellow of the Royal Anthropological Institute (London) and Docteur Honoris Causa of the University of Paris (Nanterre). His numerous publications include *Non-Renunciation: Themes and Interpretations of Hindu Culture* (Oxford University Press, 1987) and *Modern Myths, Locked Minds: Secularism and Fundamentalism in India* (Oxford University Press, 1997).

SHERRY SABBARWAL

Sherry Sabbarwal is Professor of Sociology in the Department of Sociology, Panjab University, Chandigarh.

She received her Bachelor's degree in 1977, her Master's degree in Sociology from Delhi School of Economics in 1979 and her M. Phil. and Ph. D. degrees in Sociology from Panjab University in 1981 and 1987, respectively. She worked as Lecturer in Sociology, in MCM DAV College, Chandigarh from 1981 to 1987, and then joined the Panjab University where she was Reader and then Professor.

Her areas of interest include Development Studies, Organizational Sociology, Entrepreneurship Studies, Women's Studies, Media Studies and Human Rights. She has authored *Organizational Approach to Environmental Control* and co-authored *Adolescent Reproductive Health: Using Culturally Sensitive Approaches for Communication and Advocacy in Under-Served Areas.* She is currently working on her forthcoming books entitled *Culture, Media and Development* and *Fundamentals of*

Human Rights. She has lectured in various American and European universities and has been a Visiting Scholar at the Indian Institute of Advanced Study, Shimla.

She has been the Chief Editor of the research journal *Social Sciences*, published by the Panjab University, and is at present Course Coordinator of the Post-Graduate Diploma in Human Rights and Duties. She is a member of the core committee set up by the Commonwealth Secretariat, London to formulate various courses on Human Rights and Development to be introduced in schools, colleges and universities in all commonwealth nations. Currently, she is chairperson of the Department of Sociology, Panjab University, Chandigarh.

MIHAELA GLIGOR

Mihaela Gligor studied Philosophy at Babes-Bolyai University Cluj-Napoca, Romania, where she also received her PhD in Philosophy in 2006 with a thesis *Mircea Eliade and Romanian Right Extreme*. She is the author of many reviews and studies about life and work of Mircea Eliade in international and Romanian journals. She is co-translator, in Romanian, of Mac Linscott Ricketts's monumental work, *Mircea Eliade. The Romanian Roots, 1907–1945* (Bucharest, 2004). She has coordinated, along with Mac Linscott Ricketts, the following volumes: *Intalniri cu/Encounters with Mircea Eliade* (Cluj-Napoca, Casa Cartii de Stiinta, 2005), *Intalniri cu Mircea Eliade* (Bucharest, Humanitas, 2007) and *Professor Mircea Eliade: Reminiscences* (Kolkata, Codex, 2008).

She is scientific researcher in the field of philosophy at The Romanian Academy, "George Baritiu" History Institute, Cluj-Napoca, Department of Humanities. Between February and July 2009 she was a fellow at Department of Philosophy, Jadavpur University Kolkata, India, with an ICCR postdoctoral scholarship.

She is coordinator of "*Indian Library*" *Collection* at Casa Cartii de Stiinta Publishing House, Cluj-Napoca, Collection in which she translated Amartya Sen, *The Argumentative Indian*.

She is author of volumes *Mircea Eliade. Anii tulburi. 1932–1938* (*Mircea Eliade: His Political Involvement. 1932–1938*), Bucharest, EuroPress Group, 2007 (nominated for Romanian Writers Union prizes), and *India. Insemnari, eseuri, jurnal* (*India. Writings, Essays, Journal*), Cluj-Napoca, Casa Cartii de Stiinta, 2009 (awarded with Sergiu Al-George Prize of RICA – Romanian Indian Cultural Association).

She is also editor-in-chief of *International Journal on Humanistic Ideology*, Cluj-Napoca, Cluj University Press.

DOUGLAS ALLEN

Douglas Allen is Professor of Philosophy at the University of Maine, USA. He served as Chair of the Department of Philosophy, 1998–2003. The author and editor of 13 books and over 100 scholarly articles and book chapters, his areas of research and teaching specialization are phenomenology (especially phenomenology of religion), Eliade, Indian philosophy (especially Hinduism and Buddhism), Gandhi, comparative East-West philosophy and religion, and political philosophy (especially Marx).

Professor Allen served as President of the International Society for Asian and Comparative Philosophy, 2001–2004. He is the editor of the book series, *Studies in Comparative Philosophy and Religion*, published by Lexington Books. He was the recipient of the Presidential Research and Creative Achievement Award (the outstanding Maine Research Professor) and the Distinguished Maine Professor Award (the highest honour for teaching, research and public service). His book *Structure and Creativity in Religion* was selected by the American Council of Learned Societies as best first book in history of religions. He is the editor of *Comparative Philosophy and Religion in Times of Terror* (2006) and *The Philosophy of Mahatma Gandhi for the Twenty-First Century* (2008). He is also working on his own book, *Mahatma Gandhi*, and also has book projects on the phenomenology of religion and the philosophy of Mahatma Gandhi.

Often described as one of the world's leading scholars of the phenomenology of religion in general, and the history and phenomenology of religion of Mircea Eliade in particular, Prof. Allen is the author of "The Phenomenology of Religion" monograph for *The Encyclopedia of Religion*. He has written four books focusing on the phenomenology of religion of Mircea Eliade.

Professor Allen has extensive experience in India. He spent a year at Banaras Hindu University on a Fulbright grant and returned to India on Smithsonian Institution Fellowship. He is the author or editor of *Philosophies of India, Religion and Political Conflict in South Asia*, and *Culture and Self: Philosophical and Religious Perspectives, East and West.*

SANTOSH KUMAR SINGH

Santosh Kumar Singh is an Assistant Professor of Sociology at Post Graduate Government College for Girls, Chandigarh. He holds M.A.,

M.Phil. and Ph.D. from Jawaharlal Nehru University (JNU), New Delhi. He has authored many reviews in journals of international academic repute, such as *Sociological Bulletin* and *International Journal on Humanistic Ideology*. His most recent works include "Sacred as Profane: Changing Contours of Religion in India" in *Professor Mircea Eliade: Reminiscences*, edited by Mihaela Gligor and Mac Linscott Ricketts, Codex, Kolkata, India, 2008 and "Practising Sociology on the Outside Edge" in *Sociology in India: Institutional and Intellectual Practices*, edited by Maitrayee Chaudhari, Rawat, Jaipur, India, 2010. Dr Singh has presented many papers at various national and international seminars. He contributes scholarly articles and reviews regularly in popular press in India such as *The Tribune*, *The Indian Express* and *The Herald of India* (www.heraldofindia.com). His areas of research interest include globalization and issues of identity, sociology of agribusiness, dynamics of inter-faith dialogue etc. He has been a recipient of research fellowship award by the University Grants Commission (UGC), India. Currently, he is working on a major research project funded by the UGC, on a theme "Small Farmers in Agribusiness: A Sociological Study".

RADEK CHLUP

Radek Chlup is a lecturer at the Institute for Philosophy and Religious Studies, Charles University, Prague. He specializes in ancient Greek philosophy and religion, as well as in modern methodology for the study of religion, and he has published a number of papers on all of these subjects in both Czech and international journals. His biggest project so far has been a Czech translation of the *Corpus Hermeticum*, accompanied by an introductory study and detailed commentaries on all the treatises; a summary of some of the study's conclusions has been published in the article "The Ritualization of Language in the Hermetica", *Aries* 7 (2007). At present, he is working on an introduction into the thought of the Neoplatonic philosopher Proclus, to be published by Cambridge University Press in 2011.

SANJUKTA BHATTACHARYYA

Sanjukta Bhattacharyya is a Senior Lecturer in Philosophy at the University of Calcutta, Kolkata, India. She holds a Ph.D. in Comparative Religion from the Department of Philosophy, Jadavpur University, Kolkata, and a M.A. degree in Philosophy, with specialization in Psychology, from the Department of Philosophy, University of Calcutta.

Her areas of interest are myth, religions, Mircea Eliade studies.

Among her important published titles are "Significance of Narratives of Myth in History and Culture – An Observation", *Journal of Department of Philosophy*, University of Calcutta, 2008; "Émile Durkheim' Sociological Methodology – A Tool to Understand the Significance of Myth in Society", *Journal of The Academy of Indian Philosophy*, published by The Academy of Indian Philosophy, 2008.

KEVIN SCHILBRACK

Kevin Edward Schilbrack is Professor of Philosophy and Religious Studies and Department Head at Western Carolina University. He holds a Ph.D. from University of Chicago, Divinity School.

He is contributor editor for the following books: *Thinking through Rituals: Philosophical Perspectives* (Routledge, 2004) and *Thinking through Myths: Philosophical Perspectives* (Routledge, 2002). He published several scholarly articles in journals as *Method and Theory in the Study of Religion, Journal of the American Academy of Religion, Journal of Ritual Studies, International Journal for Philosophy of Religion, American Journal of Theology and Philosophy*. He is member of Society for Philosophy of Religion and American Academy of Religion. He is doing manuscript reviews for Oxford University Press, SUNY Press, Mercer University Press, Routledge.

CARL OLSON

Carl Olson has taught at Allegheny College since 1981. The college has appointed him to the National Endowment for the Humanities Chair (1991–94), Teacher-Scholar Professorship of the Humanities (2000–03), and chairperson. During 2002, he was appointed to a Visiting Fellowship at Clare Hall, University of Cambridge, and was elected a Permanent Fellow of Clare Hall by its board of trustees.

He is member of American Asian Society, American Oriental Society, American Academy of Religion, Society for Asian and Comparative Philosophy, and North American Association for the Study of Religion.

Professor Olson has published over 200 articles and reviews for various journals. He has served as review editor for the *International Journal of Hindu Studies* since 1996. He has also published the following books: *Indian Philosophers and Postmodern Thinkers: Dialogues on the Margins of Culture* (2002); *Theory and Method in the Study of Religion: A Selection of Critical Readings* (2003); *Indian Philosophers and Postmodern Thinkers: Dialogues on the Margins of Culture,* New Delhi:

Oxford University Press, 2002, *Theory and Method in the Study of Religion,* Belmont, CA: Wadsworth Publishing, 2003.

He has edited *Original Buddhist Sources: A Reader*, Piscataway, NJ: Rutgers University Press, 2005; *The Many Colors of Hinduism: a Thematic-Historical Introduction*, Piscataway, NJ: Rutgers University Press, 2007; *Hindu Primary Sources: A Sectarian Reader,* Piscataway, NJ: Rutgers University Press, 2007; *Celibacy and Religious Traditions*, New York: Oxford University Press, 2008.

MADHUMITA CHATTOPADHYAY

Madhumita Chattopadhyay is Professor of Philosophy and Head of the Department of Philosophy from Jadavpur University, Kolkata, India.

Her numerous publications include *Walking along the Paths of Buddhist Epistemology*, D.K. Printworld, Delhi, 2008; *Interpersonal Relationship in Academy*, edited with I. Sanyal, Anjali Publishers, Calcutta, 2007; *Ethics: an Anthology*, edited with T. Bannerjee, Allied Publishers, Calcutta, 2002; *What to do with the Liar*, Allied Publishers, Calcutta, 1998.

She received, among others, the following fellowships: JSPS Fellowship for 10 months from Japan Society for the promotion of Science, for the year 2009–2010; Charles Wallace India Trust Research Fellowship in 2008; Visited Professor to Budapest, Hungary, under the Indo-Hungarian Educational Exchange Programme, 2007; Fulbright Visiting Lectureship Award in 2004 and Bukkyo Dendo Kyokai Fellowship in 2002.

Index